Podcasting

The Do-It-Yourself Guide

Podcasting
The Do-It-Yourself Guide

Todd Cochrane

Wiley Publishing, Inc.

Podcasting: The Do-It-Yourself Guide

Published by
Wiley Publishing, Inc.
10475 Crosspoint Boulevard
Indianapolis, IN 46256
www.wiley.com

Published simultaneously in Canada

ISBN-13: 978-0-7645-9778-7
ISBN-10: 0-7645-9778-7

Manufactured in the United States of America

10 9 8 7 6 5 4 3 2 1

1B/SX/QV/QV/IN

For general information on our other products and services or to obtain technical support, please contact our Customer Care Department within the U.S. at (800) 762-2974, outside the U.S. at (317) 572-3993 or fax (317) 572-4002.

Wiley also publishes its books in a variety of electronic formats. Some content that appears in print may not be available in electronic books.

Library of Congress Cataloging-in-Publication Data is Available from the Publisher

About the Author

Todd Cochrane is originally from Quincy, Michigan, but today he lives and works in Honolulu, Hawaii. His professional background is in aviation electronics. He served 21 years in the United States Navy on active duty. Married, he and his wife Shoko have four children. His ongoing professional and personal interest in new technologies keeps him abreast of the latest developments in the technology world. His interest in podcasting has its roots in nearly 15 years of participating in different online communities. Before the advent of the Internet as we know it today, he enabled people to share ideas and data by running a dial-up bulletin board. To this day, he has a hobby BBS still on the Net. Many times, these old-school BBS systems were the only connection to home and family for troops deployed to remote locations around the globe. He developed an interest in and deployed a personal weblog in 2001. In 2002, he launched the popular technology news site, Geek News Central (www.geeknewscentral.com) and has worked hard to build a significant readership. After learning about podcasting in late 2004, he quickly started his own show and now has one of the popular technology news-based podcasts, today. It complements his Geek News Central weblog. Todd's understanding of the coming of change to media distribution and consumption led him to launch Podcast Connect, Inc., in 2005. He is steadily working to implement unique podcasting opportunities that keep the podcaster's best interests at heart. He is also an active member of the Tech Podcast Network.

Credits

Executive Editor
Chris Webb

Development Editor
Sydney Jones

Technical Editor
Chris McIntyre

Production Editor
Gabrielle Nabi

Copy Editor
Jeri Freedman

Editorial Manager
Mary Beth Wakefield

Vice President & Executive Group Publisher
Richard Swadley

Vice President and Publisher
Joseph B. Wikert

Project Coordinator
Bill Ramsey

Proofreader
Jennifer Ashley

Indexer
Johnna VanHoose Dinse

*Shoko, you are my hero and
the love of my life.
Thanks for being mom and dad
while I was out doing
what I do best!*

*To Steve and Mike for
having faith in me and your support,
and to Randy for that
talk out on the flight-line
not so long ago!*

Contents at a Glance

Contents

Part IV: Hosting and Preparing to Publish Your Podcast

Part V: It's Show Time

Acknowledgments

The idea for this book started with an e-mail I received on December 6th, 2004, from Chris Webb at Wiley Publishing. What developed and has been written and published in record time is this book. It has been one of the most interesting projects I have worked on in several years. Early on, I made it clear to Chris, my acquisitions editor, that I was a geek/tech guy first and that he did not want to see my English grades. Even so, he assured me that I was their man, and I went to work.

I thoroughly enjoyed writing this book and look forward to your feedback. I told everyone from the beginning that this book has to be fun because podcasting is. I hope that you have a great time reading it. A tremendous thank you goes to my development editor, Sydney Jones. She was the best editor a first-time author could ever have. She probably pulled her hair out a few times, but she impressed me with they way she dug in and learned the material as I wrote it and then asked the tough questions someone being exposed to podcasting for the first time will ask. She brought out the absolute best in my ideas, and she is a true professional.

Chris McIntyre, my technical editor and the person behind Podcast Alley, is one of those guys that I trusted from the first moment we talked. He was my sole pick to review the content to make sure it was technically correct. Chris and I worked great together, and although the book was written under almost impossible deadlines, he dug in and made sure the finer points were technically correct. Chris, I had a great time working with you! To those I swore to silence, you have your own story to tell, and thanks for keeping a lid on things. Credit to you lies within these pages. To the Wiley team that had to scramble and get this thing published several months ahead of schedule, I want to say a huge thank you — or, as we say in Hawaii, *mahalo*.

Introduction

No doubt you've heard the podcasting buzz. What's it all about?

Podcasting is an exciting new audio medium that gives you the freedom to listen to the audio programming of your choice. Every day around the world, people are creating their own audio shows on a wide range of topics — from music to technology and everything in between. What's even more exciting is that the Podcasting Revolution, as it has been termed, enables you to subscribe to, store, and consume this audio content when and where you please. Not only that, you now have the power to create and distribute audio shows on any topic you can imagine, with the potential to reach tens of thousands of listeners worldwide. Even more exciting is that the podcasting delivery method simplifies getting your message to the masses. Call it consumption by convenience.

This book is all about podcasting. You learn how to subscribe and listen to podcasts first. Then I teach you how to create, produce, and market a podcast. Both beginners and aspiring professionals can get a lot out of this text. I touch on all aspects of podcasting, teaching you about its origins and also how to use the tools that give the podcast listener the freedom to take content they choose anywhere they can take a portable media device. I cover the equipment and software that a podcaster would need and provide options for the person on a tight budget and the individual who wants to create a professional studio.

Anyone can create a podcast. I take you through all the steps to create one and provide all the tricks and tips you will need to get you on your way to reaching a worldwide audience. I talk about what makes podcasting unique, covering Real Simple Syndication (RSS) in terms the common man can understand. I cover how to market your podcast and give you resources for publishing and hosting it.

By following my tips and guidance, you can create a polished podcast that will make your content sound like it came from a professional studio, even though your show may have been created in your very own living room.

You will realize this book is all about having fun. Whether you are simply interested in listening to podcasts and finding out what the media has been going nuts over or whether you have a creative itch to produce content unlike anything you have ever been exposed to, this is the ultimate resource — delivered to you from an actual podcaster.

Who Is This Book For?

This book was designed for you! Although the concepts and steps that I walk you through are easy, they are sophisticated enough so that everyone, including companies looking to launch their own media shows, will learn a great deal.

This book is ideal for four types of people:

- **People who want to find out what podcasting is about, its origins and history, and how to make better use of the portable media device that they may or may not have.** This book will discuss how to find new audio content on the Internet and then how to either listen to that content on a PC or fill a portable MP3 player with content that is both entertaining and informative.

- **People who want to create a podcast for fun or on a limited budget.** As a father of four with a house and car payments, I was able to create and produce a podcast that has gained worldwide listenership — without impacting family finances. I will teach you what I have learned in the process; I'll even cover how to create a podcast without a computer.

- **People who want to take their podcasts to the next level.** I will discuss how you can build a professional studio in your own home and demonstrate tools you can use to improve your production quality. I cover every feature or concept that will add a substantial Wow! factor to your podcast.

- **Companies that want to explore what's happening in the podcasting community and how to find podcasters that will market their brand.** For a company that is thinking about producing its own podcast, this book will be particularly helpful. It may preclude the necessity of hiring an expensive consulting firm.

What Does This Book Cover?

This book covers all aspects of podcasting for the prospective listener and the person who wants to create his or her own show. It's written by a podcaster who has created over 50 shows himself and has learned numerous tips and tricks along the way.

- Chapter 1 discusses the fundamentals of podcasting, its history, some of the more prominent podcasters, and the types of shows available.

- Chapters 2 and 3 discuss and review podcatcher software or podcast aggregators and how to use them to find podcasts.

- Chapters 4 and 5 discuss the concept of creating your own podcast with the steps needed to get started using gear you own, today.

- Chapter 6 discusses creating the semiprofessional studio with equipment reviews, including microphone recommendations and discussions about audio-processing gear and the purpose of that equipment.

- Chapters 7 through 9 discuss recording considerations and the actual recording of your podcast. I outline the postproduction process for creating a stellar audio recording using equipment that you own.

- Chapters 10 through 12 discuss hosting solutions and what to watch out for, including the realities of distributing audio and my secret hosting solutions. I cover publishing your podcast on the Internet and how to implement RSS feeds with or without a weblog.

- Chapters 13 through 14 cover the actual publishing and promotion of your podcast and how to integrate a marketing and promotion strategy to include advertising.

- Finally, in Chapter 15, I discuss the road ahead. How will podcasting affect traditional radio and what will the impact of commercialization be?

Listening to the Podcast Revolution

part

What Is a Podcast?

Do you have specific interests? How about triathlons? I have to admit, most radio broadcasts don't deal with those kind of subjects. But that's about to change. You can go to `http://enduranceradio.com` and download any program listed there about triathlons. You can listen to it live, you can store it and listen to it on portable media when you have time, or you can even store it on your hard drive and use it as a reference at a later date, such as when you finally start training for that iron man competition.

And it's not just triathlons. People are podcasting on more topics than you can imagine. Take, for example, the *Rock and Roll Geek Show*, a music review and commentary show; *Real Reviews*, a podcast that reviews movies and DVDs; *The Point*, a show for Mac users; and sound-seeing tours where various podcasters take you on sound tours of their parts of the world. Accessing these broadcasts is as simple as surfing the Internet.

Creating your own podcasts isn't much harder. Now you have the ability to reach listeners worldwide. You can air your ideas, share your passions, offer your music to the world, and much more.

Podcasters don't have to make advertisers happy. They don't have to worry about FCC regulations. They don't have to adhere to play lists. They don't have to pay attention to the corporate bottom line. They broadcast what they love, and you can too. The podcasting revolution has begun, and you don't want to be left behind!

You can listen to the radio, of course. You can even listen to radio while you are online. If you want to, you can record a radio program that interests you and listen to it later. So, how are the audio programs in podcasting different? Traditional radio is a business venture, governed by budget concerns and regulations. That means the information you can access is limited — probably mainstream. What if you could automatically download and listen to anything that interested you? What if, right from your home, you could broadcast programs to thousands of listeners worldwide about anything that interests you?

That's what podcasting is all about. And thousands of people are listening to and creating podcasts. You won't believe what's out there.

This chapter empowers you to take control of what you listen to. It introduces the concept of *walkaway content*. It gives you the straight story about the history of podcasting and introduces you to a sampling of podcast personalities and programs.

The Fundamentals of Podcasting

The term *podcasting*, in a way, puts you immediately into the right frame of mind. When I heard the term for the first time, the main idea that stuck in my mind was that podcasting somehow was a unique communications medium that was portable and had something to do with broadcasting.

That guess about the meaning of the term was very close, and I soon found out that podcasting represents a new way for individuals to communicate about things they love. They can actually broadcast content that comes from their hearts and are able to communicate with other people in a new and exciting way. For a long time, highly technical people have been recording and placing audio content on the Internet, but the barriers to entry were relatively high. Podcasting breaks down those barriers. The wow factor of podcasting is that the delivery vehicle has been automated for the listener and made simple enough for the person producing content so that anyone can do it.

Throughout the world today, individuals are driving to work in cars, sitting on buses, walking down the street, or waiting for a train while they listen to podcasts. Some are even tapping into podcasts while at work. Who and what are they listening to? Well, they're listening to music or to people like me talk to them about subjects we love. In Figure 1-1, I am driving down the street listening to *Tech Rag Tear Outs* via my FM-capable portable media device.

FIGURE 1-1: Listening to a podcast via my FM-capable MP3 player on the car radio.

I discovered podcasts in a hotel room in central Texas while surfing the Internet. It was like being given the keys to my first car, and being able to drive unaccompanied. The freedom we all felt the first time we drove by ourselves wasn't any different from when I listened to my first podcast. What I found intriguing was that podcasters could speak freely, without control and restrictions. The thing that also blew me away was that podcasters were regular people. Most are hardworking men and women, and it was obvious to me that everyday people with a passion were having fun creating podcasts. I immediately knew I was going to be a podcaster. It was a decision as natural as opening a door. The best part was that I didn't have to be rich to be a creator of a podcast.

I am a father of four, working a 7 to 5 job in Honolulu, Hawaii, and I've been listening to and producing podcasts since October 12, 2004. My first podcast was created in that same hotel room in Texas, where I basically taught myself how to create a show. The response and numbers of people that tuned in astounded me. I was getting comments from all over the world in a very short amount of time. Prior to this, I had my own weblog, called Geek News Central (`http://geeknewscentral.com`). Geek News Central is a site where I talk about technology and other things that interest me. I describe myself as a typical geek with a little rebel spark. I like to dig in and talk about new technologies and relevant news of the day. What drove me to podcasting was that I advocate fair use rights and had become disenchanted with the traditional broadcasting system and what I was listening to on the radio every day.

The reaction to my first podcast was nothing short of amazing. Today, the number of listeners continues to grow, and the readership of my weblog has increased dramatically. So, I can say that podcasting drew readers to my website and supplemented what I wanted to say but sometimes could not express completely with the written word. I was able for the first time to speak to readers and give them the raw emotion that is many times missing from a weblog post.

I hope to guide you in this book so that you don't make some of the mistakes I made in my early podcasts. I will cover everything I know about podcasting. I want you to feel the power of the medium as I do. The fundamental thing to remember about podcasting is to have fun and be yourself. Whether you are a listener or an aspiring podcaster, remember that the majority of podcast shows are created by average people. Sure, there are some high-end producers, but the majority are regular people having fun and creating content we love.

Podcasts are created in living rooms, cars, while walking down the street, and at home. They can be scripted or unscripted, but podcasters bring their listeners mostly unedited, real, and from-the-heart commentary. Podcasting, as a content-delivery medium, enables you to reach hundreds of thousands of listeners. You don't have to worry about licensing or government regulations. You don't have to worry about someone beating down your door or having to buy a lot of equipment. In fact, my first podcasts were created with a computer and a $7.95 microphone. Figure 1-2 shows what I used to create my first podcast.

FIGURE 1-2: A microphone and a computer are all you need to get started.

The Power of Walkaway Content

You may say, "I have heard of this medium called podcasting, but do I need to have an Apple iPod to listen to shows?" The answer to that is no. In reality, you don't even need a portable media device. You can listen to podcasts via direct downloads from the podcaster's website and listen to them directly on your PC through the media player of your choice. The power of podcasting, however, is the ability to deliver content to any MP3 player capable of synchronizing with Windows Media Player or Apple iTunes. I have used an iRiver YP790, a Samsung Yepp, iPod Shuffle, and iPod. The list of players capable of playing MP3 files is endless.

Podcasting has spun heads because you can use a very simple software utility to automatically download audio programs to which you subscribe. Your downloads are then automatically transferred to Windows Media Player or Apple iTunes, and they, in turn, load the audio file automatically to your mobile media device. The great thing about podcasts is that you're not tied to your computer. You can walk away with fresh audio loaded on your MP3 player every day.

Imagine deciding that you want a sampling of audio shows on various subjects using one of the software packages I will highlight later in this book. You subscribe to those shows for free. You then leave that application running in your computer's taskbar and go to bed.

You wake up in the morning and get ready to go to work or school. Before you leave the house, you grab your portable media device, which has been automatically synchronized with the audio content you have subscribed to — content that you want to listen to. That is the power of walkaway content: you control what you listen to, and when and where you consume it.

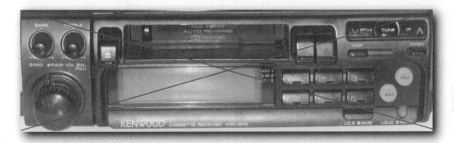

FIGURE 1-3: No radio.

What are your listening choices today? What is typically on the radio? As we browse the traditional radio dial, we are given a wide variety of programming choices, but most of those programming choices — from songs played to on-air personalities — are controlled by major media companies. You may have a choice of a dozen different types of stations in your listening area, but the same media company likely owns half those stations. These companies control what you listen to; they offer only what they want you to hear. Everything is controlled and under the watchful eyes of those who make sure ratings stay high and certain artists get promoted. Furthermore, the Federal Communication Commission (FCC) monitors traditional radio. On the one hand, this means that kids won't be exposed to pornography or other types of unsuitable content. The FCC is mandated to keep the airways relatively clean. They have, in fact, fined radio broadcasters such as Howard Stern for inappropriate content.

Podcasters are not regulated by the FCC, so a wide variety of shows exists — literally thousands of them. The majority of the podcasts are safe for work listening; but be forewarned that some aren't, so preview shows before sharing them with sensitive co-workers. Along those lines, you will also want to monitor the podcasts your kids tune in to, just as you limit other Internet content you allow your children to access. In Figure 1-4, I am listening to a podcast while taking a walk through the neighborhood.

FIGURE 1-4: Listening to a podcast while on a walk.

The History of Podcasting

The true godfathers of podcasting are Dave Winer and Adam Curry. Dave Winer (`http://scripting.com`) is a software developer and RSS evangelist; he developed the popular weblog package Radio Userland (`http://userland.com`). Today, Dave "produces" the popular podcast *Morning Coffee Notes* (`http://morningcoffeenotes.com`). Adam Curry produces the ever-popular *Daily Source Code* (`http://live.curry.com`). Adam is well-known as a mid-1980s former MTV VJ (see `http://live.curry.com`).

Note For some of you, this short history will be a trip down memory lane. But many reporters have bungled the true history behind the evolution of podcasting. I want to give you the best perspective I could obtain.

Podcasting started, before the term was even invented, with an idea from a meeting in late 2000 between Adam Curry and Dave Winer about automated media distribution. The conversation was centered around video rather than audio; Dave had some concerns about the distribution of video over the Internet.

Remember, this was the year 2000, before the world-wide growth in the number of broadband Internet subscribers. Dave felt the Internet simply hadn't evolved to the point where it would support large video downloads, not to mention the cost of delivering content. His analogy was that it was taking longer to download video than it was to play it, and many times the video was of poor and uncertain quality.

Check out `http://ipodder.org/history` for another perspective.

Adam's idea was to look at Internet connections differently and consider all the bandwidth that goes to waste when users aren't using their Internet connections. He wanted a software solution that could automatically download items that he subscribed to. This really wasn't a new idea, but there were no tools to do this in the fashion Adam desired.

I must interject that Internet service providers hope you don't use your broadband connection around the clock. In some countries, people have to pay for the amount of bandwidth they consume. The idea of millions of computers pulling content automatically while we sleep makes most ISPs shudder.

Dave was already working on *Real Simple Syndication* (RSS). For those of you not familiar with RSS, I will cover it in Chapter 12 in greater detail. Just so you won't be confused at this point, I'll give you a quick review of RSS.

Various websites, although primarily weblogs and news sites, carry an icon that might be labeled RSS, RSS .91, RSS 2.0, or XML. They are typically small icons with white letters on an orange background. These icons are linked to an XML (extensible markup language) formatted file. These files contain text that is structured in the RSS specification. Podcatchers, or podcast aggregators, are programs that run on your desktop that can interpret the data in these files. I cover these software applications in Chapters 2 and 3.

I encourage you to load `http://www.geeknewscentral.com/podcast.xml` in your web browser to see a sample of RSS 2.0. Obviously, you wouldn't want to have to read this in your web browser.

The site `http://webreference.com/authoring/languages/xml/rss/intro/` offers a detailed discussion of RSS. In the most basic terms, RSS enables you to share content across the Internet. Because an RSS file can include dynamic content as well as static content, you can use it to distribute content from your site to others.

Dave had made revisions to the original RSS 0.91 specification developed by Netscape and formalized those revisions as RSS 2.0 in 2003. The RSS 2.0 standard was released by Harvard under a Creative Commons license. More information on RSS can be found at the official site `http://blogs.law.harvard.edu/tech/rss`.

I will cover the Creative Commons license in detail in Chapter 4, but I encourage you to visit `http://creativecommons.org/` for detailed information about this exciting media/material licensing avenue.

Dave knew after his discussion with Adam that there would have to be some additional software components developed to make delivery of content happen automatically. Dave thought the process would need to be broken into three categories:

1. What software do you use when creating the content?

2. What software reads the content?

3. Where do you find the content?

Four and a half years passed from the initial meeting, and during that time, file sharing became the main vector for net audio/video distribution. Sharing technologies arrived that allowed files to be downloaded faster than they could be listened to. That, in itself, helped set the stage for what was coming.

Until the summer of 2004, progress was slow, and even though many of the individual pieces were in place, they were not tied together. There were no open source solutions — only content delivery methods that were tied to commercial solutions. This changed when Adam decided to try his hand at programming and developed the first rudimentary podcatcher application with AppleScript. He termed it *iPodder*; the original application is no longer in use today, but the premise of his code, which I will review in Chapter 2, has been improved on.

Throughout this book, I will use the word *podcatcher*. You will also hear the term *podcast aggregator* used on the Internet. It is important to know that the terms mean the same thing.

Dave initially thought that what Adam had created would not work, but with Adam's hacked-together AppleScript, Adam was able to capture and download audio posts that Dave had recently started embedding in his weblog post.

Dave's provisioning of an element called an "enclosure" within an item in RSS 2.0 allowed the tool that Adam created to understand where media files were stored and grab and download the files automatically.

Adam's program read Dave's RSS feed and interpreted the "enclosure" information and downloaded the corresponding audio file. Adam's program simply grabbed the file linked within these enclosures, downloaded it, and then utilized it in the API released for iTunes. It put the file in his iTunes play list, which then was automatically uploaded to Adam's iPod.

I cover enclosures in greater detail in Chapter 12, but essentially an enclosure contains information on the physical location, size, and type of the file. It is important to note that the file can be anything and is not restricted to audio files, as long as the RSS feed has the "enclosure tag" incorporated.

Take a look at this enclosure example:

```
<enclosure url="http://libsyn.com/media/geeknews/GNC-
2005-3-25.mp3" length=" 17191017" type="audio/mpeg"/>
```

As you can see, the enclosure provides a link only to the physical storage location on the Internet.

Adam had aspired for four years after that original meeting to automate file downloads of video and audio content and make it easy for the masses. With Adam Curry being a quasi-celebrity, his show, *The Daily Source Code,* helped launch podcasting. We must recognize Dave's outstanding evangelism of podcasting, along with the huge contribution and development of the RSS 2.0 standard. RSS enabled sites with enclosures — the glue that allows for automated distribution — to work. Adam's simple AppleScript lit the fire for the development of podcasting tools, which is today in full swing.

Adam Curry says, "Podcasting is where developers and users party together." This has been a profound battle cry and has resulted in amazing achievements in a very short time.

Literally dozens of developers and thousands of podcaster are the driving force behind the widespread number of newly created podcatcher clients, along with improvements to pre-existing weblog RSS implementations. Even developers of news aggregator software are getting onboard. The media has been following and reporting on podcasting in record numbers.

In Chapter 2, I will go into great depth and review these new software packages and improvements to existing news aggregators.

How the Podcasting Term Originated

Whenever some new media delivery method is invented, there is always a word that everyone adopts to describe it. The term *podcasting* was coined in February 2004 by Ben Hammersley, in an article in the *Guardian*. This article predates Adam's *podcatcher*. Hammersley and others did not know what to call the growing self audio publishing medium at the time and had kicked around a couple of terms, including *podcast*. People who were already embedding audio on their sites realized they had a winner, but the automated tools were not in place. Those that existed were tied to commercial enterprises, and Adam's open source tool that automated the process did not yet exist.

The creation of that program by Adam in mid-2004 made a lot of people realize how easy publishing audio for automated delivery would be. Shows sprang up and the word spread.

The term that would define this exploding medium was decided by a simple act: the first podcasting domain registered to Dannie J. Gregoire in September 2004 and hyped by Dave Slusher, who produces the Evil Genius Chronicles (`http://evilgeniuschronicles.org`), and then made popular by Adam Curry, Doc Searls, Robert Scoble, Dave Winer and the rest of the podcasters.

Some have criticized the term *podcast*, as it makes podcasting sound like it is the exclusive domain of the Apple iPod. Without a doubt, the Apple iPod is the icon of mobile media devices. Few will disagree with that, including my daughter, who worked saved every penny of her allowance, Christmas, and birthday money to buy an iPod this past year. Most podcasters would agree that the iPod has its shortcomings, like other MP3 players. It's not perfect for listening to podcasts, but it's the best we have at the moment.

We hope that the retail community will step up and listen to our needs and develop a truly revolutionary device or devices that will interact with our listeners and improve the podcasting listening and distribution process. Improvements need to be made so listeners can provide verbal recorded feedback midway through a program and even review show notes that podcasters could embed in the audio file that would help listeners quickly jump on the Net to look at a site or topic that has been discussed. Hopefully, we will soon have MP3 players with built-in WiFi and onboard software to automatically grab new podcasts.

It must be said, however, that without the millions of iPods and other media devices capable of storing large numbers of MP3 files, this medium would have never taken off in the way it has. We have given people a way to fill their iPods and other media devices with content other than music.

The Growth Rate of Podcasting

Podcasting was initially the next natural step for webloggers. In fact, many webloggers had previously been making audio posts on their sites, but because the majority of news aggregators and tools available did not recognize the audio files linked in those posts, their uptake was minimal. Audio blogging had not taken off, because only a small number of webloggers were posting audio comments. We must, of course, acknowledge that there have and continue to be a significant number of people creating audio content for streaming services, but those streams still mean you are locked to a desktop and not free to roam when listening to a podcast. Copyright concerns have also been the downfall of some of those services; the content is under strict Digital Rights Management (DRM) rules and usually can be listened to only while you are connected to the Internet. There are ways around this problem, of course, but it is still a manual process.

Forms of Digital Rights Management have been put in place by both Microsoft and Apple in order to placate organizations like the Recording Industry of America (RIAA) and Movie Producers of America (MPAA). DRM and other proprietary file formats serve to control audio and video content. Most commercial media today is under heavy copyright, and licensing control and restrictions in fair use are being encroached upon each day. DRM systems protect the copyright of materials by restricting, through software solutions, how the content can be used.

Fortunately, podcasters have largely adopted a Creative Commons License and are promoting bands and artists not under the control of the RIAA. In my opinion, the RIAA and similar organizations are probably hoping that the podcasting revolution goes away, as the medium has been generally open. Podcasters want you to share their content and are doing their best to keep the legal hand of the RIAA away by playing within the copyright rules.

As the term *podcast* began to be widely adopted, the typical land rush for domain names by early adopters began, and podcast directories started popping up. As the word got out and Google started indexing the *podcast* term, the search results went from a few hundred to 2.79 million hits within six months. The number of podcasts in the podcasting directories grew from 10 to over 4,500 in the same period. The numbers continue to grow. The podcasting revolution is truly underway.

Who Are Podcasters?

Obviously, people have been creating audio content for a very long time. The only difference is that most of that content has been available only via manual direct download. Some services stream audio content 24/7 with all varieties and types of shows, but they have been slow to adopt the podcasting delivery method. On the other hand, traditional radio is now getting onboard. Some content on such big broadcasters as the BBC and NPR are now available as podcasts. Thus, a lot of people in the corporate world have realized the power of walkaway content. By and large though, the majority of podcasters are webloggers, but it is not their sole domain. A lot of people are jumping on the bandwagon and making the necessary changes to their websites to allow listeners to download content while they sleep.

Personalities and Show Reviews

This section provides reviews of some shows I listen to. I currently subscribe to more shows than I can consume; thank goodness many of those shows are only once a week. The shows I follow range from 1 to 45 minutes. If I start a show and the topic of the day doesn't interest me, the power of walkaway content takes place as I hit the FFWD button, (just as many of you do on your TiVo). In Chapter 2, I list a large number of directories where you can find podcasts.

Review 1: Rock and Roll Geek Show

Michael Butler is a self-proclaimed rock-and-roll geek. Any geek that is as passionate as I am makes me take notice. His show (http://americanheartbreak.com/movabletype/) is a mix of music, trivia, and music reviews. Not only does Michael love rock, but he has his own band, American Heartbreak, with whom he plays bass guitar. After New Year's in 2004, Michael and his band traveled through Europe, podcasting from different locations and situations.

His band's fan base has grown because of podcasting; many listeners came to his band's shows in Europe. An interesting piece of trivia surrounds the *Rock and Roll Geek Show*. Michael was trying to get Heineken to sponsor his show for a couple cases of beer. Michael really likes Heineken and usually enjoys the beverage while doing his show. Some would consider that controversial, but it also demonstrates the fact that anything goes with podcasting.

Adam Curry tried to help Michael get Heineken to sponsor his show; instead, Heineken launched its own podcast. Most of us considered it a slap in the face. Heineken would have received a significant amount of press by simply giving Michael a couple cases of beer. Heck, I would have supported it by buying a couple for their effort. It has been rumored that Michael's podcast helped kick his band to the next level, and I'm sure they're on their way to bigger and better things.

I foresee a time in the near future when podcasters are the driving force behind the signing of an unknown band to a major label. In conclusion, Michael's *Rock and Roll Geek Show* is a great one to listen to and has been on my subscription list for a long time.

Review 2: Endurance Radio

Endurance Radio (http://enduranceradio.com), hosted by Tim Bourquin, is one of the podcasts that started as a streaming audio program. When Tim realized the potential growth of podcasting, he added the necessary code to his website and offered the content as podcast. Tim does a great job and has already produced nearly 100 shows. *Endurance Radio* is all about endurance sports, triathletes, adventure racers, cyclists, marathon runners, and mountain bikers. I am not much of an athlete, but I get motivated when I hear these people tell their stories. So, if you're into extreme sports, this is a podcast you will want to tune in to.

Review 3: Manic Minute

Michael Lehman does several podcasts, but a favorite of mine is his daily *Manic Minute* (`manicminute.net/`), a one-minute podcast in which he uses an audio trick to compress 2 to 3 minutes of fast-paced news and commentary into a show no longer than a minute. I listen as I am driving home from work, and there is always a gem or two in the podcast that galvanizes me to rush to my computer when I get home to look at the site he's talked about. This is one of the best short-format podcasts — it is like drinking from a fire hose; you get a quick blast and you're all filled up.

Review 4: IndieFeed

Looking for music on the Internet that is free of control by the Recording Industry Association of America and similar organizations? The *IndieFeed* podcasts provide just that. They highlight a variety of music styles, and, on an almost daily basis, bring to our listening palate two or three new songs. We can listen to the songs, and then go to the respective website and either download them for free, or better yet, support the independent artist they highlight and buy their music. With most radio stations today using the same boring play lists, *IndieFeed* provides fresh acts. *IndieFeed* features genres acceptable to any age group and music you would most likely not find anywhere else.

Summary

Podcasting began as an idea two people shared. They wanted a system that provided automatic delivery of audio content. They wanted it to synchronize automatically so their listeners weren't trapped behind a computer while enjoying their show.

The open source community jumped in, and now you can listen to any show you choose while you drive to work, jog through the park, or browse the aisles of a grocery store. Not only that, you can produce a show about anything you love and expose your thoughts and ideas to thousands of listeners.

The podcasting revolution has begun. Podcasting enables you to listen to any content you want about any subject that interests you, and there is a lot of it out there.

If nothing else, I want you to walk away from this chapter with two ideas:

- Podcasting is about having fun.
- Podcasting is generally unscripted and includes life's real moments.

Excited yet? In Chapter 2, you learn everything you need to know about choosing podcasting software.

Choosing Podcatcher Software

A number of software packages are available for use in downloading podcasts. In this chapter, I discuss a variety of them so that you can make an informed choice and select the software package that is best suited for you and the operating system you use. Because all of these software packages are in continual development and new software solutions are becoming available all the time, you will want to check out the website resources page that we reference at the end of this chapter. These sites will help you find info on all the newest releases of podcatcher software clients available today.

Some of the standard news aggregators available today are also starting to support the download of podcasts. You may already be using a news aggregator that has podcast download support built in. I will cover a few of these applications as well.

What Is Podcatcher Software?

A podcatcher is a software tool that you use to subscribe to and manage all the podcast feeds that you want to have downloaded automatically. Generally, good podcatcher clients allow you to manage when and how often they check for updates as well as automatically download new shows and put them in the media player of your choice. Some simply place them on your hard drive for your manual intervention. I have done my best to give you a large sampling of available software packages.

Note *Podcatchers* and *podcast aggregators* are the same thing. You will see these software applications referred to in both ways on the Internet. I use the term *podcatcher* because I personally prefer it.

Podcatcher client interfaces have been designed thus far for the following operating systems:

- Windows
- Mac
- Linux
- Pocket PC
- Several MP3-capable mobile phones

Generally, the podcatcher clients have been designed to work with Windows Media Player and Apple iTunes. If you use another media player, there are optional command-line commands that you can input to run scripts or launch other media players to catalog new shows.

During the installation or within the preference settings, you will be given the option to choose the media player to which you would like the podcatcher client to add downloaded files. Apple iTunes is almost universally supported. Be sure to check Table 2-1 in the next section to find out whether the podcatcher client you choose supports the media player you plan to use.

The more advanced clients available today also support management of files, so if you choose, they will automatically remove old shows you do not want cluttering up your media player. Some of the clients offer a travel or vacation function, ensuring that when you are away from your broadband connection, the client is smart enough not to try to download two weeks' worth of shows in one shot. I will overview a handful of the clients in this chapter, and in Chapter 3, I will go into detail about using specific clients.

Determining Which Software Is Right for You

I recommend that you test drive several of the podcatcher clients to see what best suits your needs. To get a complete list of all podcatcher clients available today, visit `http://podcastalley.com/software/`.

I will refer to BitTorrent as I review these clients. BitTorrent is a peer-to-peer (P2P) protocol designed to download and help distribute files. At this time, adoption of BitTorrent as a download protocol has not been widely implemented. In almost all cases, podcasts have made subscribing to a BitTorrent feed voluntary, as some are not comfortable with P2P applications. If you do choose a BitTorrent-enabled feed, once you have completed the download your client will help in the distribution of that podcast to other listeners while your podcatcher client remains running. The distribution of that file to other listeners by BitTorrent programs is known as *seeding*. The term is derived from the process of throwing small pieces of the file to others downloading the file, then those clients putting the pieces back together.

Because some podcasters are facing mounting bandwidth concerns, they are asking listeners to help them out by using the P2P-enabled feeds. This is something you will have to keep in mind when determining which feed you will subscribe to, whether it is a direct download or a BitTorrent-enabled download. For more information on BitTorrent, visit http://dessent.net/btfaq/#what.

I refer often to Real Simple Syndication (RSS) as an RSS feed. As an example, view my site's RSS feed, at http://geeknewscentral.com/index.xml. In your computer browser, the text is formatted in a way that is not easily readable; now, if you back up to my home page at http://geeknewscentral.com, you will see, on the right border of the page, an icon that simply says "RSS 2.0." This is the direct link to the preceding index.xml file. So, whenever you want to subscribe to a website's RSS feed, all you have to do is copy that URL and paste the information into the podcast-supported client's Add Feed window. Many podcasters have set up podcast-specific RSS feeds, so look for those specific icons. On my site, my podcast-specific feeds are labeled.

I will refer to *Outline Processor Markup Language (OPML)* in this chapter as well. OPML is XML-based code that provides an outline of content on a website that can be shared with other people and computers. OPML files are used to create notes, play lists, and other detailed lists that need to be organized in an outline format.

As an example, an OPML file could contain all of the podcasts someone subscribes to. Many of these clients support importing OPML files; these files are located on personal websites and are linked in the same way as RSS pages. Using software like Radio Userland (http://userland.com), you can build an entire website with content from another site's OPML files. OPML is great for projects like podcasting in which people want to share lists of the podcasts they listen to.

Podcast Features

Many of the podcatcher clients today are using some of the same base source code, so I have done my best in the upcoming reviews to give you a broad spectrum of choices. As the code matures, you will see more divergence among clients. If I could wave a magic wand over all the podcatcher applications, I would probably want a podcatcher client that had all of the following features:

- **Active directory:** This is where the clients can query. It would include all the podcasting directories and make available multiple lists within the clients. Currently, the majority of the podcatchers look at only a small number of the actual directories available. With some directories in the podcatcher clients becoming commercially driven, it is important that listeners are able to review unbiased directory layouts — not to suggest this is happening, but the potential exists.

There is some momentum in developing what is called the *Open Podcast Directory Application*. I am hoping that by this book's publishing date, there will be forward momentum on this project. The Open Podcast Directory Application will allow anyone to create an independent list without needing large amounts of technical knowledge.

- **Support for Windows Media:** Many of the podcatcher clients support Windows Media Player, but you still have to do a small amount of work to manage what gets uploaded to your media player. This process needs improvement. The current podcatcher clients that support Windows Media Player add the shows and the files to the player's library only, and you must still select what will be uploaded to your media device. As more Windows Media Player–supported MP3 players reach the market, developers will need to pay a little more attention to the Windows Media Player interface.

- **Support for Apple iTunes:** Because Apple iTunes supports the high-capacity Apple iPods, podcatcher support for this media player is almost universal. With the clients adding podcasts to the play list, integration and synchronization is the easiest on Apple iTunes between the two media players.

- **BitTorrent functionality:** For general users, there is some mystery about how BitTorrent works and the players that implement it and have the BitTorrent client embedded in their source code; thus, no secondary applications are needed. It is important as you read my reviews to give podcatcher clients a higher score when the BitTorrent functionality is built into the client.

- **Import OPML:** I have a list of podcasts that I listen to that I make available to people via my website or e-mail. Those of you who want a great starter list can e-mail me at podcastbook@gmail.com, and I will provide a website link where you can import my starter list with the Import OPML feature into your podcatcher. Then you can pick and choose which shows you like and manage your subscriptions (I'll outline this in the next section).

- **Export OPML:** Just as I share my list, you can do the same with family and friends. This feature also allows you to back up your subscription list so that if you want to change podcatcher clients in the future, you have an easy transition path.

- **Displays show notes:** When most podcasters publish their podcasts, they provide a website post with everything covered in the show, along with website links to the featured sites. Some podcatcher clients allow you to read those posts directly in the application. As podcatcher clients and media players improve, the show notes may advance across our portable media player's screen as the host talks about each topic, and the relevant link for content being talked about will be viewable and immediately accessible.

- **Free:** The majority of podcatcher clients are free, but some companies are starting to create podcatcher clients that require registration. I am all for improvements, and like many of you, I am willing to pay for them.

- **File management capability:** I subscribe to a large number of podcasts as I try to keep abreast of new and innovative ways to do podcasts. With that in mind, I download a significant number of files per month. Some podcatcher clients manage these files by cleaning up after themselves based on settings I have set in the preferences of the application. It would be great in the future if I could tag a program to be kept, because some podcasts are so good that I don't want them erased.

- **Settings for limiting downloads:** Whether you are on vacation or on a limited dial-up connection, a time will come when you don't want your podcatcher client to download 200 mgs of new show data each day. The best podcatcher clients have features to limit downloads based on show size and the number of previous shows to download when first subscribing to a show. If you're a new subscriber, you don't want to download two months of old information.

In Table 2-1, I lay out the features of each podcatcher client; some of the clients may or may not do everything exactly as I have described here.

Table 2-1 Summary of Podcatcher Features

	Active Directory	Windows Media	Apple iTunes	BitTorrent	Import OPML	Export OPML	View Show Notes	Free	Manage Files	Limit Downloads
Windows										
Doppler	x	x	x	x	x	x	x	x	x	x
iPodder	x	x	x	x	x	x		x	x	
jPodder	x	x	x	x				x		x
Nimiq	x	x	x	x	x	x		x		x
Mac										
iPodder	x		x	x	x	x		x	x	
iPodderX	x		x	x		x				
PoddumFeeder	x		x		x	x				x
Linux										
Bash iPodder		n/a	n/a	x	x			x		
jPodder	x	n/a	n/a	x				x		x
PocketPC										
Egress		x			x			x	x	x
FeederReeder	x	x			x			x	x	x
Standard Aggregator										
BlogMatrix Sparks	x	x	x		x			x		
FeedDemon		x			x	x	x		x	x
NewsGator					x	x	x			x

Podcatcher Software for Windows

Each team that develops clients needs to be acknowledged for their hard work. Inclusion or exclusion from this book doesn't mean that the client didn't meet my specifications. Many clients were in early development, and I simply had no information; in a few instances, requests for information were ignored.

I reviewed all of the clients and personally chose those that embody the best implementation of the feature list in Table 2-1. I realize that many developers are working to implement additional features. But at this time, I picked the review candidates based upon my experience and what excited me. In Table 2-2, I list the respective websites for all known Windows podcatcher clients.

Table 2-2   Podcatcher Software (Windows)

Software Title	URL	Reviewed	Price
Armangil's Podcatcher	http://podcatcher.rubyforge.org/	No	Free
Doppler Radio	dopplerradio.net/	Yes	Free
Happy Fish	http://thirstycrow.net/happyfish/	No	Free
iPodder	http://ipodder.sourceforge.net/index.php	Yes	Free
Jager	http://jaeger.blogmatrix.com/	No	Free
jPodder	http://jpodder.com/	Yes	Free
Nimiq	http://nimiq.nl/	Yes	Free
PrimeTime Podcast Receiver	http://primetimepodcast.com/	No	Free

Doppler

Doppler (version 2.0.0.1), at `http://dopplerradio.net/`, is in my opinion one of the best podcatcher clients available today. It was developed, as are many of the other clients, as open source.

Note   *Open source* simply means that the source code to the program is publicly available, allowing programmers to modify and improve the code. The most widely known open-source software is the Linux operating system.

The client supports importing to Windows Media Player and Apple iTunes. You can easily search for podcasts or browse the active directories of podcast shows.

Note Doppler used the `http://ipodder.org` and `http://allpodcasts.com` directories for its list of podcasts. These aren't the only directories, but they are good starting points. In Chapter 3, I provide a list of all podcast directories available.

This enables you to subscribe to a podcast from within the application itself. After you subscribe to a show, you can easily review it, because the client has a built-in feed parser, which allows you to read the latest podcast show notes within the application. Subscribing manually is as easy as clicking the Add Feed button and pasting in the URL of the site's RSS or XML feed. Figure 2-1 shows the Doppler main window.

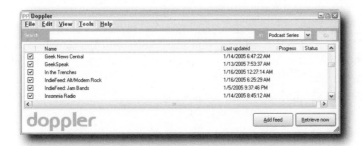

FIGURE 2-1: Doppler main window.

If you want to add multiple sites at a time, you can do so through the Import an OPML function. The feature list of this program is impressive; you can customize the play list names to help keep your media player's play list organized. Doppler has a feature that allows you to download only the last podcast. This comes in handy when you're traveling or checking out a podcast for the first time and aren't yet sure whether you'll become a permanent subscriber.

If you are traveling and on a dial-up connection, you can change a setting to force the system to put a limit on the file download size until you are back on broadband.

One of the best features is the client's ability to clean up after itself. It removes files older than a preconfigured date you choose, managing the amount of old data that remains on your media player.

Some podcasters do not implement ID3 tags info in their MP3 files, so you have the ability to change several of the tag variables for better organization of the data once it's on your MP3 player.

You can set the maximum number of downloads that are permitted at the same time. One of the unique features allows you to direct by file extension what media player to which you want files added. This is nice because you could, in effect, synchronize two devices with one application. Overall, Doppler is one of the most feature-rich podcatcher clients available today.

iPodder

iPodder (version 2.0), at `http://ipodder.sourceforge.net/`, is being developed as open source and is free. iPodder currently offers stable Windows and Mac versions, and a Linux version is in beta testing. The product supports Apple iTunes only.

You can easily subscribe to new podcasts within the application because it links to a categorized daily updated directory of podcasts. Adding feeds manually is as simple as copying the location of the RSS or XML and pasting it into the pop-up Add Feed window. iPodder supports background automated scheduling of downloads, with settings for three unique times each day to look for new feeds, or you can choose to have it scan sites after a set period of time.

iPodder supports BitTorrent downloads. It ships with BitTorrent software included and will launch the separate BitTorrent application during BitTorrent downloads. You are able to import and export OPML files, a welcome addition to version 2.0. The podcatcher client has a file management system but requires manual intervention.

The podcatcher is simple and effective. iPodder remains one of the most favorite podcatcher applications and has a very active development team. Figure 2-2 shows the iPodder main operating screen.

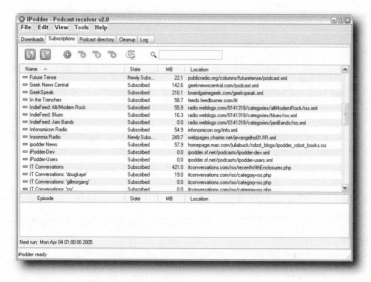

FIGURE 2-2: The iPodder operating screen.

jPodder

jPodder (beta version 8), at http://jpodder.com/, is being developed as open source and is free. This program supports both Windows Media Player and Apple iTunes. Figure 2-3 shows the jPodder main operating screen.

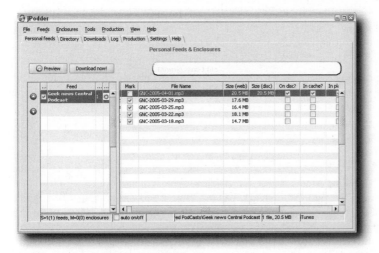

FIGURE 2-3: The jPodder operating screen.

jPodder uses a Java engine, but with that implementation, it can also be used on Linux machines. In my test, jPodder was the most processor-demanding podcatcher client. With jPodder, you can easily browse podcast listings and links through an internal active podcast directory. jPodder uses the iPodderX directory; the directory would be perfect if it connected to other podcast directories. You can search for topics of interest via the client, then subscribe to shows within the application.

The client is BitTorrent-capable and requires an external BitTorrent application. This program is capable of downloading more than one podcast at a time, and you can set the maximum number of podcasts to download at one time, so, when you are on a broadband connection, you can speed up your synchronization times.

One of the features I really like about jPodder is its display. The interface shows you which podcasts have been downloaded or are available for download from each subscribed show. One positive thing about this client is that it has an option to download a set number of podcasts on a feed-by-feed basis. This prevents the program from downloading 20 previous shows when you initially subscribe to a podcast.

What Is an ID3 Tag?

Most audio formats, whether they are MP3, WMA, or OGG, allow a small amount of text to be added to the file. The text includes extended information about what is on the audio file. If you have ever used Apple iTunes and right-clicked an audio file, you have seen a Get Info selection. Clicking that brings up the information the artist has chosen to include about the content. See this reference for more info: `http://id3.org/id3v1.html`.

The main thing missing from jPodder is media player file management. This is painful when you want to free up space on your mobile media device, because this program does not manage files it has already added to your mobile media device.

Nimiq

Nimiq (version 1.2), at `http://nimiq.nl/`, is a very simple podcatcher client. The client is free; it supports Windows Media Player and Apple iTunes. Nimiq has a built-in feed browser that is linked to an active podcast directory. You can browse and subscribe to a podcast directly from the client. Nimiq has a periodic scheduler that allows you to schedule how often you want it to check for new podcasts. If you are on a limited connection, it gives you the option to limit the number of downloads it does at one time, which is useful when subscribing to a site for the first time. Figure 2-4 shows the Nimiq main operating screen.

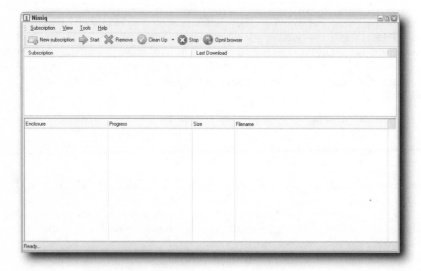

FIGURE 2-4: The Nimiq operating screen.

One feature I really like is Nimiq's ability to export and import subscriptions to and from an OPML file. This allows you to easily back up your subscribed feeds and to share what you are subscribed to with other people or different podcatchers.

This client, unlike others, has a BitTorrent client built into it, which eliminates the need to install a separate BitTorrent client. My only concern with Nimiq is that I have not found a way to turn off the seeding of the file once it is downloaded.

Podcatcher Software for Macs

With Windows users outnumbering Mac users, you would think there would be fewer clients available for the Mac platform, but this isn't the case. Some of the Windows clients have been ported to the Mac, and overall, most of the features are the same except done the Mac way. Having purchased a Mac Mini for the specific purpose of writing this book, it was not a big leap to see the differences and general similarities. The biggest difference I have seen thus far is that some of the Mac podcatcher clients are not free. In Table 2-3, I list the Mac podcatcher clients.

Table 2-3   Podcatcher Software (Mac)

Software Title	URL	Reviewed	Price
BashPodder	http://linc.homeunix.org:8080/scripts/bashpodder/	No	Free
iPodder	http://ipodder.sourceforge.net/index.php	Yes	Free
iPodderX	http://ipodderx.com/	Yes	$19.95
PlayPod	http://iggsoftware.com/playpod/	No	Free
POD2GO	http://kainjow.com/pod2go/	No	$12
PoddumFeeder	http://ifthensoft.com/poddumfeeder.html	Yes	$4.95
Podcast Tuner	http://podcasttuner.com/	No	Unknown

iPodderX

The iPodderX (version 2.2.8), at http://ipodderx.com/, for $19.95, is designed for the Mac and was tested using OS X. The program supports Apple iTunes. iPodderX is linked to its own active directory. This directory organization leaves a lot to be desired and doesn't lend itself well to finding new podcasts, as it doesn't employ subdirectories under major categories. I recommend that you use the Search function.

When I tried searching for my own feed, I couldn't find it, nor could I find it when browsing directly in the application. But when I went to the website via a web browser, the link to my show was listed on page 16 of the technology section.

They list the top 10 subscribed to shows on initial startup of a fresh install. This is a bit dubious in that it helps keep those shows listed in the top 10. Subscribing to shows manually is simple. It does have a feature that will copy new shows directly to the iTunes music folder and erase them from the iPodderX directory, but this doesn't eliminate anything or clean up all files in the list. Even though the program has some issues, it is still a very popular choice among Mac users. Figure 2-5 shows the iPodderX main screen.

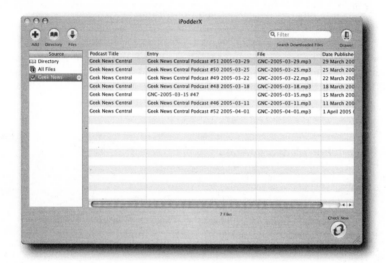

FIGURE 2-5: The iPodderX operating screen.

Honestly, for an application that isn't free, iPodderX is extremely far behind in development compared to its Windows counterparts. Response to the iPodderX support line went unanswered for over two weeks on simple questions.

PoddumFeeder

PoddumFeeder (version 1.11) is offered at http://ifthensoft.com/ for $4.95. I was very surprised when I reviewed this client, because I had not heard a lot about it. It is feature-packed and uses the http://iPodder.org active directory with an option to get extended info about a particular feed. It checks for new podcasts on a scheduled basis and comes with an option to convert all the MP3 downloads to AAC, which then allows people to bookmark sections of shows.

Note AAC is another audio format similar to MP3 with security and better sound quality at lower bit rates. In Chapter 4, I will discuss bit rates in detail. For a detailed definition of AAC, visit www. apple.com/mpeg4/aac/.

The client will automatically update iTunes and forces a synchronization of your iPod. You can import and export OPML files. At times, you will want to force an update on a single feed, and this application has that option. Something unique on this software application is that you can share a notable podcast and e-mail the embedded URL with a click of a button. This client is tightly integrated with iTunes. Overall, this is a terrific application and can be registered for $4.95. Figure 2-6 shows the main program screen.

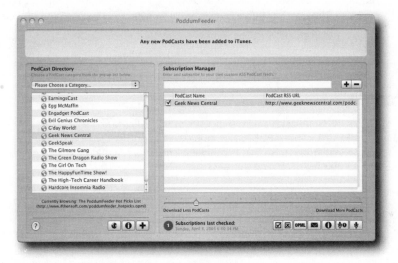

FIGURE 2-6: The PoddumFeeder operating screen.

Podcatcher Software for Linux

Many of the clients we have already discussed are Linux-capable and are at the same revision level as their Windows counterparts. There are several independent, open-source teams working on standalone Linux podcatcher clients. Because I am not a Linux guru, I am basing my review on the online documentation, reviews, and screen shots that were available. Linux users will want to visit these developers' websites for further information, as most of these programs are being developed as open source. Table 2-4 lists all sites that have or had active Linux podcatcher development.

Table 2-4   Podcatcher Software (Linux)

Software Title	URL	Reviewed	Price
Armangils Podcatcher	http://podcatcher.rubyforge.org/ No		Free
Bash iPodder	http://linc.homeunix.org:8080/scripts/bashpodder/	Yes	Free
CastGrab	http://fubarpa.com/projects/castgrab	No	Free
iPodder	http://ipodder.sourceforge.net/index.php	No	Free
jPodder	http://jpodder.com/	Yes	Free
Perl Podder	http://sourceforge.net/projects/perlpodder/	No	Free
PodGet	http://sourceforge.net/projects/podget/	No	Free

Bash iPodder

Bash iPodder (no version number) is a bare-bones podcatcher client. The support website (`http://linc.homeunix.org:8080/scripts/bashpodder/`) has detailed instructions on how to install the program so that even a new Linux user should be able to get the package installed and running.

Bash has an easy-to-use menu interface and is very self-explanatory. This program has one of the best online tutorials I have seen for installing and using the application. The application is lacking an active podcast directory to search, but I am told that that is forthcoming. You will have to use the resources at the end of this chapter to find podcasts. The application allows you to set up a cron job so that you can schedule downloads of subscribed shows as often as you want.

Note A *cron* job is a process that runs in all flavors of Unix. It scans a file that contains scheduled processes, then executes commands listed on a preconfigured schedule.

Bash supports BitTorrent, but you will need to have the Linux program `btdownload curses.py` installed. This is a very straightforward podcatcher client. Linux users will have to set the download path manually and then arrange through third-party applications to get the podcasts onto their mobile media devices. Figure 2-7 shows the main operating screen of the application.

jPodder Linux

The review for jPodder Linux is the same as that for the Windows version. You can find the application at `http://jpodder.com/`. The layout is the same as the Windows version. Obviously, it doesn't have support for Windows Media Player, so you will have to use third-party applications to get the downloaded podcast to your mobile media devices. You get all the regular features that are available in the Windows version. It is unclear how they have implemented BitTorrent support in this version. Figure 2-8 shows jPodder running on Linux.

FIGURE 2-7: The Bash iPodder Linux client.

FIGURE 2-8: jPodder Linux.

Podcatcher Software for Pocket PCs

Several existing Pocket PC applications that were originally designed to download news headlines from RSS-enabled websites have adapted their programs to support the downloading of podcasts and synchronization with a Pocket PC.

Listening to a podcast on a Pocket PC makes sense. With devices now able to accept larger external storage cards, they are well-suited to handle a day's worth of podcast. Pocket PCs serve as the perfect playback device for those who do not have a media player like the Apple iPod. Those who have wireless connectivity to their device can download new shows wirelessly, getting the latest shows from almost anywhere.

A word of caution: Check to see if the shows you subscribe to offer lower bit-rate files. If you are using a Pocket PCs or a mobile phone that has a Pocket PC embedded in it, you would not want the unit to download a 20 MB file and rack up untold connectivity charges.

As an alternative to using the following applications, if you are synchronizing from home or at work on a broadband connection, consider this: You can also use some of the regular podcatcher clients already reviewed versus using the following applications, because most of the podcatcher clients allow you to select the directory you want downloaded shows to be placed in. The Pocket PC's synchronization program allows files that are dumped to a specific directory on the desktop to be synchronized to your Pocket PC.

If your Pocket PC is not capable of synchronizing with a directory on your desktop, or you prefer the flexibility of having your subscriptions all on your Pocket PCs, try one of the applications listed in the following table. Table 2-5 outlines all Pocket PC podcatcher-capable applications.

Table 2-5   Podcatcher Software (Pocket PC)

Software Title	URL	Reviewed	Price
Egress	newsguy.com/GarishKernels/egress.html	Yes	$12
Feeder Reeder	feederreader.com/	No	Unknown
iPodderSP	equin.co.uk/ipoddersp/	No	$10
PIP	equin.co.uk/pip/	No	Unknown
Playlist Sync	freewareppc.com/multimedia/playlistsync.shtml	No	Free
PPC Tunes	pocketmac.net/products/ppctunes/	No	$9.95
iPodder for PPC	ipportunities.nl/wordpress/index.php?p=19	No	Free
PocketRSS	happyjackroad.net/pocketpc/pocketRSS/pocketRSS.asp	Yes	$5.95

Egress

Egress (version 2.0.2) is offered at http://newsguy.com/GarishKernels/egress. html for $12. I loaded Egress on my IPAQ Pocket PC and discovered a functional news aggregator with podcast download capability. Egress queues new podcasts automatically when you sync with your laptop or connect to a wireless network. They really thought this through. The podcatcher will download the podcast only after you click the file and authorize it to download the file. This gives you the opportunity not to download a file that is too big over your Pocket PC wireless connections. Figure 2-9 shows the Egress main operating screen.

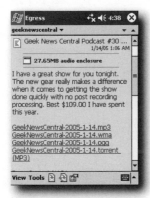

FIGURE 2-9: Egress Pocket PC
aggregator and podcatcher.

There is an additional option to set storage location, and I was able to indicate easily where the file should reside. I then used the Windows Media Player on the Pocket PC to play the podcast. The interface for navigating the news and podcast feeds is simple.

PocketRSS

PocketRSS (version 2.0.18) is offered at http://happyjackroad.net/pocketpc/ pocketRSS/pocketRSS.asp for $5.95. It is a feature-rich Pocket PC news aggregator and podcatcher. This small application is packed with features. I was surprised when I found an option to import an OPML file. This option allows you to load hundreds of podcast feeds automatically; after the shows are downloaded, they can be stored on the Pocket PC memory stick.

The interface was completely manageable by the buttons on the screen—a big plus. I hate having to open pull-down windows to make a selection. One of the main features I liked was that I could select on a site-by-site basis which sites I wanted to enable the podcast support for. I was also able to set a maximum file size that would be downloaded automatically, which prevents downloading a 20 MB podcast while connected to commercial wireless service. The program needs no further prompting to download the podcast, in contrast to Egress. Overall, I was very impressed by PocketRSS. Figure 2-10 shows the main screen of the PocketRSS.

FIGURE 2-10: Pocket RSS aggregator and podcatcher.

Aggregators

Up to this point, we have been talking about podcatcher applications. The previously reviewed Pocket PC applications are a sort of combination news aggregator and podcatcher. The traditional news aggregators that I will review now have been updated to support the automatic downloads of podcasts.

These existing software applications have had additional code added to make them do what the standalone podcatcher clients can do minus a lot of the features.

To avoid confusion, the applications I am about to review are dual-purpose applications. For those of you that have never used a news aggregator, I will explain their function.

In the same way podcatcher clients download podcast files by reading information contained in a RSS file, news aggregators downloads news by extracting different information from the same RSS file and displaying it on the software interface in human-readable format. This allows people to read a large number of websites without ever physically visiting the site. If you have never used a news aggregator before, I recommend that you give one a try.

The following applications all have trial versions; each present the information in their own unique ways and your decision to stick with one or the other will depend on personal preference.

In Table 2-6, I list only those news aggregators that have added the ability to download podcasts.

Table 2-6   News Aggregators (Podcast Download–Capable)

Software Title	OS	URL	Review	Price
BlogMatrix Sparks	Windows, Mac, and Linux	http://sparks.blogmatrix.com/	Yes	Free
FeedDemon	Windows	http://bradsoft.com/	Yes	$29.95
NewsGator Outlook Edition	Windows	http://newsgator.com/ngs/default.aspx	Yes	$29
NewzCrawler	Windows	http://newzcrawler.com/	No	$24.95

BlogMatrix Sparks

BlogMatrix Sparks (version 2.0), at `http://sparks.blogmatrix.com/`, is free. This application is unique: it's more than a podcatcher. BlogMatrix Sparks has been designed to be a podcast recorder, podcast publisher, podcatcher, news aggregator, streaming audio receiver, and much more.

The author's goal is to build an application that does it all. Quite honestly, I had a hard time classifying this application, as it almost deserves a category of its own. The development of this application indicates where a lot of developers are headed as they try to create all-in-one solutions. By my basic description, you see that the application can do a lot more than download podcasts.

In the context of its performance as a podcatcher, BlogMatrix Sparks supports both Apple iTunes and Windows Media Player. It runs on Windows, Mac, and Linux. The application has a prebuilt directory, and you can import your own or other OPML files. It is lacking in management of the files it has downloaded, but overall the application is very robust. Figure 2-11 shows BlogMatrix Sparks opened to the Podcatcher window.

For those of you who want the convenience of listening to streaming audio when you are connected to the Internet in front of a computer and then listening to a podcast later on the go, this program would be a natural extension. It is in active development and the interface needs improvement, but so far, it's made a great start.

FIGURE 2-11: BlogMatrix Sparks Podcatcher window.

FeedDemon

FeedDemon (version 1.5), at `http://bradsoft.com/`, sells for $29.95. This is one of the most popular commercial news aggregators on the market and is a feature-rich application. FeedDemon was one of the first commercial news aggregators to implement podcast-download support. FeedDemon supports automatic updates to your media player and works with both Windows Media Player and Apple iTunes. You may visit sites and read the news, but if you don't want to listen to their podcasts, you can specify on a site-by-site basis whether you want the application to automatically download podcasts.

This aggregator has a separate download client, appropriately called FeedStation. Within FeedStation, you can configure where your files will be stored and which media player to use. Those of you already using FeedDemon have all the tools you need to start downloading podcasts immediately (see Figure 2-12).

NewsGator

NewsGator (version 2.0.3), at `http://newsgator.com/ngs/default.aspx`, is available for $29. NewsGator is a unique news aggregator in that it is designed to work within Microsoft Outlook—you read the news as you would regular e-mail. As you can see by the screen shot, the podcast is downloaded and displayed as a regular file attachment. Unlike FeedDemon, it does not support any media player, so you have to manually manipulate the file.

NewsGator has a unique service that synchronizes what you read via Outlook and a web-based news aggregator service. This enables you to leave your computer at home and go to work and not read the same news twice. The premium services they offer are quite expensive. If you like Outlook and don't mind manipulating the way the files are added to your media player, this would be a good fit for you. Otherwise, it does not automate the process used to get a podcast onto a mobile media device. Figure 2-13 shows the NewsGator main operating page.

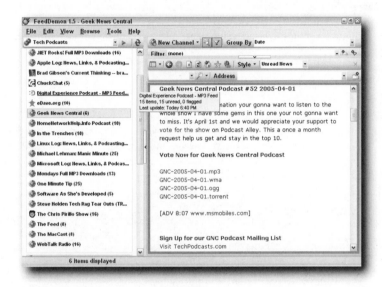

FIGURE 2-12: FeedDemon RSS aggregator.

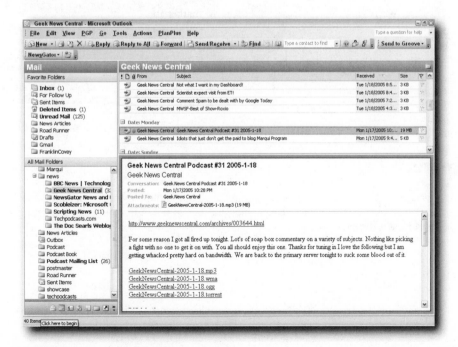

FIGURE 2-13: NewsGator main operating page.

Smart Phones

I did not have a smart phone to test, and to date, there is only one software package available for owners of smart phones — iPodderSP. You can find that software at `http://equin.co.uk/ipoddersp`. I recommend that you check with `http://podcastalley.com/software` to determine whether further developments have been made with smart phone podcatcher clients.

Podcatcher Resources

Phew! You've gotten a lot of information about the software you need to download and enjoy podcasts. Table 2-7 lists some resources to help you gather more information on the podcatchers that are out there.

Table 2-7   Podcatcher Websites

Site Name	Purpose	URL
Podcast Alley	Podcatcher user forums	http://www.podcastalley.com/phpBB2/index.php
iPodderX	Mac iPodderX support forum	http://ipodderx.com:16080/forum/
Doppler	Doppler support forum	http://forum.dopplerradio.net/
iPodder Dev	iPodder devleopment team	http://groups.yahoo.com/group/ipodder-dev/
Podcasters	User/Podcaster discussion	http://groups.yahoo.com/group/podcasters/
Tech Podcasters	Tech-based podcast discussion	http://groups.yahoo.com/group/techpodcasts/
Software	Podcatcher client list	http://ipodder.org/directory/4/ipodderSoftware
Software	Podcatcher client list	www.podcastalley.com/software

Summary

In this chapter, I covered the basics of podcatcher clients and their various features. We all want the podcasting experience to be an enjoyable one, so not only should the podcast be good, so should the software.

Let's review some minimum features for PC users:

- An active directory so that you can find podcasts quickly with up-to-date lists.
- The ability to import other people's play lists with the Import OPML feature.
- The capability to clean up old shows and manage your downloaded podcast.
- Support for Windows Media Player and Apple iTunes.

Those of you using Pocket PC will want these features:

- The client package must be able to limit downloads by file size.
- The client must be easy to navigate.
- The client must offer you the ability to easily change storage locations.

I want to leave you with this thought. Although my standard news aggregator is on the reviews list, I still use a standalone podcatcher client to control my subscriptions more closely. Thus, I have a news aggregator for news and a podcatcher for podcasting. Obviously, for downloading podcasts, all you need is the podcatcher software. In the next chapter, I walk you through the process of getting a podcatcher client set up and some podcasts onto your mobile media device.

Whether you are a Windows, Mac, Linux, Pocket PC, or smart phone user, there is a way today to automate the loading of podcasts onto almost every mobile device. In the next chapter, we discuss how to use these podcatcher clients.

Finding and Subscribing to Podcasts

It's time to subscribe to some podcasts to start enjoying content on your computer or your MP3 player. This chapter takes a close look at several of the podcast directories available. I will provide you with a comprehensive list of those directories so that you can find the podcast you want to listen to quickly. I will walk you through the set-up of a few of the popular podcatcher clients. With the enormous number of shows available, I will give you some tips on avoiding podcast overload and some tips on managing all those subscriptions. I will talk about various portable media devices and discuss limitations and future growth challenges.

I am about to empower you and get you tapped into the power of the Podcast Revolution so that you can enjoy the power of walkaway content.

Finding Podcasts

With any new innovation, enablers jump in to help consumers organize information and create content. Scores of individuals have set up websites to list, categorize, rank, and review podcasts. A significant number of sites are developing lists of podcasts. Some of these sites simply duplicate information found on other sites, but they present a lot of great content and present those podcasts in unique ways.

Each person has his or her own hobbies and interests. All of us have our own listening preferences. Podcast topics span from agriculture to wine. Some of the more popular categories include technology, music, politics, movie reviews, sex, comedy, and computer gaming. New podcasts are starting on a regular basis.

Top-Level Podcast Directories

The podcast directories are the best place to begin looking for shows that may interest you. Two of my favorites are covered in the following sections. A comprehensive list of additional directories is available at the end of this section.

iPodder.org

iPodder.org (`http://ipodder.org`) is the original website that Adam Curry started to centralize information about podcasting. This site continues to be one of the central points to which new podcasters go to have their shows added to the primary directory others build from. The iPodder.org directory is maintained by podcasters, but is owned by Adam's commercial company; Adam assigns volunteers to specific categories to maintain the site listings, ensuring that links stay up-to-date and that new podcasts are categorized correctly. The number of people dedicated to maintaining the site is amazing. Figure 3-1 shows the main page of the iPodder.org website.

FIGURE 3-1: The main page at iPodder.org.

The iPodder.org main page always has a listing of new shows and information about what is happening in the podcasting scene. This page is maintained by Adam Curry, and typically, he links all the new shows. If you are using a news aggregator, you will want to subscribe to the page content (`http://ipodder.org/xml/rss.xml`) so that you can see what new shows are available.

Note As I discussed in Chapter 2, if you haven't yet started using a news aggregator, I would encourage you to try out my favorite aggregator—FeedDemon, at `http://feeddemon.com`—or search Google for "list of news aggregators." You will find a variety of aggregators available today.

Those of you not using an aggregator will want to visit the site often because there is new content daily. The iPodder.org site's content is highly dynamic. To get a quick look at new shows, you should scan through the main page before progressing to the categorized directory. Figure 3-2 shows the actual category listings available at `http://ipodder.org/directory/4/podcasts/categories`.

FIGURE 3-2: iPodder category listings.

As you can see, the page lists categories for different show subjects. If you find a podcast on the Internet and it isn't listed in a particular category, be sure to encourage the podcaster to get it listed. That said, this category list is not inclusive; Adam will add categories as new types of shows are produced. With the wide variety of shows and limited information available about each show, you will have to do a little research at this site to find shows that interest you. Figure 3-3 shows the Technology/General News listing.

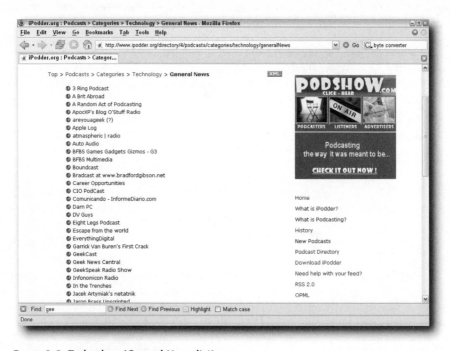

FIGURE 3-3: Technology/General News listing.

I drilled down into the Technology sublisting located at `http://ipodder.org/directory/4/podcasts/categories/technology/generalNews` and found 65 + podcasts from which to choose.

If you go to `http://ipodder.org/directory/4/podcasts/categories/technology`, you will find that the technology category is broken down into more subsections to include new technology, operating systems, podcasting, smart phones, software, text-speech, usability, and website builders. The managers of the directory have done a great job of categorizing the podcast listings.

Keep in mind that this directory is just a big list with no details. It has only the show name or site name with links to the respective RSS files. To find details on a show, you will need to visit the referenced site directly, but because of the structure of this list you may not even be able to find the home page of the show in question. Often times, the show's RSS feed is hosted by a third party. So you may have to do a Google search on the site's show name. Thus far, I have been able to find original home pages of every site I looked for that way. This list is great for people who generally know what they are looking for, but it isn't useful for finding specific information.

The globe by the name of the show has the link to the RSS feed. If you are using Internet Explorer, you can right-click the globe and select Capture shortcut. This will capture the podcast RSS feed URL, which enables you to paste it into your podcatcher software client. In Firefox, my browser of choice, right-click and choose Copy link location.

If you want to stay abreast of the changes to any specific category listings, you can add category-specific RSS feeds to your news aggregator by capturing the link to the XML icon on each page. At the top of the page is the orange and white button with XML stamped on it. That file is linked to the raw OPML that contains all the listings on the specific page you have loaded. By capturing and adding this link to your news aggregator, you will essentially be subscribing to all the shows in the list. What's even more fun is if you choose to save that linked file versus copying the location. That way, you can import the file into your podcatcher using the Import OPML feature, which will subscribe you to all the shows at once.

Podcast Alley

Podcast Alley (http://podcastalley.com) is one of my favorite directories. The creator is innovative, and under his leadership, the site has evolved to be the leading podcast directory. Podcast Alley was the first directory that allowed listeners to make centralized publicly viewable comments about shows. The site also allows fans and podcasters alike to vote once a month for shows they support. The owner of the site says he sees tens of thousands of daily hits. Most importantly, the site was also the first to provide information about each show in the directory. Rumor has it that he will be adding a subscription module where you can build custom subscriptions.

If you want detailed information about a podcast before subscribing, this is the site to stop at first. The interface allows you to see detailed information about each podcast, such as how many people have voted for it.

Not only that, the site has regular categorized listings that allow you to drill down and find the specific category you are looking for. A lot of great shows are waiting to be discovered. Just because a site is in the Top 50 list doesn't mean it's the best podcast; it only means that the listeners have voted. I've found great shows from digging into the listings and viewing the show details. Figure 3-4 shows the Podcast Alley main page.

FIGURE 3-4: Podcast Alley main page.

Not only does this site have an extensive directory, but it also has interviews with podcasters, and it showcases a new site every week. One of the best features of the site is the weekly featured podcast site where the featured podcaster answers questions that site administrator Chris McIntyre has put together.

The site also features a message board where you can talk about shows and podcasting in general. Resources are being added to the site on a regular basis. The site administrator takes greater care than other site administrators in that he makes sure each and every show listed has a valid website link and compliant RSS feed. Figure 3-5 shows a detailed listing of my site's entry.

What I like about the detailed site info is that the description is provided by the owner registering the site. Then Chris actually pulls data via the podcaster's RSS feed and imports that information from every website. Thus, you can see the latest show information on each and every podcast including show notes. You can even listen to podcasts from this main screen. Features are being added weekly, so be sure to check out Podcast Alley.

Using Topic-Specific Directories

Emerging sites are focusing on specific topics. Podcasters are forming alliances, or, as I like to call them, umbrella groups, to build subject-specific sites and support one another. Several have already formed; the Association of Music Podcasting and Tech Podcasts Network have organized associations. Figure 3-6 shows the Association of Music Podcasting (www.music podcasting.com).

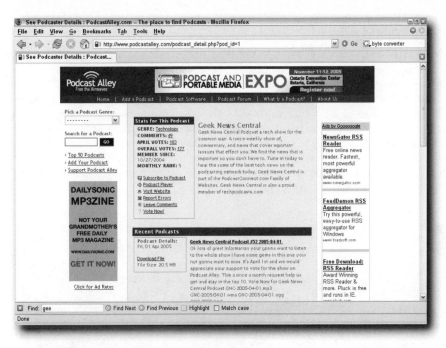

FIGURE 3-5: Podcast Alley detailed listing of my site.

FIGURE 3-6: Association of Music Podcasting.

The AMP has gathered a group of like-minded music podcasters who are dedicated to promoting independent labels.

Techpodcasts.com (`http://techpodcasts.com`) is a website where those interested in technology can review a centralized directory of technology podcasts covering a wide variety of topics. You will find detailed descriptions of the shows, biographies of the affiliates, and a calendar of scheduled tech podcast releases. The site imports participants' show notes and has links to their sites. In addition, many of the tech podcasters are available to help individuals and groups launch their own podcasts. Members provide feedback and advice to fellow members. As I am a member of the website, I do have some bias about the site's usefulness, but overall, it is great to see what can be accomplished when a group of like-minded people work together and share common values and goals that will attract sponsors and underwriters. Figure 3-7 shows the front page of their extensive site.

FIGURE 3-7: Tech Podcasts Network,

Exploring Podcast Directories

Each of the directories online today has something a little different to offer, so I encourage you to visit each of the following directories. The majority of podcast sites work very hard to bring you detailed information.

- **iPodder (`http://ipodder.org`):** A decentralized list of podcasts broken down into categories. Daily announcements of new shows and information on the podcasting scene. The majority of podcatcher applications use this list as their master directory.

- **Podcast Alley (`http://podcastalley.com`):** A directory with detailed show information, voting, comments, and show notes, with a great forum area.

- **Podcast Net (`http://podcasting.net`):** A standard directory that relies on tags and categories to organize podcast listings.

- **iPodderX (`http://ipodderx.com/directory`):** A top-level directory with no sub-categories, which results in hundreds of shows listed in a particular category. Primarily used with the iPodderX podcatcher application.

- **Podcast Directory (`http://podcastdirectory.com`):** Has nearly 300 sub-categories, which allows listeners to hone in on subject-specific podcasts. Unfortunately, there is no search function, so it is almost impossible to find specific shows. Otherwise, a decent directory.

- **Podcast Bunker (`http://podcastbunker.com`):** The Bunker reviews each show before it allows it into the directory. If the show does not meet the site's standards, it is not added. Typically, I have found that the podcasts listed are of superior quality.

- **Tech Podcasts (`http://techpodcasts.com`):** If it's tech, it's here. You will find the top tech podcasts on this site. Every podcast is work- and child-safe.

- **Music Podcast Association (`http://musicpodcasting.org`):** A list of music podcasts that play nothing but independent music.

Using Podcatcher Software

In Chapter 2, I reviewed some of the podcatcher clients. In this section, I walk you through the process of setting up several of the podcatcher clients that we reviewed in Chapter 2.

Doppler

If you have not downloaded and installed Doppler, you need to do so (`http://doppler radio.net`) in order to follow the steps outlined here. After you install the application, I will walk you through setting up default settings and subscribing to a new podcast. Figure 3-8 shows the window that is displayed upon running the Doppler program.

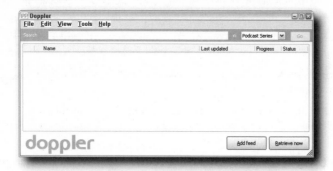

FIGURE 3-8: Doppler startup window.

As you can see, the initial startup page is fairly basic, but looks can be deceiving. This screen has a Search feature, and buttons for adding and retrieving feeds. But first you must set the default options.

Step 1: Setting Options on the Main Screen

Start by clicking Tools and then Options. Figure 3-9 shows the main tab in the Options menu that you just opened.

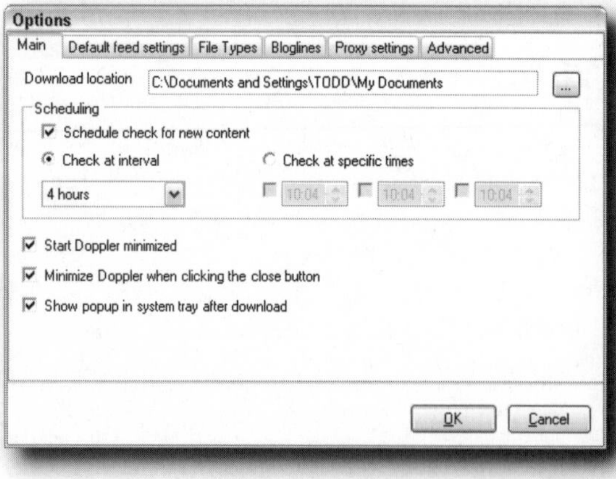

FIGURE 3-9: Primary Options menu.

The Differences between RSS Feeds and Regular Web Pages

As you get ready to subscribe to a podcast, it's important that you understand what a Real Simple Syndication (RSS) feed is. These podcatcher clients all have an Add feed menu item. If you add a feed manually and try to use the podcast's main website URL versus the RSS 2.0 feed link, the application will oftentimes not even allow you to save the entry, let alone download the podcast automatically.

Luckily, the majority of podcatcher applications have built-in podcast directories, so this will be a concern only when you are manually adding a podcast to your subscription list. The raw data contained in a RSS 2.0 file, as shown in the following figure, is the language that podcatcher applications require.

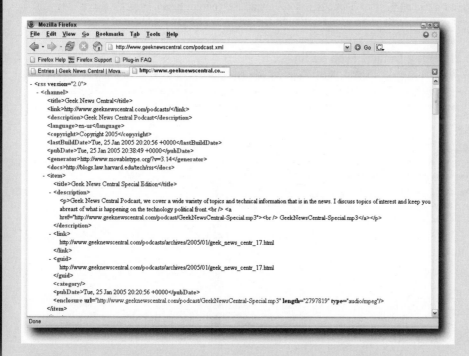

You don't need to worry about the structure of this RSS feed now. But it's obvious that this isn't something you would read in your web browser. I wanted to show you an example of RSS information; we all know what a website looks like.

Thus, it is important, as we discussed in Chapter 1, that you look for the white-on-orange icons on the sites you are visiting to find the links to the RSS feed that you will need to add shows manually to your podcatcher application. You can look at my RSS, MP3 feed at http://geeknewscentral.com/podcast.xml.

On the Main screen, you need to determine how often you want the application to poll the sites you subscribe to. Think about this carefully. Every time you scan a site, you are using its bandwidth; so if your computer is running autonomously at home while you are at work, you can save the podcasters some bandwidth and schedule Doppler to check for new feeds every 8 to 12 hours.

Note You should keep an eye on hard drive space on the drive that you indicated for all downloads to be sent to. Depending on the number of podcasts you subscribe to, you could end up with several gigs of shows within a couple of weeks.

Caution If you change the default download location after you have downloaded some podcasts, then you must move the content of the old directories to the new location. So, you should do your best to pick a drive that has the most available free space. If you change the download directory and don't move all the files, Doppler will download the content again. Doppler also allows you to override these settings on a feed-by-feed basis, which will be covered later in this section.

Step 2: Setting Default Feed Settings

Figure 3-10 shows the Default Feed Settings tab. By choosing a maximum number of podcasts to download, you will avoid downloading the past 15 shows a site has produced. This can prevent you from getting content that could be weeks or even months old.

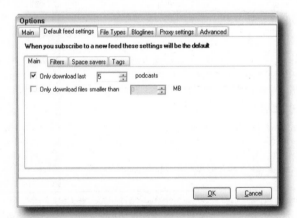

FIGURE 3-10: Default Feed settings.

In some cases, you will want all of a site's content because the content may contain music reviews and so on. You can revise this setting on a feed-by-feed basis (covered later in this section).

Most shows run between 5 and 25 MB, so choose wisely if you fill in the Only download files smaller than box. This feature comes in handy when you are traveling or if you are on a limited connection.

Step 3: Setting Space Savers, Filters, and Tags

One of the most powerful features of Doppler is the Space Saver option shown in Figure 3-11. Enabling Space Saver allows Doppler to clean up after itself. Most podcatcher clients don't offer this feature. Because I download a large number of podcasts, I set up Doppler to remove files older than 15 days. I also have it remove the listings from my media player so that when I sync my MP3 player, the files are also removed from my portable media device.

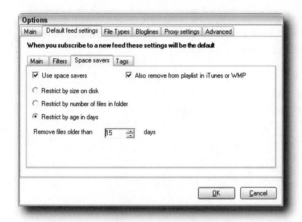

FIGURE 3-11: Default Options: Space Savers.

If you want to limit shows that are downloaded to keyword association only, from information contained in the written podcast post or show notes that are embedded in the RSS 2.0 feed, you can use the Filter tab. Be forewarned: entering a word or phrase will limit downloads to an exact match. I would use this feature with great caution!

Because there is no set standard and podcasters have not had a reference book such as this to consult, many new podcasters put strange information in their ID3 tags when they produce their shows. Doppler offers a Tag tab so you can adjust settings as needed. This allows you to manage what is added to either Apple iTunes or Windows Media Player.

Note   ID3 tags contain the embedded information inside MP3 files that allows your media player to display the artist, genre, album name, track number, and so on displayed on your media player.

I like to build play lists for my media player based on Genre tags, so in the Genre setting I enter the word "podcast." This ensures that I'll be able to find all podcasts easily in my media player and my mobile media device if I decide that I want to do some preliminary cleanup before Doppler does it for me.

Step 4: Setting File Types

Doppler is flexible enough to allow updates to both Apple iTunes and Windows Media Player. In Figure 3-12, you see two windows. In the first, I opened the File Types tab, then I opened the overlapping window with the MP3 extension selection information; I selected both Apple iTunes and Windows Media Player. This allows me to synchronize my Apple iPod with Apple iTunes and my Samsung Yepp with Windows Media Player. This way, my wife can listen to content she wants to on her MP3 player, and I get to listen to my own.

Note   To date, I have seen podcasts that are produced in MP3, WAV, OGG, and WMA, as well as other formats, including a couple that are sending video via MOV format. So you may have to add a format based on the types of content you are subscribed to.

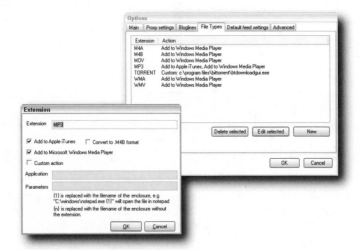

FIGURE 3-12: Default Options: File Types.

Step 5: Setting Bloglines

Bloglines is an online news aggregator (http://bloglines.com). If you use this service and have categorized all of your podcast feeds, you can synchronize your bloglines feed with Doppler, as shown in Figure 3-13.

Finally, you can make changes to the two remaining tabs that we have not displayed.

- **Proxy Settings tab:** For those of you running Doppler behind a proxy server, you can enter your proxy information on the Proxy Settings tab.

- **Advanced Settings tab:** There is an option that enables you to select the number of concurrent downloads, a logging option, and a selection on what to do when the application encounters duplicate files.

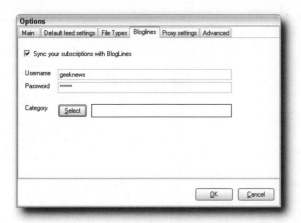

FIGURE 3-13: Default Options: Bloglines.

Click OK to close the Options window. It is now time to find and subscribe to a podcast.

Step 6: Searching for and Adding a Feed

I know all of you will want to listen to the *Geek News Central* podcast, so I have shown you the way, by searching for "Geek News." When the main screen opens in Doppler, you type **Geek News** in the Search box. Doppler queries the directory and locates the show, along with a number of others. Highlight it and click Subscribe Selected. This will add the feed to the main window. Figure 3-14 displays the results of these steps.

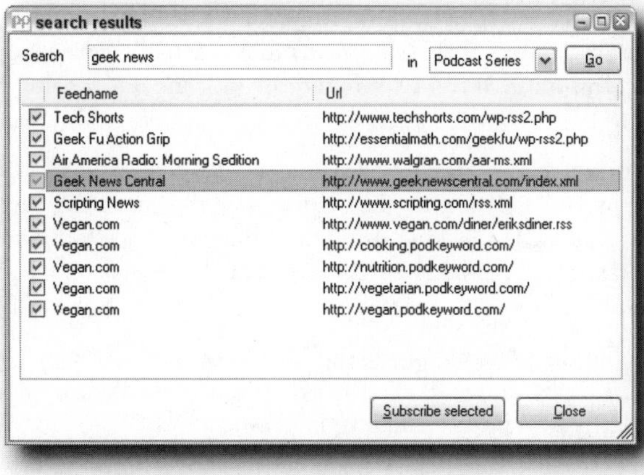

FIGURE 3-14: Search and subscribe.

To add shows manually, you click the Add feed button on the Main screen. A menu pops up, called the Feed screen (see Figure 3-15).

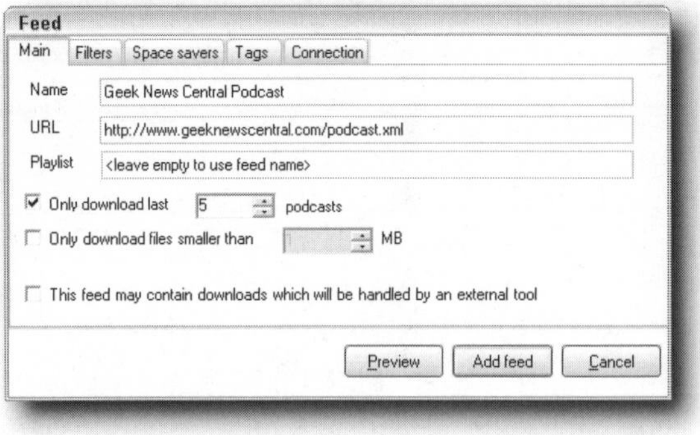

FIGURE 3-15: Feed window.

This window looks a little like the Tools Options window, but it isn't. Doppler enables you to make changes on a feed-by-feed basis to the default settings you have already configured This allows you great flexibility in the configuration if you want to change a single feed's settings.

The Preview function will actually download a small segment of the latest podcast and play it in your default media player on your computer. This allows you to sample a minute or so of the podcast before subscribing.

In many cases, you will have checked out the podcaster's website before you subscribe. Or, if a friend provides you with a link, you may just want to add the link manually. Sometimes you will have to look around the page to try and find the link. It may not always be a RSS 2.0 icon and could be text. Because I offer four different types of media files, I actually have independent RSS feeds for each file type. In Figure 3-16 I have found the link and am copying the location.

In the Firefox browser window, I right-clicked the link and selected Copy link location, then I pasted that URL for the RSS file into the URL entry in Figure 3-15; thus, I do not have to use the directory built into Doppler to add feeds. Clicking Add Feed brings you back to Figure 3-17, which is the main screen. You can see that the podcast has been added.

If you are online, go ahead and click Retrieve Now. Doppler will download the newest podcast or the number you have indicated in the preferences and add those podcasts to the play list of Windows Media Player or Apple iTunes. Apple iPod users just need to sync their iPods and the downloaded file with their playlist will be uploaded to the iPod.

Windows Media Player users need to choose which play list to synchronize to their MP3 players. Add the show's play list to your sync settings, and let windows synchronize your device.

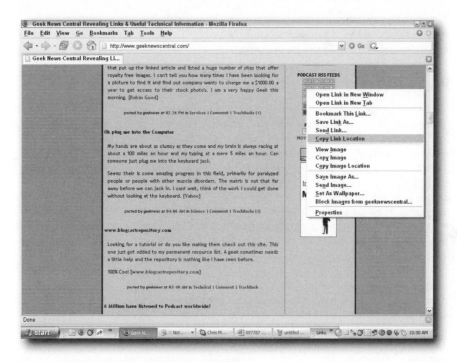

FIGURE 3-16: RSS link being copied from website.

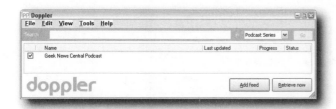

FIGURE 3-17: Success—your first subscription.

Note If you do not know how to synchronize your portable media device, please consult your operator's manual or visit your respective manufacturer to find the correct procedure.

At any rate, almost every portable media device being sold today can be synchronized.

Note Doppler does not synchronize your MP3 player. Windows Media Player and Apple iTunes do.

From the Doppler Main window, you can check to see what has been posted on the websites you have subscribed to. If you double-click the description of *Geek News Central*, a window will open with the show notes from the website.

iPodder Version 2.0

iPodder 2.0 brings to the table the same level of excellence as Doppler in terms of popularity and features. There are Windows and Mac editions; plus the fact that it is free helps the popularity contest. This application probably accounts for the majority of the downloads I see in my log files. Until version 2.0 was released, it did not support Windows Media Player, but with the release of version 2.0, it now supports both Apple iTunes and Windows Media Player.

Note Because there are both Windows and Mac versions available, and the basic functions for both operating systems are nearly the same, I only review the Windows version; the only real difference is that the skins have been changed to reflect the differences between operating systems. Those of you who are Mac users should try this client in addition to the clients I review later in this section.

You can download the iPodder software at `http://ipodder.sourceforge.net/index.php`. After you have installed iPodder, start the application. Figure 3-18 shows the default startup window.

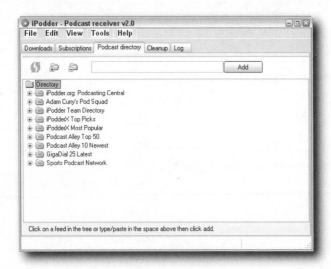

FIGURE 3-18: iPodder version 2.0 Startup window.

Step 1: Configuring General Settings in iPodder

The tabbed layout is very clean. All of the controls have dialog boxes tied to them. Select File ⇨ Preferences so that you can configure the client. Figure 3-19 shows the Preferences window.

FIGURE 3-19: General Preferences tab.

You can choose to have the program load at startup, and minimize. You should choose your download folder location. A nice feature is that iPodder will watch your hard-drive space, and you can set the level at which you want it to stop downloading.

Step 2: Configuring Thread Settings

Click Threading to bring up the window shown in Figure 3-20.

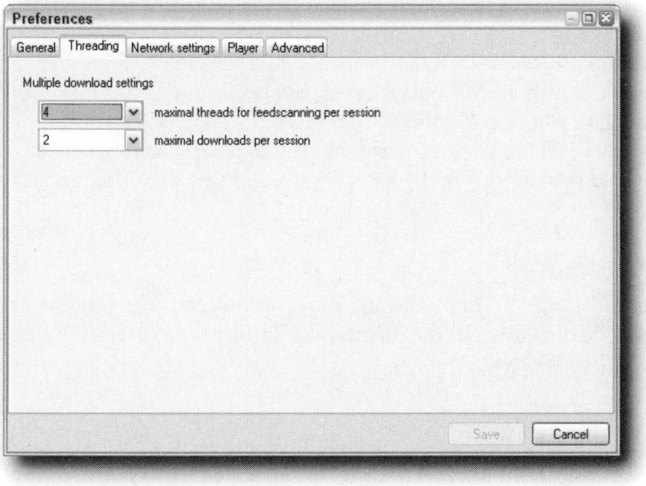

FIGURE 3-20: Threading preference level.

You can select the maximum number of feeds it scans at a time along with the maximum number of downloads at one time. Dial-up users will likely want to set Maximum downloads per session to one. The Network setting tab is for those who may have to use a proxy server, and you can enter that proxy server information in that window.

Step 3: Configuring Player Settings in iPodder

Click Player Settings on the Preference tab, and you will see the windows displayed in Figure 3-21.

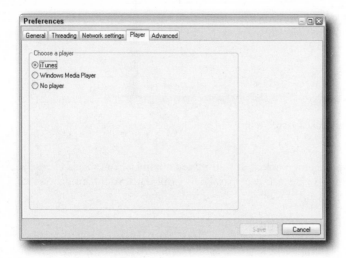

FIGURE 3-21: The Player Selection window.

The selections are pretty straightforward. Choose which media player you would like to use or none at all. Even if you do not own an MP3 player, these applications can still make your life much more enjoyable, because you can download programs to listen to when you choose with the media player of your choice. The Advance tab allows you to enter a command-line entry to run after each audio file download. Click the Save button, and this will bring us back to the main screen.

Step 4: Subscribing to a Podcast

You can view all podcast directories listed by clicking the Directory tab. The window in Figure 3-22 opens. Subscribe directly from the directory or add a podcast website's RSS 2.0 feed directly into the Add feed window.

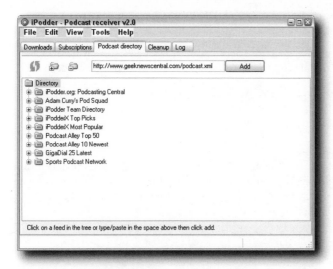

FIGURE 3-22: Directory window.

In version 2.0 the iPodder team added a significant number of new directories, and I anticipate over time they will add more. After you add a feed, the Subscription window opens. Figure 3-23 shows the Subscription window.

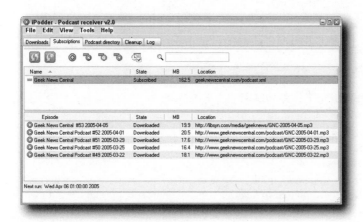

FIGURE 3-23: The Subscription window.

The Subscription window shows you all the shows that are currently subscribed to and the location of the download.

The check mark indicates what you have selected to be downloaded. You will notice that it gives you the location of the file and the size of the file that will be downloaded.

Note You do not have to manually intervene after this point because the client will automatically download all new shows.

Step 5: Downloading Files

The Download window, shown in Figure 3-24, shows you the progress of the download while the file is being downloaded and the status of downloaded files. Upon completion of a download, Apple iTunes will automatically open, and you will see that the show and file have been added to the program's play list.

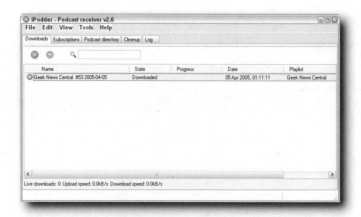

FIGURE **3-24:** The Download window.

A cleanup function is a new feature in iPodder version 2.0.

Using the Cleanup Window

iPodder has the best Cleanup window I have seen to date. This interface gives you the option to save a show of interest as opposed to deleting it based on a set date. The Cleanup window allows you to go through each of your shows and check which of the files you want removed from iTunes. In addition, it also removes files from your hard drive. Figure 3-25 shows the Cleanup window.

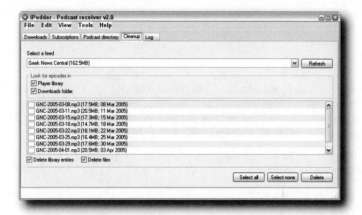

FIGURE 3-25: Cleanup window.

Using Media Player Play Lists and Your MP3 Player

Some of you have huge music collections, and often keeping music collections organized can be difficult. With the help of Compact Disk Database (CDDB), you generally are presented with all kinds of information about a specific music track. Many applications will actually connect to the Internet and automatically update the information about a particular song and even download album art.

This is not the case with podcasts. No database contains master information about each show. In fact, it is not even practical, because many times you are getting the podcast shortly after it was created. So, as you are browsing your downloaded podcast you may see a wide disparity in the information that the producer of the podcast has provided.

Podcasters have to populate their own ID3 tags, and believe me no one has standardized what they should be putting in these ID3 tag fields. You may find that some new podcasters are not entering anything into the ID3 fields during their postproduction process. Thus you end up with incomplete information in your media player information fields. This is why I have found it beneficial to use the Doppler option that updates the ID3 tag once it is downloaded by naming the genre to something that allows you to keep your soon-to-be fast-growing library of podcasts organized.

Because podcasts come in a variety of show lengths, and no one adheres to a standard bit rate, shows can range from 500K to 25 MB. Depending on the storage size of your portable media device, you will have to pay attention to what is on it and clean it from time to time. Fortunately, the pricing for high-storage devices is on the decline.

If you are using Doppler or iPodder v 2.0, the management of show files is easier. Most of the podcatcher developers have realized that they need to improve their podcatcher clients so that they clean up after themselves.

Using iTunes

Apple has a unique place in today's marketplace. The Apple iPod and the Apple iTunes media player are joined at the hip. Popularized by both Mac and Windows users, many Windows users use iTunes not just because they have an iPod but because they may be buying music online from Apple, and of course Apple packages this on their Mac products,

For those of you with iPods, Apple iTunes will already be joined at the hip and you have very little to do but manage your subscriptions.

Figure 3-26 shows how play lists are arranged in Apple iTunes after Doppler has automatically inserted the play list.

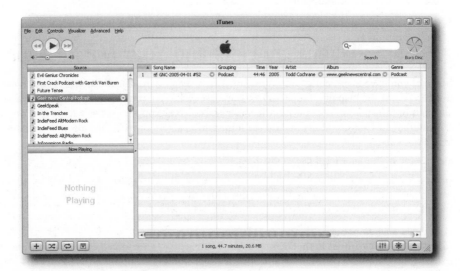

FIGURE 3-26: Apple iTunes typical podcast play list.

Because I sample a lot of shows, my play list can run 100 entries. This can result in a lot of podcasts being stored on my hard drive and added to my portable media device. So I simply create some playlist rules to make it easier to navigate after the podcasts are loaded on my iPod.

Additionally I have my music selection loaded, so being able to find podcast listings in the library is crucial to making sure that the podcatcher clients do not leave any files in the library after the cleanup process. Figure 3-27 shows a typical Apple iTunes library.

FIGURE 3-27: iTunes Library.

If your podcatcher client does not clean up after itself, you will need to remove shows manually after you have listened to them. As I write this, most of the clients do not clean up after themselves, so keep this in mind, or you could start running out of hard-drive space and room on your portable media device. You will see that genre shown in Figure 3-27 is primarily podcast. I have seen podcasts labeled Podcast, Speech, Talk, Other, and Show. The genre can also be blank.

 Note Depending on the iTunes Preferences settings, when you remove files from the Library, iTunes may not delete the files from your hard drive, so you may have to do this manually. You can do this by searching out old files with " * . * " and setting a modified date parameter. Then run that search in the top-level podcast storage folder. This will locate all files older than the prescribed date, and then you can simply remove them from the hard drive

 Caution Deleting files from the play list shown in Figure 3-26 will not remove them from the library displayed in Figure 3-27. Those of you with portable media devices with lower amounts of memory will have to pay particular attention to the management of your files as you probably already do with music.

Using Windows Media Player

My wife and I each have our own MP3 players, and because she is not a geek I synchronize her MP3 player from selections on Windows Media Player. I synchronize my selections to my iPod via iTunes. Figure 3-28 shows a typical podcast play list in Windows Media Player.

FIGURE 3-28: Windows Media Player play list.

Your media player's storage limit will determine whether you sync all the play list or pick and choose with the synchronization manager. Figure 3-29 shows a postsynchronization of my iRiver IFP-790.

Most of the MP3 players that are recognized by a USB drive when plugged in show up as a standard drive letter. Building a permanent play list is important so you can automate the process and not have to manually move the files each time.

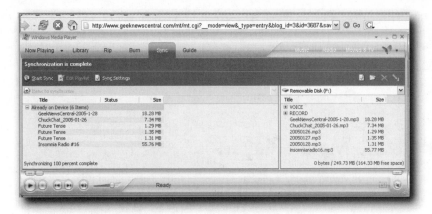

FIGURE 3-29: Windows Media Player Synchronization window.

If you choose not to use the Windows Media Player, you can always copy the files manually with Windows Explorer. I do not recommend this because the whole process is supposed to be fun and should require little work on your part after you set up your subscriptions and organize your play list.

Note Because some of the MP3 players today use proprietary synchronization interfaces, you may have to load podcasts manually.

Do You Really Need an MP3 Player?

The answer to that question is No! But you now have the opportunity to free yourself from the corporate media machine, so consider this: Some media players are very basic with no display; they may have simple Play, Fast Forward, Reverse, and Stop buttons. These devices may not have all of the fancy settings that are on some of the advanced players, but they are more than capable of playing podcasts.

Do not think that you have to spend a great deal of money to get a capable MP3 player with a fair amount of storage. With the introduction of the iPod Shuffle, the iRiver IFP-700 series, the Samsung Yepp series, and similar high-capacity MP3 players, players are available at very reasonable prices. We will continue to see prices come down and storage capacities go up.

It has become obvious that the market is ripe to enable those who may have been intimidated by prior prices of these devices. You may save some money by using that PDA you have lying around.

If you choose to listen to podcasts via your PC from work or home, I encourage you to do so. After all, I recommend that you still subscribe and listen to podcasts via direct download on the Internet if an MP3 player is not within your budget today.

Using Portable Media Players

You will find a wide variety of MP3 players available on the commercial market, today. The number of players and manufacturers are growing. As the Podcasting Revolution continues, automatic synchronization of proprietary media devices will improve daily. Following is a short list of questions you should ask to avoid buying something that will not work well with podcatcher clients:

1. Does this MP3 player synchronize with Windows Media Player?

   The answer to this question should be yes. Remember you don't want to have to load podcasts manually. You want to subscribe, synchronize, and go.

2. Is this MP3 player recognized as a USB drive?

   The answer should be yes. It is easier to synchronize an MP3 player automatically that does not need a third-party application to load files on it.

3. Is this MP3 player USB 2.0–capable?

   If the MP3 player is USB 2.0–capable it will load files more quickly, and when you're in a hurry there is nothing more frustrating than waiting for data to load.

4. What is the total storage of this device?

   You want 256/512 MB minimum with 512 MB or greater being best.

5. What is the battery life of this MP3 player?

   You want at least eight hours.

6. Will this MP3 player play files other than MP3?

   This would certainly be preferable. Check to see which other file types the model can play. Podcasters are creating content primarily in MP3 format but some also create in AAC, WMA, and OGG. Some of these audio formats take up less space, so you can get more data onto MP3 players that have lower storage amounts.

Those are just the very basic questions you should ask and should suffice for finding a good MP3 player or a phone or other media device that is capable of playing MP3s.

One MP3 Player Accessory That Empowers Freedom of the Airways

Obviously, having an MP3 player is a luxury. Equipping that MP3 player with an add-on device like iTrip (http://griffintechnology.com/) allows you to transmit whatever you are playing on your iPod via an FM signal to your car radio. A wide variety of add-on devices can be found simply by searching for "MP3 FM transmitter" on Google. I found 20 different manufacturers with this search. One of my favorites is the Belkin F8V3080-APL, a perfect device for those living in dense FM areas.

Future Possibilities (Multidistribution Paths)

It seems every company that has an electronics division has released its own MP3 player or device that will play MP3s. Currently, the Apple iPod rules in units sold, although a lot of companies are trying to make their mark. As more companies compete for consumer dollars, we will see a wider variety of products. We are already seeing MP3-capable mobile phones and watches. Car radios have been able to play CDs with MP3s on them for a while, but why not a car radio with WiFi built in with the necessary storage available to handle the large number of media files that people are consuming? PDAs are already capable of handling large amounts of memory via external memory sticks, so in the near term it will not be a matter of storage concerns but connectivity and interoperability.

Hopefully, we will see wide variety of devices capable of using high-capacity memory sticks that are WiFi-enabled so that they can synchronize podcasts and other types of media content remotely. Just look at how the public has fallen in love with digital video recorders such as TiVo. Such devices have changed the way we watch television. This does not come without concern from the major networks, because people are now fast forwarding through commercials. In response, networks are shifting start and stop time of programming to try to force people to watch live television.

This and tactics like it will be short-lived as the enablers of technology adapt the software tools we use to give the consumers what they want. The same is true of podcatcher clients and portable media devices. Give programming teams a little time, and all the features that I and others evangelize about will come to be.

As this medium grows and the tools improve, I can see a day when the following scenario will play out: In the morning as you are getting ready for work, you start listening to a subscribed podcast on your media center computer. As you are leaving the house, you hit the pause button. You then jump in your car, and as you are leaving the driveway, you hit the play button on your car stereo, and it picks up where you left off in the house. Upon reaching work, your mobile phone picks up the queue, and you are able to listen to programming through your Bluetooth-enabled headset or other media device.

This allows consumers to program whatever they wish to listen to in advance without having to deal with the programming decisions of the corporate media moguls.

Summary

In this chapter, I have provided you with the following:

- A list of resources from which to find podcasts
- Instructions for subscribing to a podcast
- Tips on managing podcasts on your MP3 player and your hard drive
- Tips on purchasing the correct media player
- A look at the future of podcasting

In the next chapter, I will outline the way for you to join the production of the Podcasting Revolution and the steps you need to take to prepare for a successful podcast.

Joining the Revolution: Your Own Podcast

part

Choosing Your Podcast Format

Y ou have the opportunity now to reach hundreds and thousands of people without leaving the privacy of your home. Pull up a chair, sit down on the couch, or lie in bed in your pajamas and talk to the world. The best part is that no one will know, or care, if you tell them you're doing your podcast in your pajamas. There is showmanship in each and every one of us. I'm excited that you want to create your own podcast, and even if I can't be there with you, I want to help you prepare for your first one.

Professional syndicated, nationwide radio shows have large research staffs that feed hosts information and help them prepare. Podcasters generally are a staff of one. I hope to give you some ideas that you can use to prepare for a successful launch of your show.

In this chapter, I teach you how to choose a show topic, I talk about format ideas, and I tell you how to find answers to legal questions you might have before launching your first podcast.

Get out your paper and pencil. You might want to take some notes so that you can capitalize on the ideas that come to mind as you go through this chapter.

Deciding on the Podcast Format

So you have decided to produce your own show! You now have a lot more decisions to make. You have to decide whether your show will have a set topic. If so, what will that topic be? Where will you get your content? You need to determine whether you'll do your show alone or with others. You need to decide the length of your show and how often it will run. You need to decide where you'll be producing it, and you need to know how to determine whether broadcasting the content you choose violates copyright laws. The following sections are filled with information that can help you make these decisions.

What Type of Show Should I Produce?

Pencils ready? When deciding on the type of podcast to produce, ask these questions:

- What do I enjoy the most?
- What subject am I passionate about?
- What topics can I speak about as an expert?
- What are subjects that people seek me out for?
- What do I do for fun?
- What topics do I have a lot of fun talking about?

Take some time and answer those questions thoroughly. The subjects people are discussing in podcasts cover all topics. I am sure that by purchasing this book, you have made a preliminary commitment to do this for the long haul. It does not matter if you want to reach 1 person or a 100,000; all of these questions apply. The main thing to keep in mind is that you must be able to have fun with the format you choose.

If you are a company wanting to start a podcast, you must also think this process through. As a consumer, I would probably check out podcasts produced by companies I buy products from. So you need to ask yourselves the following questions:

- What message do we want to convey?
- Will we turn off our customers if they think we are pushing for a sale?
- Should we talk about product development?
- Can we promote new products?
- Will we want to offer incentives to listeners?

Companies that decide to produce a podcast will be on the cutting edge. Your content will represent your company, so you must make sure that what is produced passes this litmus test. Consumers will listen to content that adds value to products they own, but will have little patience for an infomercial. If you're a small company, podcasting is a great way to get the word out about your product. If you do not want to produce the podcast, why not hire one of the existing podcasters to produce your promo?

Obviously, I love technology; I also have an almost equal passion for food. My wife and I always seem to get into deep discussions about the quality of food served at the places we eat. We have talked of doing restaurant reviews here in Hawaii as we sample new venues and places that catch our eye. I am sure it would be a successful podcast with the number of tourists coming to Hawaii. Tourists want to eat where the locals eat. After all, locals know the best restaurants. So, you see, finding ideas for your podcasts is as simple as finding the things you enjoy talking about and doing.

You may even want to consider doing a show that isn't a solo podcast. Some of the most popular podcasts are husband-and-wife teams. I like participating in podcasts where a group of four to five people do one together, because these types of podcasts are dynamic and develop a life of their own.

Solo acts make up the vast majority of podcasts. They are recorded in a variety of places. Don't think that you have to have a professional studio to do this; in fact, you will be surprised by how little equipment you need.

Note In Chapter 5, I discuss podcasting equipment and what you need to record a podcast.

Where you will be recording your podcast is something you should consider before you get into the actual recording process. Background noise is a consideration. If you plan to record in a noisy environment, don't fear. I have some solutions for you in Chapter 8.

We all have busy lives, and mine is no exception. I currently record my shows after the kids have gone to bed on Mondays and Thursdays. This works out well for my show format, as fresh technology news seems to come out on Monday. Then I do a wrap-up of the week's events on Thursday. I try to produce my shows on a schedule, and my regular listeners know that at about 5:00 EST the next morning, my show will be online.

Where you live, or the podcast subject, especially if it has a short shelf-life, will sometimes dictate what time you do your podcast. You can record your podcasts in your car, while riding the bus, while walking to work, and so on. Virtually any venue will support the recording of a podcast. Now, you may have trouble if you're trying to record something next to a jackhammer, but you get my drift. Let your imagination flow regarding where and when you will produce your show.

The majority of podcasts are theme-oriented; typically, a podcaster will cover the same subject. It is important to remember that nothing can stop you from changing your theme, and there are no rules on what you can do or what you can say. Some podcasters discuss topics that are not appropriate for work and will make some people uncomfortable. So pick a topic, any topic, and be passionate about what you have to say. It is important to be yourself, because if you are not yourself, people have a sense about those sort of things and will let you know if they think you are being disingenuous.

Note If you produce a regular show in which you represent yourself as something that you are not, then it is best to disclose to your listeners that you are producing a parody or that you are using a character to put the audience in the correct frame of mind.

Your listeners will grow to expect a podcast on the schedule you commit to. We're all human, and life throws curve balls every once in a while. If something comes up, try to put out either a weblog post or a 2-minute "hey, folks, sorry no show today" statement. Your listeners will understand. Random podcasts are okay, but be upfront about your show production plans.

How Long Should My Podcast Be?

An important part of deciding what your podcast will cover is determining the amount of time you are willing to commit to produce it. I can speak only from personal experience and will give you some ideas about how long it takes to produce a single *Geek News Central* podcast.

My podcast typically runs 35 to 45 minutes; I usually cover 15 to 20 news stories. After the kids have gone off to bed, I fire up my news aggregator and scan over 200 news sites looking for gems I want to discuss. I use FeedDemon to review the last two to three days of news, loading all those stories into Firefox. Once I feel I have enough content, I read the articles I have picked in full, and make a decision about whether the news item is show-worthy. I usually throw out more than half the original choices. Some of the stories may not make the cut because I am not familiar enough with the subject, or the story does not light some sort of fire in me. This process takes about an hour.

I then prepare my show notes, which we will talk about in depth later in this chapter. At the 90-minute mark, I am usually ready to record. I do my sound checks and record the program. Typically at about the two-hour mark, I am finished (or just about) with the recording.

Because I have opted to invest some money in my setup, I do no show postproduction. (I will go into production and postproduction in Chapters 8 and 9.) I then compress my recording and produce the audio files I make available to my listeners. I edit the ID3 tags, upload the files to my web server, and transpose the show notes entries to my weblog and publish the show. So, in all, I have about two and a half hours in total production time to produce a 45-minute show.

Obviously, the amount of preparation time you need will be tied to the subject and length of the show. I have found that I can get a show out more quickly now than when I started. Don't be discouraged if the first couple of shows take you longer — eventually, you'll get into the rhythm of things. By reading the upcoming chapters, you will be armed with all the information you need to produce a quality podcast from day one.

Another consideration related to show length is bandwidth usage. The content you publish to the Internet will be downloaded by your listeners. Bandwidth download costs are not free, unless you have a well-placed connection.

I go into hosting and the cost of bandwidth in Chapter 10 in detail. Luckily, I have solutions that I will detail in Chapter 11. If you are hesitant to produce a podcast because of the perceived high cost of entry, my solutions will make such concerns irrelevant. You must realize, though, that all hosting providers give you a fixed amount of storage and a fixed amount of useable bandwidth.

When I say *bandwidth* I mean that hosting providers measure each and every byte that comes and goes through your website. You will be transferring audio files from your website to your listener's hard drives, and that counts against your allowable bandwidth.

Typically, my shows are 45 minutes long, and I encode the file at 64K bits per second (bps). The majority of podcasters encode at 48K bps, which results in a file that is approximately 20 MB.

Note 20 MB does not equal 20 million bytes. There is a conversion factor. 1 MB is 1,048,576 bytes or 1,024 kilobytes. Okay, I know it is confusing. There is a conversion calculator you can use at `www.t1shopper.com/tools/calculate/byteconverter.shtml` that will make it easier for you to visualize the conversion.

So, for theoretical purposes, let's imagine that I am allowed on my host a maximum bandwidth allowance of 75 GB. If I produce only one show for the entire month, then I would do this conversion: 75 GB = 76,800 MB. (Remember, I said my typical show is 20 MB.) It's a simple matter of division. Hypothetically, if the transfers are pure downloads, that show could be downloaded approximately 3,840 times.

As I discuss next, using a lower encoding rate reduces the size of your audio file. Typical podcasters have between 300 and 2,000 listeners.

Obviously, another factor is show length. A podcaster who produces a 10-minute show at a lower encoding bit rate will be able to stretch the total number of downloads a lot farther before reaching the bandwidth allowance.

Some have dreams of creating a popular show with lots of listeners. As your show grows and gets more popular, these examples can become trivial. In March 2005, my website traffic and the downloads of my show's audio file combined consumed 1.6 terabytes of bandwidth.

I am sure some of you just said, wow! I estimated through log files that nearly 100 GB of that traffic was duplicated. All of you will have a certain amount of traffic for one reason or another that is waste. I will let you do the math. I do eight shows a month, with the average show size being 20 MB. Deduct 200 GB for duplicate traffic and normal website usage, and you get a rough number of how many people are listening to the *Geek News Central* podcast. What is even more amazing is how little I spend to support that type of traffic. You will get my secrets in Chapter 11.

Remember, I told you that I am a dad with four kids ranging from 1 to 14 years. Those of us with kids, house payments, car payments, and so on usually have a budget. My wife keeps tabs on mine, but do not despair. Many podcasters are producing high-quality shows on a budget.

Caution Exceeding your bandwidth on your hosting service can be extremely expensive. We will give you the info you need to protect your wallet in Chapter 10.

So, to summarize these points: Think seriously about show length because the longer the show, the larger the audio file size. Not only do you have to consider show length, but also how much emphasis you want to put on quality. You should be able to keep audio quality at acceptable levels through the magic of good production and postproduction procedures I will lay out in future chapters.

Note Show Length and Audio Quality = File Size x Audience = Bandwidth Considerations

Audio quality is very subjective. When you listen to a music CD, you have paid for a quality digital master that has an industry standard sample rate of 44,100 samples per second.

Note *Sample rate* is how often an analog audio signal is sampled as it is converted into digital data. 44.1 kHz is the sample rate for compact disks, but you will find games and some multimedia recorded at 22.050 kHz. The higher the sample rate, the higher the frequency response.

Due to the way the encoding of a recorded audio file works, you should always set your sample rate to 44 kHz, as the encoded file will have a dynamic range of 22.050. Setting the sample rate to 22.050 kHz would result in an encoded file having a sample rate of 11.025.

So as not to confuse you, you need to know about bit rate. Due to pure physics, the lower bit rate at which you encode your audio files, the lower the allowable sample rate.

Note *Bit rate* is the number of bits that one second of audio will produce. Because we are dealing with digital audio, the encoder has to smash a lot of information into a single second. How high you set the bit rate will depend on the amount of data that is needed to accurately reconstruct that bit rate.

The higher the bit rate, the larger the amount of physical data. Podcasters have used a variety of bit and sample rates in the creation of their MP3 files. Music on CDs is encoded with a bit rate of 112,000 to 128,000 bps.

Table 4-1 shows examples of typical file sizes for a podcast that is 10 minutes long. You need to realize that trade offs have to be made. Higher quality recordings will have higher bandwidth demands.

Note I used Adobe Audition version 1.5 with a recording sample rate of 44,100 Hz stereo at 32-bit resolution and converted that recording into MP3-Pro format at the following bit rates. There will be some variation of file size depending upon the software package you use to encode the MP3 files.

Table 4-1   MP3-Encoded File Sizes Comparison for a 10-Minute Recording

Bit Rate/Sample Rate	File Size	Relative Quality
128,000/44,100 Hz	9.44 MB	CD Quality
96,000/44,100 Hz	7.08 MB	Near CD Quality
64,000/22,050 Hz	4.72 MB	Similar to FM
56,000/22,050 Hz	4.13 MB	Similar to FM
48,000/22,050 Hz	3.54 MB	Better than AM
32,000/12,000 Hz	2.36 MB	Better than AM

As the bit rate decreases, the sample rate also decreases; this cannot be avoided. I have found from personal experience that my podcasts sound very good when recorded with the sample rate set to 44.100 kHz and encoded at 64,000/22,050, although I do incur a larger bandwidth bill because my shows are characteristically 40 minutes or more. Thus, a 40-minute show would result in 18 MB `audio.mp3` files. Using the calculator from above, assume you have

1,000 listeners and a single show consuming 17.58 GB of bandwidth. If my audience grows, I can exercise some cost savings by lowering the encoding rate to 48,000/22,050. The audio quality is not as good as 64,000/22.050, but it is a fair trade-off in that I lower my bandwidth allotment by approximately 4 GB per listener.

Note I am sure most of you understand what a *gigabyte* or *megabyte* represents. Those who do not, please go to www.google.com and enter the search term "define: gigabyte".

Again, I am sure some of you are in a mild panic about the file sizes you see here. There are significant numbers of hosting plans available today for less than $10 a month. Most of these will support podcasters. My audience grew at an exponential rate, and I was worried about being able to handle the bandwidth. Fortunately, some hosting providers like Libsyn (www.libsyn.org) are offering unlimited bandwidth and charge strictly based upon storage. We will get into hosting in depth in Chapter 10, and I will lay out how you can do a 40-minute show several times a week and keep the audio quality high without breaking the bank. I will go into strategies for having your listeners help you with your bandwidth concerns using popular peer-to-peer (P2P) solutions.

Note P2P was made popular by exchanging files via the Internet from people who had already downloaded a file. Although P2P has taken a terrible rap for all the illegal file trading, it is a great method for legally distributing podcasts.

How Often Should I Produce a Show?

Many times, podcasters start by saying they will produce a set number of shows per week only to find out later that they can't keep up the pace. Your listeners will appreciate quality shows versus quantity. When I started I thought I would do three shows a week and found my schedule did not support that type of commitment. If I were doing this as a full-time job, I could easily create a new show five days a week. But few of us are independently wealthy. Celebrities like Adam Curry, who produce shows Monday through Friday, set a bar that a lot of podcasters wish they could match. But Curry is independently wealthy and can afford to do a show every day.

Here are some questions you need to ask yourself:

- How many shows a week will people want to listen to?
- How many other shows are being created with the same subject?
- Can I find enough fresh material to support the number of shows I want to create?
- Based on what I know now, will my plans fit my budget?
- Can I create the content within the constraints of my family?
- Can I create the content without impacting my job?
- Can I create a show if a team member is not available?

My listeners have been my number-one source of feedback, but for the first month you may have to only go on what I have told you, because the feedback may be minimal as you build your audience. Ask for feedback during every show: be prepared for the feedback you may get!

Podcast Show Preparation Tips

You have decided on a show theme, and now it is time to think about show format. Developing a show format will help you in the delivery of your content, which will allow you to stay organized and develop a professional dialogue. Because the majority of us are not professional broadcasters, nor have we had any experience in radio, you are likely to experience a certain level of dread at hearing your own voice when you play back a recording. I'll be honest with you; hearing my own voice played back is weird and makes me self-conscious.

When I am recording a podcast, I try to envision standing in front of 10,000 people and speaking to them (just kidding). I think if I were actually speaking to a live audience it would almost be easier. Humans have the ability to read a crowd, but when you are talking into the microphone during a podcast, you will generally be by yourself. So you won't be able to see how your words are being received by your audience.

 Note There is hot debate in the podcasting community about whether people should edit their podcasts after they are finished. I don't, but that is a personal choice. It's your show, and you edit any way you see fit. If you follow the guidelines I lay out in Chapter 9, your audience will never be able to tell when you have edited a section of your podcast.

You will find as you start listening to other podcasts and developing your own, that most podcasters stick to a format. I know that some podcasters reading this book will cringe when I say "format," as it goes against the grain of the free-flowing podcast. But to produce consistent good quality you need a plan. The key is conveying the content of that plan so the material does not sound scripted.

Podcasters may follow a show format, but this does not stop them from deviating when they want to. I find that I digress from time to time, because a thought that I want to explore will come to me midstream, but I always find myself coming back to my show format and picking up where I left off.

Sticking to Format

I try to stick to the format I have developed for my show for a simple reason. By the third or fourth time you listen to my show, you will know what to expect and approximately when. Like everyone else, I experimented with the format of the show, and, still to this day, solicit feedback from the audience. Some podcasters have changed format without warning their audiences and have found their e-mail inboxes full. So it is important as you develop your format that you tell your audience in advance when you are going to make a change.

I hate to say it, but people love structure. Just don't get hung up on the structure. Have fun. If you feel something isn't working, it probably isn't jiving with your audience either.

As an example, I will show you how I laid out my show format:

1. **Day and date:** I announce at the very beginning the day and date of the podcast so listeners will know when it was recorded without looking at the screen.

2. **Preintro:** Having announced the day and date, I usually give a quick three-second or less welcome message. I try to vary it and keep it witty, for example, "Better turn up the volume; we have a hot one for you today."

3. **Intro music queue:** Those of you who listen to late-night talk shows will notice the host is always introduced. I have some short intros that have been recorded with music or background sound effects.

4. **My full intro:** I tell everyone who I am, where I am, what I have been up to, and generally welcome them to the podcast and deliver some messages to new and longstanding listeners. This is usually under 1 to 2 minutes in length and usually a teaser for what I am going to talk about that day.

5. **Website location:** People are finding podcasts in a variety of directories and may be playing the show from a website other than my own. Thus, I always tell people where they can go to find the actual website and an archive of old shows (30 seconds maximum).

6. **Promotions:** Periodically I will run a promotion for prizes, and if so I will announce winners or remind people of the promotion.

7. **Sponsor:** I cover finding sponsors in Chapter 14. If I have a sponsor, I either insert their clip or read the advertisement at this time (maximum 20 to 30 seconds).

8. **Announcements:** (4 to 6 minutes)

    1. **Rants and raves:** I may have found something I really want to spend extended time on, and I will do this in the rant and rave section. It usually focuses on a big event in the tech news sector or something that is going on with me. It can be a mix of topics, or a personal and one-topic discussion.

    2. **Podcast promotions:** I always promote at least one other podcast per show. This is generally someone I listen to and think my listeners will like.

9. **News reviews:** This is where I go into the meat of the tech news I want to cover—usually 10 to 15 articles. Getting through this material typically lasts about 25 to 30 minutes.

10. **Closing remarks:** This is usually a minute of dialogue: me thanking everyone for tuning in, mentioning when the next podcast is going to be, and any other administrative stuff I may have forgotten to talk about before.

11. **Contact info email, skype, voice mail:** I give all of my contact info. (For those who have not used skype, it is a great VOIP service that all geeks love, found at www.skype.com.)

12. **Website location:** I remind my listeners to visit the website a final time and give the site URL.

13. **Featured non-RIAA music artist** (time allowing)

Creating Show or Crib Notes

Now you've seen how I lay my show out. I print this outline with a lot of spaces in between. Some podcasters prefer to just leave the format up on the computer screen, but I find that other windows have a tendency to get in the way.

Putting together the crib notes is relatively easy. Here is an example of exactly what I had written down for a podcast I did last night:

1. Tue Feb 1 2005, Preintro

2. Theme

3. Welcome, raining, back pain, big storm hitting Hawaii

3. www.geeknewscentral.com

4. Four-day extension to contest

5. Wife packed ready for Japan, pain meds evil, Ground Hog Day

6. Issue I had with Volvo

7. Promote *Rock and Roll Geek Show*

8. News review (I use a tabbed browser and have that open on my desktop)

9. Closing comments

10. E-mail, skype, voice mail

11. www.geeknewscentral.com

12. No music this show

Obviously, these are just talking points. During the recording of that show, I did stray from format once, but I was able to get back on track when I was ready because I had my show laid out. Some of you will never need crib notes and will free-style it. Whatever works for you and fits your personality best. In Figure 4-1, you see how these notes transposed into the weblog post that I put up on my website.

In Chapter 11, I cover publishing your show and the steps to make sure your podcast is set up correctly for distribution. If you review the posting for the show, you will notice I did not include everything that was in my show notes. Typically, I will highlight a couple of announcements and then provide links to all the websites and articles I discussed.

It will be very important to have a website your listeners can go to if they are listening to the podcast at the gym or at work. This way, as you talk about subjects, they won't have to be carrying a pen to write down info. I put up links to the sites I talk about on the podcast. The traffic I get after producing a podcast is predictable. People want to look at what I discussed in more detail. Weblogs are not required, but they make the publication process very straightforward.

In a nutshell, having a format and crib notes gives you something to refer to when your brain misfires and you forget what you're supposed to be talking about. But hey, if that happens, keep on recording, because life is like that sometimes.

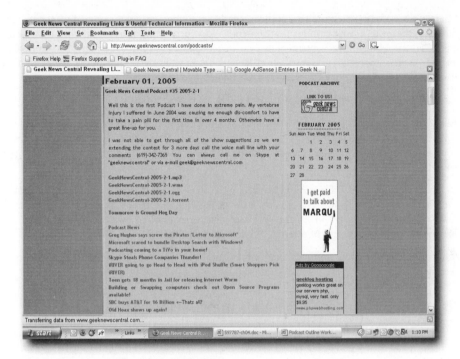

FIGURE 4-1: Weblog post from show notes.

Understanding Basic Copyrights

According to Merriam-Webster online (www.webster.com) *copyright* "is the exclusive right of a creator to reproduce, prepare derivative works, distribute, perform, display, sell, lend or rent their creations."

Over the years, there have been a substantial number of court cases that outline fair use of materials, which determines what you may talk about or publish on your website. The subject can be exhaustive, and I recommend that if you have concerns about copyright material you use in your podcast, refer to http://copyright.gov/.

Note   I am not a lawyer and the comments in this section are my opinions and should not be taken as legal advice. If you have legal concerns, consult an attorney in your jurisdiction.

Typically, you will be speaking in your own words during your podcast. If you do happen to quote a website, always be sure to give credit to the author and, if possible, tell which website it came from during the show and provide the URL or source of information. Additionally, provide a link to the website in the show notes.

I personally do both when quoting someone verbatim. After all, if you are reading the material directly, you are repeating content that someone else created, and you need to give that person credit. To try and claim the statement as your own could result in legal action. Most authors and website owners appreciate the traffic to their sites when you give proper credit, although if you have made negative comments, they may not be inclined to be nice.

As long as you give credit to the source you quote, you should have no reason for concern.

Everything you say is protected by copyright, but you can also be subject to libel, as I will discuss later in this section. You do have certain rights under the protection of the law. You should consult an attorney if you have any doubts as to whether the subject you are covering can get you into trouble.

In recent court cases, certain webloggers have been taken to court to reveal sources that provided them with trademark issues. We can argue till we are blue in the face about the privilege that reporters have with their sources. But it is becoming more evident that companies are taking a harder stance on the release of internal intellectual property.

You will know when you approach that line, because you may get that should-I-be-saying-this? feeling.

Recording Industry Association of America

When I produced my first podcast, I was not familiar with the rules surrounding playing copyrighted music on my podcast. In early November 2004, I was reading a mailing list devoted to podcasting (http://groups.yahoo.com/group/podcasters). A very serious discussion started on whether it was safe to play music without permission by labels that were members of the RIAA. It became clear to me — and I should have known better from the start — that it was not legal. I figured, hey, background music is safe right? Well it wasn't.

I immediately put a stop to playing background music that I did not have explicit permission to play, and removed the three shows from the server I had concerns with.

We are all familiar with how the Recording Industry Association of America (RIAA) has taken a very aggressive legal stance against people who share music over the peer-to-peer file sharing networks. Because the desire of the podcasting community is not to paint a target on our foreheads, we have come up with alternate solutions.

One solution is to use independent artists, but you must understand more of the legalities of playing independent artists. I am very serious when it comes to respecting the copyright of musicians.

Obviously podcasters are creating programming for public consumption. Radio stations and websites that stream music fall under very strict licensing and royalty payment rules. You may say "hey, I want to do this as a hobby. I'm not out to make any money. I'm encoding the music at a bit-rate below CD quality, so there should be no issues when I play music from today's Top-40 list for my listeners."

As much as it pains me to say this, it is not legal to do so. To date, only ASCAP has come out with a specific license for podcasters (http://ascap.com/weblicense/). The RIAA and other associations surrounding the distribution and licensing of music have not taken a public stance on podcasting, but I would not want to risk a lawsuit for playing copyrighted music without a license.

I believe that RIAA is taking a watch-and-see stance to see how far podcasters are going to self-regulate before they start issuing cease-and-desist letters or worse. Most podcasters are playing by the rules. However, I have listened to podcasts that use copyrighted songs in their programs. It is not my job to tell another podcaster what to do. Each person assumes liability, and for all I know, each podcaster has gone through all the proper licensing channels.

Organizations such as the RIAA, through heavy lobbying in Congress and in part the signing into law of the Digital Millennium Copyright Act (DMCA), have caused the gap of fair-use rights to narrow so that you cannot legally play music to the public in almost any forum without the correct licenses. Through heavy lobbying efforts, the RIAA has assured that artists get the micro-royalty payments from the music that is being played on a variety of mediums.

As an alternative to playing music controlled by the RIAA, podcasters are largely promoting bands who are not signed to a label and are not members of the RIAA. Podcasters have scoured the net for music that can legally be played under a Creative Commons License (`http://creativecommons.org/`) or have received explicit permission from bands or recording artists in writing.

Some of this music is being found on `http://GarageBand.com` with bands that display a Creative Commons License. Not all GarageBand.com artists have a Creative Commons License, and permission must be requested directly.

Copyright and Licensing Your Podcast

According to Creative Commons (`http://creativecommons.org`), "The Creative Commons License is very straightforward; they offer a flexible range of protections and freedoms for authors and artists. They have built upon the 'all rights reserved' of traditional copyright to create a voluntary 'some rights reserved' copyright."

The Road Ahead for Fair Use

I can rant for hours about the RIAA. We must realize they are paid untold millions of dollars to protect the interests of the major labels. They serve their masters well and have continued to erode the fair use of material that many of us have purchased and own. I have been very outspoken in saying that if people in the United States don't wake up and smell the coffee, it will not be long before they find themselves paying multiple times for the same medium they purchased years before. In a way, it has already happened.

I am going to show my age here a little. When I was in high school, 8-track tapes were popular; they were phased out to cassettes, followed by CDs. I remember buying the same late 70s album three times due to media changes. Now we are faced with the same dilemma, as companies push to introduce new formats that in the future will make CDs obsolete, while at the same time introducing DRM technologies to consumer equipment.

So what happens in 10 years when I want to copy a single song from that 70s album to my computer, MP3 player, or home media center, and I have to pay a new license fee for each copy because of the continual efforts of organizations like the RIAA and others?

Readers may laugh, scoff, and say it will never happen, but folks, it is happening. Wake up!

I encourage you to determine the Creative Commons License that is best for your podcast. This will help you understand what issues musicians face. The primary thing to remember about the license is that it is just a license. Creative Commons allows you the flexibility to retain a full copyright for the material you create in the format of a conditional license that makes it clear how people can reuse your content. The *Geek News Central* podcast is produced under the following license: Attribution-NonCommercial-ShareAlike 2.0.

So, what does that all mean? Figure 4-2 shows you what the basic license looks like.

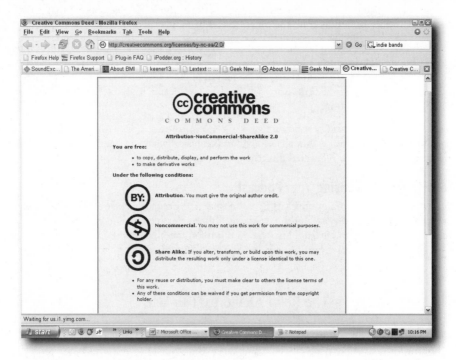

FIGURE 4-2: A typical Creative Commons License.

This license can be viewed in full at `http://creativecommons.org/licenses/by-nc-sa/2.0/`. There are multiple variations of the license, and all you have to do is visit their website and create a license that is best suited for you.

In the license shown, I retain the original copyright, and in very plain language, indicate what people can do with my content. All that is required of individuals who use my content is that they must give me credit, and the content cannot be used for commercial purposes. Others are welcome to share that content as long as it is distributed under the same license.

Creative Commons has created a specific license for musicians. When I go to `http://Garageband.com` and see that an artist has a license with a "Noncommercial-No Derivative Works-Attribution," that artist has said that I can download, copy, file-share, trade, distribute, and publicly perform (webcast/podcast) it under the following conditions:

- **Noncommercial:** You may not sell copies of this music or make any other commercial use of it.

- **No Derivative Works:** You may not sample or remix this music. You may not alter, transform, or build upon this music. (This includes synching the music to a moving image.)

- **Attribution:** You must give the original author credit.

This is podcast-safe music that you are free to use and promote. Give credit to the artist in your podcast and in your show notes. If you do not find a Creative Commons License for an artist on any music site including Garageband.com, then you need to get written permission from the band or artist to play their music. Be sure to encourage them to license their material under Creative Commons.

Note Magnatune (www.magnatune.com), a progressive music label, has been responsive to podcasters and has a sensible and fair-use policy. They have said that they consider podcasts a noncommercial use of their library, and as such, they are covered by the Creative Commons use of Magnatune's catalog, requiring no fee or further permissions. They have a unique philosophy that I wish in my heart we would see from the big labels; regardless, the Magnatune's catalog of music is a great source of podcast-safe music.

Getting Permission

I have been very vocal about the RIAA over the past few years, so I have been aggressive in writing e-mails to bands I like and simply introducing myself and explaining what my podcast is all about. I offer them some free publicity and promise to link to their website and/or their commerce site. Heck, if I like something I will buy it, and I encourage my listeners to visit the artist's site and buy a track or two if they like a tune. Do they all answer? No, but to play in the sand box you have to play within the rules.

Licensing

You have decided you are going to play music that is controlled by the man (RIAA), and you want to apply for a license. Because I am not a lawyer, I want to point you to some resources and suggest a few Google search terms to help you find the info you need to become properly licensed. A number of podcasters are licensed, and they are fairly confident that they have abided by all the rules.

It is imperative that you read the FAQ at the RIAA website (http://riaa.com/issues/licensing/webcasting_faq.asp). This is the place to start, and it lays out all the rules. You will see references to a *statutory license*. There are specific guidelines that you have to abide by in order to qualify for that license.

The following list provides resources that will help you sort out music licensing issues:

- **RIAA (Recording Industry Association of America):** http://riaa.com

- **RIAA Webcasting FAQ:** http://riaa.com/issues/licensing/webcasting_faq.asp

- **SoundExchange:** http://soundexchange.com/

- **ASCAP (American Society of Composers, Authors and Publishers):** `http://ascap.com/index.html`
- **ASCAP Specific Podcast License:** `http://scap.com/weblicense/`
- **BMI (Broadcast Music Inc.):** `http://bmi.com/`
- **SEASAC:** `http://sesac.com/home.asp`
- **United States Copyright Office:** `http://copyright.gov/`

Rules vary from country to country, so ensure that you comply with laws in your jurisdictions.

There have been several podcaster discussions about this licensing issue. I cannot endorse those discussions without legal ramifications. You should be able to find useful commentary by searching for "How to Podcast RIAA Music Under License." As always, when in doubt, seek legal advice.

Note The best solution is to support independent bands and artists who are trying to break through and help them become stars.

Legal Concerns

Copyright concerns are not the only legal matters of which podcasters must be aware. For example, you need to be aware of the concept of libel. The Webster definition of libel can be found at www.webster.com. We all should have a pretty good idea what *libel* means. But as a friendly reminder, in all public mediums, what you say and write about a company, person, group, and so on could be used against you in a court of law. I have had to temper my comments at times, and you will sense when you have stepped over the line. As this medium is about having fun, I would hate to see a podcaster be hauled into court for slandering someone. Americans are guaranteed freedom of speech and freedom of the press, but that is not to say that you can malign someone with a false or exaggerated statement.

Summary

You learned that to decide on your show's topic, you should make lists of the things you love to do and the topics that interest you. Just about anything goes in the world of podcasting. I have also given you some tips on how to format your shows. As for length, you must take into account the amount of bandwidth you will use and the amount of time you have in which to prepare your podcasts.

The legal issues surrounding podcasting can be sticky, but this chapter has given you some websites that explain licenses and offer licenses you can use to protect your own work. We have covered basic copyrights and provided you with a number of legal concerns that you need to be aware of to ensure an enjoyable podcasting experience.

As we move into the equipment portion of the book, you now have the building blocks to prepare you to step up to the microphone and press Record.

Producing a Podcast with Gear You Own Today

I have talked to a lot of people about podcasting, and they are surprised when I talk about the basic podcasting hardware requirements. Most think they need a studio setup, but this couldn't be farther from the truth.

You're probably asking yourself, what do I need to get started today? A computer, a microphone, and a website, along with software that can be downloaded from the Internet. It's really that simple.

In this chapter I will cover the very basic equipment and software that you need to start podcasting almost immediately with the gear you own, today. Remember, I recorded my first podcast in a hotel room using my laptop and a $7.95 headset microphone, along with some software downloaded from the Internet and some that already resided on my computer.

Note Some of you will want to take your productions to the next level, and in Chapter 6, I will go through what I characterize as the semi-professional studio. But the focus of this chapter is getting started with basic, inexpensive equipment and software.

Computer Requirements

If you have purchased a computer within the last two or three years, you probably have a PC that is capable of recording a podcast. This is a general statement; if you have a PC running Windows XP or a Mac running OSX, you should be good to go. Recording audio on PCs has been going on for a long time, and there are many variations in equipment setups in the world today. In the following sections, I cover computer basics for Windows and Mac users.

Windows XP/2000

The majority of the computers in the world are running a Windows operating system. Windows machines today come in many different styles, including laptops, desktops, tablets, mini PCs, and so on. These machines or their components run the gambit in performance. Typically, you would not expect your $399 rebate special to perform at the same level as a $2,000-plus gaming machine. This is not to say the $399 rebate special will not work, but you will have to minimize the number of programs running so as not to interfere with the recording process. Sometimes by simply increasing a computer's Random Access Memory (RAM) and not overtasking, you can record a podcast on an entry-level PC.

In recent years most brand-name manufacturers have been selling computers at rock-bottom prices, targeting price-conscious shoppers. I love a good deal just like the next person, and my kids have benefited from these lower-priced PCs, sharing a $399 rebate special between them. I, on the other hand, have always built my own desktop servers, so, being a geek/power user, I typically let performance win over price. If you are concerned your machine may not be up to the task of processing audio efficiently, you will simply have to experiment and see. The only way you will know for certain is by installing the software I recommend here and then seeing how well recording a podcast goes.

I will generalize and say that if you have a Pentium 4 or equivalent processor with 512MB of ram, 3 to 4 GB of available space on your hard drive, and audio ports for line in and line out, you can start podcasting today. *Line in* and *line out* refer to where microphone and headphones are connected to your computer.

PC and Mac users have found that from time to time, operating systems do weird things. Even those of you with $3,500 super computers can lose a show before you have saved it to the hard drive during recording or postprocessing. I will thoroughly cover this to help mitigate that risk in Chapter 8.

For Windows users, basic requirements are as follows:

- Windows XP/2000
- Pentium 4 processor
- 512 MB of RAM
- 3 to 4 GB of free space on the hard drive
- Line Out/Line In

Not too tough so far, is it?

Apple

Prior to writing this book, the closest I ever got to a Mac was when I walked by someone with one. Sure, I joked with co-workers who were Mac users and dealt with the typical PC-versus-Mac mindset. In researching materials for this book, I found I could not do the reviews justice unless I had a Mac, so I purchased a Mac Mini. I knew that the Mac Mini, Apple's introductory machine, has the lowest possible performance specifications of any machine on the Apple G4 product line. I knew that if I could record a podcast on a Mac Mini, it would probably make the Mac fans happy.

The Mac Mini that I used was the 1.42 GHz machine, with 512 MB of RAM and a USB Griffin iMic microphone and headphones. The iMic can be purchased online at (http://griffintechnology.com) or through any major computer store that carries Apple products.

The Mac Mini does not have a built-in microphone jack, even though it does have a headphone plug, which I did not use. The unit came with 256 MB of RAM, but from the very start, that was not enough. I installed 512 MB, but to have achieved the best performance, I should have installed a 1GB chip.

I used the basic software setup that a beginner user probably would. I did have to purchase one application to upload my first Mac Mini podcast — a file transfer protocol (FTP) application. I chose Captain FTP from the Apple software resource list, available at (www.captainftp.com) for under $30. I used this program to transfer files to my website.

The biggest disappointment was with the delayed audio feedback through MAC OS X. This is an issue that even users of Powerbooks are finding, because there are latency issues that build up the longer you record.

Note

Audio latency tests with the Mac Mini revealed that as I spoke, I incurred a delay of up to about a second before I would hear feedback (my voice) through the headphones. It was very irritating and distracting. (Apple — if you're reading this, you need to fix it.) I hear this as a complaint from almost every Mac podcaster out there.)

To date, I have not heard of any workarounds, but I do have a solution — I recommend that you not listen to the audio feedback. This has some drawbacks, but I personally was beyond irritated with the latency issue. In Chapter 6, I will outline some hardware you can acquire to help avoid this issue.

There is no reason to think that it would not be just as easy to record podcasts on OS 9. The recording software that I explain how to use in Chapter 9 has release versions for OS 9. I personally would consider the Mac Mini with 512 MB of RAM a minimum standard.

Microphone and Headset Requirements

In the next chapter, I will discuss the extreme importance of choosing a professional microphone. Those of you wishing to build a semi-professional studio will need to take some time and make an informed decision.

I must emphasize that, today, as you prepare to produce your first podcast with what you have, you do not need a fancy microphone. My first was a $7.95 headset/microphone combination from Labtec (http://labtec.com). Almost any microphone that you have in your home that will plug into your microphone jack will work. The same goes for headphones; as I stated earlier, I used a headphone/mic combo, but almost any headphone that will plug into your computer's line out will work. So dig around and see what you have on hand.

Software

I have done my best to find software solutions that are free, but in some cases, this hasn't been possible. In the software reviews that follow, I have reviewed only software that I have used or that I know is being used in the world of podcasting today. If you don't want to purchase any software, you don't have to. I've simply pointed you to software resources and given you guidelines to follow.

Note In this section, I will cover the software that you need for your computer, not what you will need on your website. That will be covered in detail in Chapter 10.

Here's what you need:

- Recording/editing software
- Audio conversion programs (optional)
- FTP program for file transfers
- Audio routing tools (for Mac only)

I will say this; there has been a lot of movement by developers to produce tools to make it simple for people to create podcasts. There are even developments by new companies, such as Odeo (http://odeo.com), to create a service that will allow you to listen, create, and distribute podcasts through tools built into a web browser. These solutions will require careful development. It is tough enough to get a quality recording on software residing on your computer, let alone a tool that will run in your browser.

The following software tools are tried-and-true and, without a reasonable doubt, will give you a quality recording. I will be keeping an eye on these new services as they roll out. You will want to stay informed of the latest developments by checking websites that have active forums like Podcast Alley (http://podcastalley.com) and the earlier adopters/testers of these new services. A number of tech podcasters at `http://techpodcasts.com` are involved in test-ing some of these new tools, so you should make sure you check out their shows for the latest developments.

Recording Software

A wide variety of recording software packages are available on the market. I will review only the most popular choices. If you have a recording package you are familiar with then go ahead and use it. If not, pick one from the reviews in the following sections.

The following are critical features to look for in a recording package:

- Configurable bit rate
- Configurable sample rate
- Capability of saving to MP3 without using secondary applications
- Noise reduction utilities
- Audio amplification utilities
- Audio normalization utilities

Audacity for Windows, Mac, and GNU/Linux

Audacity is an audio editor and recorder. This software package is developed under open source and is free. Audacity is the editor's choice application to be used with the Mac and Linux. You can find Audacity at `http://audacity.sourceforge.net/`. Podcasters worldwide are using Audacity with its full feature set. Figure 5-1 shows the basic interface for Audacity.

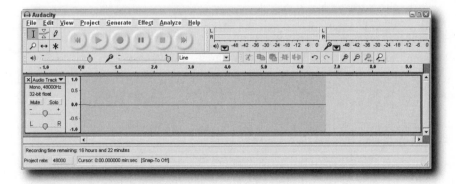

FIGURE 5-1: Audacity basic interface.

I have highlighted a few items from Audacity's long list of features that I feel are good for any recording software package. I have found these particular features to be key to producing and editing a podcast. The complete list can be viewed at `http://audacity.sourceforge.net/about/features`. The following information was derived from the Audacity website with permission under the Creative Commons License.

Audacity enables you to perform the following tasks:

- Record from microphone, line input, or other sources
- Dub over existing tracks to create multitrack recordings
- Monitor volume levels, using its level meters, before, during, and after recording
- Import and export WAV, AIFF, AU, and OGG Vorbis files
- Import MPEG audio (including MP2 and MP3 files)
- Export MP3s with the optional LAME encoder library
- Create WAV or AIFF files suitable for burning to CD
- Edit with cut, copy, paste, and delete
- Use unlimited undo (and redo) to go back any number of steps
- Rapidly edit large files
- Fade the volume up or down with the Envelope tool
- Remove static, hiss, hum, or other constant background noises
- Adjust volumes with compressor, amplify, and normalize effects
- Record at up to 96 kHz
- Mix tracks with different sample rates or formats, with Audacity converting them automatically in real time
- Load various sound enhancement and effects plug-ins

Other built-in effects include Echo, Phaser, Wahwah, and Reverse.

Audacity is licensed under the GNU General Public License (GPL) on Mac OSX, Windows, and GNU/Linux

Note GNU is a License vehicle for open-source software. For more information, visit `http://gnu.org/licenses/licenses.html#Intro`.

The features I have listed will help you create a great podcast. Even though this list is not exhaustive, it shows you the diversity and power of an open-source program.

As with any open-source project, the developers, due to software patent concerns, had to be careful about which functionalities they included in the base code, especially when supporting the MP3 format.

Note

To convert a recording to MP3 in Audacity, you need to install a software add-on called LAME. (LAME ain't an MP3 encoder.) The project's name, which is actually represented in parentheses, seems to contradict what you think it should do. LAME was intended to be a MP3 educational tool, but it just so happens that a lot of audio recording programs use the program to convert many types of file formats to MP3. You will find the URL links to LAME and other recommended additional software add-ons via the respective operating system link on the Audacity download page (http://audacity.sourceforge.net/download/).

I will discuss many of these features as I get into the tutorials in Chapters 8 and 9.

Adobe Audition for Windows

Adobe Audition is a commercial recording and editing software program which you can find at http://adobe.com/products/audition/main.html, and retails for $299. Figure 5-2 shows the multi-track view of Adobe Audition.

FIGURE 5-2: Adobe Audition — the multitrack view.

I did my first podcast using Adobe Audition, partly because I already owned Audition. Audition is the editor's pick for Windows users. The price may scare some of you, but it is worth every penny.

Adobe Audition is feature-packed but very simple to use. Audition has a large number of the audio conversion routines built in. This means that when you record, it does so in WAV format. When you save the file, you convert it to the file format you want to publish—in my case, MP3.

Audition is great for those of you considering doing podcasts with multiple parties in separate locations. (In Chapter 7 we will talk about multiparty recordings.) Adobe, the creator of Audition, does offer a trial version. You can find the link to the tryout page on the Audition main page on Adobe's website (referenced above).

Audition contains the following primary features:

- Audio effects and Digital Signal Processing (DSP) tools
- Multitrack mixing
- 5,000 royalty-free music loops
- Highly accurate editing tools
- Built-in sound effects tools
- Automatic click/pop reduction

Adobe Audition is well suited for those of you with some shows under your belt who want to do more fancy editing. I use it as my default application.

Audio Hijack Pro Mac

You can find Audio Hijack Pro at http://rogueamoeba.com/audiohijackpro/. They have a free trial period for the product, but there is a $32 registration fee if you continue using it. Figure 5-3 shows the Audio Hijack default startup screen.

Audio Hijack Pro's purpose is to hijack audio streams from various applications on the desktop. The program has been adopted as the Mac podcaster's best friend. RogueAmoeba, the parent company, has been proactive in meeting podcasters' feature requests, and rumors are that they are making changes to make Audio Hijack more podcast-friendly.

Experienced Mac users will say that this application is not intended for podcasting, so why not use GarageBand? I agree that GarageBand brings to the table the same advanced features as Adobe Audition and Audacity, but for someone who has never experimented with audio before, GarageBand can be intimidating. Keeping podcasting on the KISS (Keep-it-Simple-Stupid) mentality is better, and Audio Hijack Pro is very simple to use.

Because Audio Hijack Pro will capture any kind of audio, it is much like a digital video recorded for audio. Many of us have listened to a streaming audio show and wished we had a tool that could capture the audio to listen to later. I like to listen to *Coast to Coast AM* (http://coasttocoastam.com/) with George Noory, which is a syndicated late-night talk show that explores supernatural and out-of-this-world topics. I subscribe to the streaming service, which until recently had no archive service; thus, there was no way to listen to shows later. Fortunately, within the last couple of years, Windows and Mac users have been offered similar tools to do the same thing. Audio Hijack Pro is the king of the hill and has hit a home run with this product.

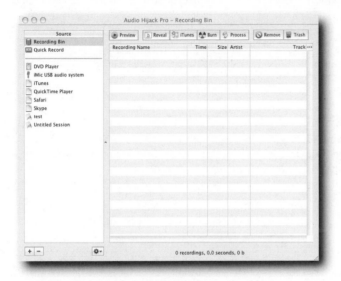

FIGURE 5-3: Audio Hijack Pro default startup screen.

I can capture any audio stream with Audio Hijack; thus, I have the perfect podcast recording tool. I can save in several different file formats, and if need be, I can load files to Audacity for editing. (Audio Hijack Pro is not an editor; it is only a recording software package.)

Additionally Audio Hijack Pro comes with a number of preloaded audio plug-ins so that you can apply filters and effects directly to the recorded stream.

Audio Hijack contains the following features:

- Nearly 50 audio effects plug-ins
- Gives you the ability to work with VST, Audio Unit, and LADSPA plug-ins
- 10-band equalizer
- Lets you create MP3, AIFF, AAC, or the Apple Lossless formats
- Gives you the ability to block system alerts and beeps

Table 5-1   Audio Plug-ins and Other Resources

Website Name	Format Supported	URL
KVR Audio	Open Source VST, DX, AU	http://kvraudio.com/
Audio Units	Mac OS X audio units	http://audio-units.com/
LADSAP	LADSAP	http://adspa.org/
MHC	VST and audio units	http://mhc.se/software/plugins/
Sound Exchange	Multiple	http://sox.sourceforge.net/

Wiretap (Mac)

Some podcasters are having success with Wiretap (`http://ambrosiasw.com/utilities/wiretap/`), a record-only application for $19. Figure 5-4 shows Wiretap opened, along with its recording session window.

FIGURE 5-4: Wiretap and its
recording session window.

Michael Butler of *The Rock and Roll Geek Show* came up with a recording recipe that works well with this application. You can see it at `http://americanheartbreak.com/movabletype/archives/000160.html`.

What I like about Wiretap is its ability to record by default everything going on inside the Mac. Using this application requires you to use Audacity to edit after you are finished recording. For those of you who want a quick-start application, this (or Audio Hijack Pro) is the way to go.

Podcast All-in-One Recording Solutions

I did my best to get into beta testing on some recording solutions that were being released at the time I was doing final wrap up on this chapter. A unique tool with great promise made it out in time to be included — Mix Cast Live (`www.mixcastlive.com`). Figure 5-5 shows the control panel for Mix Cast Live 0.9.4.

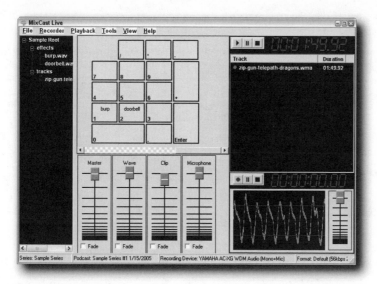

FIGURE 5-5: Mixcast Live.

This application is very straightforward. It allows you to load all your audio clips to be played while you are recording your show, and has some tools built in so that you can do post-show editing. It does not have any plug-in support, but for the beginning podcaster, it is an easy-to-use recording program. After you're finished, it gets your file encoded and ready to upload to your web server.

Audio Conversion Applications

As we get into the actual recording process in later chapters and start listening to the quality of the MP3 files you create, you may not be happy with the way your program encoded the file. It is always best, when getting started, to save the initial recordings you make in a high-quality lossless format—WAV for PC/Mac or M4A for the Mac.

Once you have saved in lossless format, you can save a file to MP3 format and check its quality. The only complaints I've heard about conversion are from individuals using Audacity and the LAME converter. You will most likely not need an audio conversion program at all if you use any of the other applications I have reviewed to this point. Audio converters would only be used if you decided to save your recording in a lossless format upon completion of all postproduction editing.

I have tried a number of encoders, from the commercial-licensed encoder in Audition to LAME in Audacity, and have found little difference. Audacity and Audition allow you to store your recordings in WAV format. This gives you the opportunity to convert, using the audio conversion tool of your choice, a WAV file to MP3 or any other format.

I do like Razor Lame, a Windows graphical interface front end to LAME. This tool gives you more control over the conversion of WAV files to MP3 than what you normally would have using the direct Audacity interface (http://dors.de/razorlame/index.php). Razor Lame is fast and allows you to set encoding variables that you can't in Audacity.

Table 5-2 shows a list of resources for audio conversion applications.

Table 5-2   Audio Conversion Directories

Directory	Operating System	URL
Tucows	Windows	http://tucows.com/audiocon95_default.html
Tucows	Linux	http://linux.tucows.com/audioconversion_default.html
Tucows	Mac	http://mac.tucows.com/converters_default.html
Shareware.com	Multiple	http://shareware.com/
Razor Lame	Windows	http://dors.de/razorlame/index.php

FTP Clients

Once your podcast is complete, you will need a file transfer protocol (FTP) utility to upload your podcast to your web host. Many people use Internet Explorer to download files from FTP sites, but I have personally never used this built-in functionality.

Note

I have not used Internet Explorer version 6 for some time, because of security concerns.

Due to the fact that you will be uploading your audio file to a website, you want a robust FTP program that is capable of error checking to ensure that the file transferred is an exact copy of what is on your hard drive.

I cover transferring the file to your web server in detail in Chapter 13. Most of you will probably be familiar with FTP and may have a client on your desktop already. For those that have not been initiated, an FTP program simply moves a file on your computer to the file directory of your web host, where it can be accessed by the public.

It should be noted that there are literally a hundred or more FTP clients available. Table 5-3 lists sites from which you can download an FTP client.

Table 5-3   FTP Client Directory

Directory	Operating System	URL
Tucows	Windows	http://tucows.com/networkadministration_ftp_default.html
Tucows	Mac	http://mac.tucows.com/networkprot_ftp_default.html
Tucows	Linux	http://linux.tucows.com/ftp_default.html

Audio Plug-ins

An *audio plug-in* is a tool that runs in your audio editor or recorder. These tools are either actual instruments or sound effects. Thus, instrument plug-ins replicate the sound of an instrument, and "effects" are used to modify or process audio. Literally thousands of different types of effects can be found all over the Internet. They fall into the following general categories:

- VST, which replicates special effects and sound synthesizers

- Audio Unit (Mac), which replicates instruments

- Linux Audio Developers Simple Plug-in API (LADSPA), which is a combination of instruments, effects, and synthesizers

As you become used to the applications, you can start experimenting with plug-ins. All the software packages reviewed so far can use them. Many of the best tools are commercialized and require purchase. Table 5-1 includes a list of a few audio plug-in resources.

WS_FTP Pro (Windows)

For a number of years, I have used WS_FTP Professional. It can be found at www.ipswitch. com/Products/WS_FTP/ for $49.95. (Many of the FTP programs that you will find on the resource list are free.) In Figure 5-6 you can see what the application looks like when logged into a web server.

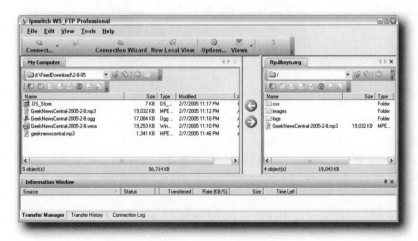

FIGURE 5-6: WS-FTP professional basic operating page.

Because there are so many FTP clients out there, you have a wide selection of choices both free and commercial to choose from. Here are some basic features you should look for:

- **Auto reconnect:** The client will reconnect when it loses a connection with your host.

- **Auto retry:** The client will continue to try and connect after failure to connect to your host.

- **Auto resume:** The client will resume where it left off if your connection is interrupted during a file transfer.

Captain FTP (Mac OS X)

The Mac operating system has an equally high number of FTP clients available. I particularly like Captain FTP version 4.0, which is feature-rich. You can find Captain FTP at www.captain ftp.com/. The program is free for trial for 15 days, but it does require a registration of $34. Figure 5-7 shows Captain FTP in default startup mode.

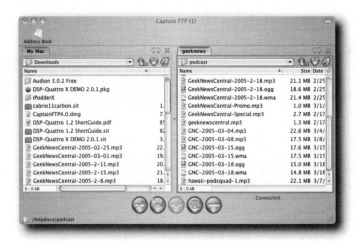

FIGURE 5-7: Captain FTP.

Captain FTP has all the primary features that a good FTP program needs. Having tested six or seven Mac applications for price versus features, I have to say that this program is on the right track, and I highly recommend it.

Some other popular Mac FTP programs include Fetch (http://fetchsoftworks.com), for $25, and Transmit3 (http://panic.com) for $29.95.

FTP Clients for Linux

The built-in FTP client native with Linux is a great application and should serve the purpose. I will not even insult Linux users with a description of the best application to use, as the majority of Linux users are power users to begin with.

Media Players

You will find as you create podcasts that you will need an audio player to organize introductions, audio clips, or any bumper music you may have.

Windows users may want to use an MP3 player with a lower memory requirement. I have found that Winamp works very well and does not impact the audio recorder software. You can find Winamp at `http://winamp.com/`. The best part is that it's free.

Note You will find that some media players are much more capable and thus, typically require more computer RAM and consume more processor resources. For those of you with machines with a smaller amount of RAM, this can be a concern because recording audio is processor- and RAM-intensive. So, it is important that you use a media player that is simply a media player, without a lot of excessive features that could rob valuable processor and RAM resources.

Mac users will want to stick to the old faithful: iTunes. I tested a number of media players and was not able to find anything better for podcasting than the standard installed iTunes.

Note If you have large libraries loaded in iTunes, you might see a performance drag on the system while it is loading and switching play lists. Make sure you have all your extra audio clips set up and ready before you hit Play.

Because I am not a Linux guru and do not claim to be, I point any Linux users to the Tucows directory (`http://tucows.com/`.) You will want to pick a media player that does not use a lot of system resources and has a play list capability.

Mac Specialty Applications

The Mac requires some special applications for you to be able to pass audio to other applications. Audio Hijack Pro does a good job without having to use the following applications. But those who decide that they will be using Audacity to record podcast will indeed need SoundFlower and SoundFlowerBed.

Mac is configured differently than a PC, and it is not as easy to capture audio you may want at the same time you produce your podcast. Using Audacity without the following applications will make it impossible to insert audio clips from iTunes into the recording live. You can splice them in later, but that is extra work. The following applications act as a big switchboard and allow you to route all audio into the recording application.

SoundFlower and SoundFlowerBed

SoundFlower and SoundFlowerBed can be downloaded via `http://cycling74.com/products/soundflower.html`.

SoundFlower is an extension for Mac OS X (10.2 and later). Once installed, SoundFlower presents itself as an audio device. Therefore, any audio application can send and receive audio. SoundFlower is free and open source.

Some of you may have a hard time understanding this concept, so I want to give an alternate description: In order for music or other audio you play in iTunes to be recorded into Audacity along with your voice, you need an application to link the two applications.

Note

iTunes does not allow you to choose an audio output device. It defaults its output to the default setting in the Audio Configurations settings. Thus, if you want to record what is being played on iTunes in Audacity, there is no way to capture that audio. By going in and setting the default audio output to the two-channel selection for SoundFlower, you can, in a sense, route the audio. Think of SoundFlower as an audio patch panel.

SoundFlowerBed is useful when you are trying to send audio to and from an application but cannot send it through audio monitor devices. SoundFlowerBed is part of SunFlower and can be accessed from the Finder's menu bar. When using it, you can access any SunFlower channels and direct them through an audio device.

Note

When you have SoundFlower set as the primary audio output device, you may not be able to physically hear what iTunes is playing and what Audacity is recording, so you use SoundFlowerBed to tap into the SoundFlower channel.

Many people have had a hard time getting their heads wrapped around these two utilities. Please visit their home pages for more information.

A very good reference on using these two tools can be found at `http://macdevcenter.com/pub/a/mac/2005/01/25/podcast.html`. You can always ask for help directly from the podcasters via a mailing list, which you can sign up for at `http://groups.yahoo.com/group/podcasters/`.

Line In

This is the final application that you will need for Mac OS X. It is free and can be found at `http://rogueamoeba.com/freebies.com/`.

This application for OS X enables the "playing of audio from input devices through the output," which will allow you to have a headset feedback loop. This feature was available in OS 9's "Play input through output device" option.

Summary

You are one step closer to putting all the pieces together. In this chapter, I covered the minimum hardware and software you will need for podcasting and gave you some choices for both. As you move towards turning on the microphone and saying, "Welcome to my podcast," I have armed you with information that you can use to load up your PC with the necessary software tools.

Mac users will need at least a Mac Mini, although I am sure there are Mac users out there who will be able to create a podcast on older models. Through my testing, I discovered that a Mac Mini is more than capable of creating a podcast. Those of you using Windows will need to realize that using a $399 special may require that you add some RAM or make sure you have minimized the number of applications running on the taskbar. Typically, though, you will be safe with a PC with a Pentium 4 or equivalent processor with 512 MB of RAM, 3 to 4 GB of available space on your hard drive, and an audio port for line in and line out.

In addition, you will need recording/editing software, along with an FTP client and a media player. Mac users may need SunFlower, SunFlowerBed, and line in as well.

This chapter has provided URLs and resources for finding the software. To continue on the way towards joining the podcasting revolution, you need to

- Download and install the software that you feel best fits your plans

- Test, evaluate, and purchase any of the software tools that you may need

In Chapter 6, I will review hardware that you can use to transform your basic podcast setup into a semi-professional studio.

The Semiprofessional Podcast Studio

Podcasting is the hottest new medium to hit the Internet in many years, and you have decided to jump in with both feet and your wallet. Some of you will find that recording to your personal PC with an inexpensive microphone is fun. Others may be ready to take their podcasting to the next level. I will point you at some tools that will make your podcast sound as if it were created in a professional studio instead of your living room.

As with any venture, there may be some sticker shock about the price of some of the equipment I'm about to recommend. I have tried hard to find the best mix of equipment for everyone. Those of you on a budget will find components that are affordable so you can create that professional sound you're looking for.

Okay. Enough talk; let's get into the hardware.

What Is Really Important

In this chapter I cover many different types of equipment. Only a few of you will need everything that I review here. But this chapter provides enough solutions to cover almost every contingency. Specifically, it covers:

- Software
- Sound cards
- Microphones
- Mixers
- Audio processing
- Digital recording devices
- Portable recording devices
- Telephone recording solutions

Be advised that I have stuck a lot of real-life issues and solutions into this chapter, along with equipment recommendations, so don't skip areas because you will find a bunch of gems. If you focus in on the suggestions I make and understand why I suggest them, you will be able to create a studio that will make your podcast sound like it came out of a professional recording studio. Remember, most of these solutions are for those who want to kick it up a notch. Because I also have to live within a budget, I cover value-priced solutions that should leave you in a position to create superb sound.

Professional Podcast Software Recording Solutions

Broadcast studios invest thousands of dollars in software recording solutions. The software solutions I present here are for those who want to take their podcast production to the next level. These solutions may not match what's in your pocketbook, but we are striving for the semiprofessional podcasting studio.

Windows Users

I will stick with Adobe Audition version 1.5 (`http://adobe.com`) as my number-one choice for Windows users. With a price tag of $299, you get almost as many options as there are dollars in the price. Adobe Audition is a powerful recording package.

Sony's Soundforge 7.0 is a world-class recording solution for Windows users and can be found at `http://mediasoftware.sonypictures.com`. It is priced at $399, and it complements a number of their media offerings.

Mac Users

DSP Quattro is a new but amazing audio-recording and editing package. The price of the software package is equally as amazing, at $149. You can find DSP Quattro at `http://i3net.it/Products/dspQuattro`. This product won an Electronic Musicians 2005 Editor's Choice Award. Playing with the limited edition demo, I was beyond impressed with the application's capabilities. My Mac Mini will have a registered copy of this running on it shortly.

Figure 6-1 shows DSP Quattro loaded up and set to record a podcast.

FIGURE 6-1: DSP Quattro main operating screen.

Hardware Components

Selecting the best components for building your home or mobile studio can prove to be a challenge because of the great number of choices out there. I have used many of the components I review and recommend. You should be able to mix and match to come up with a recording solution that fits your recording location along with production goals you may have for your show.

Choosing a Sound Card

Nearly all computers today come with a sound card built into the motherboard. Unless you have purchased a computer with a media package you can almost be assured that the computer does not have a very good sound card. I found that the sound card that came on my laptop was quite noisy.

I did a simple experiment to determine my baseline computer/microphone/background noise level by sitting in my office with only my microphone plugged in and my other computers turned off. The reading on the software-controlled meter in my audio-recording package showed nearly 40 dB of baseline noise. Figure 6-2 shows the computerized meter sound levels of my laptop sound card.

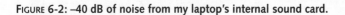

FIGURE 6-2: –40 dB of noise from my laptop's internal sound card.

I didn't realize how noisy my computer's sound circuitry really was until I changed the sound card. Folks, that was one very noisy piece of electronics! My reading was taken in virtually a silent room.

Note One decibel is the amount by which the pressure of a pure sine wave of sound must be varied in order for the change to be detected by the average human ear.

So, even before I could start recording I was dealing with a significant amount of noise. Performance sound cards have superior noise isolation.

I purchased the Sound Blaster Audigy 2 ZS PCMCIA card for my laptop. You can find product details on this card at `http://soundblaster.com/products/Audigy2zs notebook`. This product retails for around $100.

The PCMCIA sound card is amazing. I set this card up and ran the same test as before. Look at the difference in noise levels. Figure 6-3 shows the noise levels of the Sound Blaster Audigy 2 ZS notebook card.

You can see the amazing difference in terms of background noise that was being generated by the manufacturer's sound card. This noise was making it onto the recording. The superior sound card made a world of difference. Both of these tests were done in my office at the same time, and although far from scientific, they demonstrated to me that the sound card built into my laptop was definitely not a selling point.

Note I ran the test by simply setting up my equipment as if I were ready to record and by doing an audio sampling to see the audio levels. It is best to run this test in the configuration in which you will be recording.

Some of you already own high-end sound cards; those of you who don't will want to seriously consider investing in one. You can run this same test yourself to see what kind of noise your factory-stock sound card is making. Your recordings will come out much cleaner and will not require as much post-production editing.

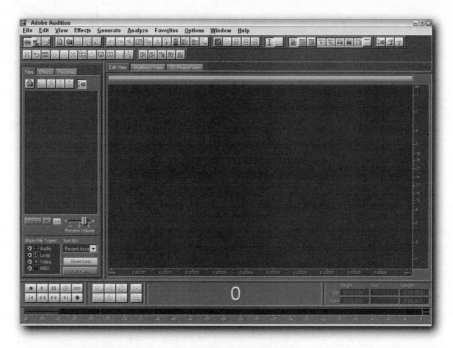

FIGURE 6-3: –66 dB of noise from the Audigy 2 ZS notebook card.

Laptop users do not have as many sound card choices. For desktop users, there are quite a few good choices. Please be sure that the sound card you purchase has these minimum recording standards:

- **Cards should be capable of 24-bit, 96-kHz recording:** A 24-bit card will give you more dynamic range. Typically, you will only sample at 44.1kHz, so the important thing to watch for on a card spec is the 24 bit; you will get the 96 kHz sample rate by default.

- **ASIO 2.0 support with drivers for low latency:** ASIO-compliant programs are able to communicate directly with the sound card or interface device. Thus, you can make changes on the software interface, and it will make a change to the actual hardware components without you having to make changes within the OS.

- **High-quality A/D converters:** A/D refers to *audio-to-digital converters*. On their web-site, manufacturers usually list the A/D converter's specs.

As with anything else, you get what you pay for. This just may be the excuse you have been look-ing for to pick up that good surround-sound, audio card for podcast recording that you can also use to enjoy your gaming experience. Table 6-1 lists the sound cards that I am recommending.

Table 6-1   Sound Card Recommendations

Manufacturer	Model	Price	URL	Operating System
Creative	Audigy 2 ZS Series	$85	http://soundblaster.com	Windows
M-Audio	Audiophile 192	$199	http://maudio.co.uk	Windows/Mac/Linux
M-Audio	Audiophile 2496	$99	http://maudio.co.uk	Windows/Mac/Linux
E-MU	1212M	$199	http://emu.com/	Windows

Eliminating Computer Case, Fan, and Component Noise

You may ask why I cover computer cases. Computer desktops, and at times even laptops, can generate a lot of noise via power supply and cooling fan noise. Typically, the fans that are shipped with standard PCs are as noisy as airplanes.

My computers are in a small office, thus the fan noise is unbearable. If you have more than one computer, you will probably find that you need to turn one of the computers off during the recording of your podcast. The distinct hum of fans is easy to hear, and although it can be reduced by adding some audio-processing components or doing recording noise reduction, it is better to kill the noise source than have to throw hardware at the solution. If fixing fan noise is not an option, I discuss some hardware solutions later in this chapter and talk about postproduction noise reduction in Chapter 9.

Some of you have your computers in a central part of your homes; thus, the fan noise may not be as noticeable. In general though, fans increase the background noise. I had thought of building a computer case enclosure with soundproof materials, but this was not a viable option for me. I chose, instead, to purchase a new computer case for my desktop and replace some fans in my wife's computer and a web server that I have here. The server needed to be on all the time, plus I did not want to have to shut it down during the show.

The small investment I made resulted in a dramatic improvement and reduced overall room noise by 35 dB. There are companies that even specialize in building custom PC solutions that are designed to be used in studios.

Note   The majority of the references here are for Windows and Linux users. Mac users typically have very quiet computers, and thus far, I have heard no complaints from Mac users on issues with background noise.

Table 6-2 lists some of the best resources for quieting your PC, with links to manufacturers of a full line of quiet PC components.

Table 6-2   Quiet PC Components

Website	URL	Topics
QuietPC USA	http://quietpcusa.com	Component reviews and suggestions
Acousti Products	http://acoustiproducts.com	Cases, fans, materials
End PC Noise	http://endpcnoise.com	Component review and suggestions
Silicon Acoustics	http://siliconacoustics.com	Component review and suggestions
Daw Box	http://dawbox.com	Custom PCs
CompuQuiet	www.directron.com/silence.html	Component review and specifications

Microphones

Microphone upgrades are the number-one purchase in which you can invest your hard-earned dollars toward improving the quality of your show. Let's say you have a budget of $1000 toward improving your sound quality. At a minimum, at least 50 percent of that budget should be put toward your microphone purchase.

Microphones are broken down into two types: dynamic and condenser.

- *Dynamic microphones* usually require no power source. Dynamic microphones are the most common type people use today. You will find inexpensive dynamic mikes at most stores. The category of professional dynamic microphones contains some of the best microphones in the world.

- A *condenser microphone* is generally never found in households. People might have them, but they usually are not aware that they do. Microphones that require a battery are condenser mikes. Professional broadcasters, bands, and even some of the better public address systems use professional condenser mikes.

Typically, professional condenser microphones cannot be used without what is called *phantom power* (external power), so if you run down to your local music store and buy a top-of-the-line condenser microphone and run home and plug it into your computer, it will not work. Some of the best condenser microphones come with their own separate power supply. You will want to ask your salesperson if the microphone needs a phantom power source. You should take very good care of any condenser microphones you own; store them in a safe place when not in use because they are delicate and should be handled as a musical instrument would be.

Note For phantom power, the majority of condenser microphones use an external 48-volt DC power source. The majority of audio mixers have switched (turn it on or off) phantom power incorporated into them. This will be an important factor to remember as we discuss mixers and FireWire microphone interfaces later in this segment.

When I decided to really get on the podcast bandwagon, I started looking for a microphone, and because my budget at the time was very small (less than $200) I opted for a microphone that a lot of podcasters on a budget are purchasing. As with anything, the higher the price, the better the product. But there are a few things you should pay attention to when making any microphone purchase:

- Frequency response
- Maximum SPL (sound pressure level)
- Sensitivity
- Signal-to-noise ratio (SNR)
- Equivalent noise

All of these items are tied together. You want a microphone with a wide frequency response, and at the same time you want it to be equally sensitive across that frequency range. You do not want a microphone that has a significantly better sensitivity at certain frequencies. The higher the signal-to-noise ratio (SNR), the better. Typically, the microphones you find around home have a 20 dB SNR. The microphones I review in this section are all 75 to 85 SNR. SNR is simply the physical measure of signal strength relative to background noise. Equivalent noise is essentially how noisy the microphone itself is. Thus, the lower the number, the better.

All the microphones that I have reviewed are excellent, and although some are better than others, you cannot go wrong with any of these selections. There are noticeable differences in sound quality as you go up the price scale, however.

MXL 990 Cardioid (Condenser)

The MXL 990 is a condenser microphone and should be considered a starter mike. It can be found at http://mxlmics.com. The best thing about this mike is that it gives you a lot of bang for the buck and can be found online for as little as $60. This is the microphone that I started with, and it is great for those of you on a budget. Figure 6-4 shows a picture of the Marshall MXL-990.

It has the following specifications:

- 30 Hz to 20 kHz frequency response
- 130 dB maximum SPL
- Sensitivity 15 mV/pa
- SNR 80 dB
- Equivalent noise 20 dB

FIGURE 6-4: Marshall MXL-990.

Audio Technica AT2020 (Condenser)

The Audio Technica AT2020 microphone does not get a lot of coverage but it does give you great sound at a great price. You can find detailed specifications about this mike at `http://audiotechnica.com`. It retails for around $99.

It has the following specifications:

- 20 to 20 kHz frequency response
- 144 dB maximum SPL
- Sensitivity 14.1 mV
- SNR 74 dB
- Equivalent noise 20 dB

Audio Technica AT3035 (Condenser)

This microphone has very dynamic sound and comes highly rated on multiple websites. It has a large diaphragm and low self-noise. You can find detailed specifications at `http://audiotechnica.com`. This mike retails for $199.

It has the following specifications:

- 20 to 20 kHz frequency response
- 148 dB maximum SPL
- Sensitivity 25.1 mV
- SNR 82 dB
- Equivalent noise 12 dB

SM7B (Dynamic)

This professional microphone is one of the few dynamic microphones that have become an industry broadcast standard. When you have a Shure (`http://shure.com`) SM7B microphone on your desktop, people know you mean business. This mike can be found for as low as $350, but typically you will see prices near $600. Figure 6-5 shows the Shure SM7B.

Because there have been extensive tests on this microphone, visit Shure's website and review their FAQ Sheet and extensive laboratory testing results.

Electrovoice RE20 (Dynamic)

The Electrovoice RE20 is another world-class microphone. You can find information on this mike at `http://electrovoice.com`. You can find this microphone on sale for $399, with prices as high as $799. With its wide frequency response, it is perfect for broadcast recordings. Figure 6-6 shows the Electrovoice RE20.

For specifications, refer to the manufacturer's website (`www.electrovoice.com/`).

Figure 6-5: Shure SM7B.

Figure 6-6: Electro-Voice RE20.

Photo courtesy of Electro-Voice 2005 Telex Communications, Inc.

Headsets

Headsets come in a variety of forms and sizes. The main issue I had with my inexpensive headset was that if I had the audio turned up too high, I would get some audio feedback. This was with an open-cuff earpiece. I found that using a headset that covered my ears completely solved my feedback issue.

Any full-cuff headset will work fine. I do like the noise-canceling headsets because they enable you to hear the noise that is being introduced in the recordings. This allows you to get a real sense of what is being recorded. Having the noise-canceling headset has helped me isolate noises because I am able to cancel out exterior sounds.

Most people have a particular type of headset that they hate or love. I have even used the ear buds that came with my iPod, but found that the headset was the best option. Very few people can talk into a microphone without a headset.

Obviously, if you are driving down the highway while recording your podcast, you are not going to be as concerned with background noise, so this mainly applies to those trying to control their environment.

A full line of headsets and headset reviews can be found at `http://headphones.com`.

Audio FireWire Interfaces

Mac users who are experiencing audio latency problems will want to move away from a USB microphone solution. If you are not having latency issues on the USB microphone combination, then you would not need an audio FireWire interface, with a couple of exceptions, which I cover shortly. Obviously, many USB microphone interfaces are available on the market. Not all are created equal, and you may be fine with your current interface.

To date, I have yet to talk to a Mac user who is not experiencing latency issues, and many times the problem crops up as soon as you start recording and adding filters and effects to your recording. The only sure way to solve the issue is to go with a FireWire audio interface.

I have not personally used any of these devices and can only go on recommendations that were made to me by other podcasters who use the Mac exclusively. I encourage you to ask other Mac podcasters what they are using and how they have dealt with the latency problem.

Clearly, audio FireWire devices are not cheap. The devices convert analog audio to digital audio and transfer that info at FireWire bus speeds to the PC. You still record the audio on your PC. FireWire devices can be used in conjunction with a mixer. Some of them are almost mini-mixers.

When shopping for a FireWire device, look for the following features:

- Compact
- Multiple power sources (battery, FireWire bus, external power)
- Multiple audio jacks

- Phantom power

- 24-bit, 96 kHz digital signal processing

- High signal-to-noise ratio

Note

Mac users utilizing an audio FireWire interface do not need to purchase a superior sound card.

PC users in all likelihood will not need to purchase a FireWire audio interface.

The following are my recommendations, and although they may not fit every budget, you can find a variety of products and price ranges by searching the Internet for "audio FireWire interfaces."

Phaser 24

Phaser 24 by Terratec, which can be found at `http://audioen.terratec.net/`, is an audio FireWire interface that retails for $249.95 and can be found online at most music stores.

Following are some of the Phaser 24 features:

- FireWire audio interface

- Two analog inputs/outputs, balanced 1/4-inch jacks

- One analog stereo output, balanced 1/4-inch jack with line level

- One coax digital I/O

- One MIDI I/O

- 24-bit, 192 kHz analog signal processing

- 24-bit, 96 kHz digital signal processing

- 109 dB SNR analog input

- 111 dB SNR analog outputs

This is a great box with an impressive signal-to-noise ratio and a significant number of input/output connections. This list includes only a small portion of the features this product offers. Please visit the manufacturer's website for full product specifications.

Note

The Phaser 24 does not come with phantom power and is a great solution for those of you selecting a dynamic microphone.

EDIROL FA-66 Portable FireWire Audio Interface

This is an amazing Audio FireWire interface loaded with features. The best part is that it is designed to be portable, and it does not take up a lot of space. It can even be powered by your FireWire bus. This product packs a lot of punch for its size. The FA-66 can be found at `http://edirol.com` and retails for between $399 and $499 online.

Following are some of the FA-66 features:

- 6-in/6-out 24-bit, 96 kHz simultaneous performance
- 4-in/4-out 24-bit/192 kHz simultaneous performance
- Compatible with Mac OS X standard driver provided by Apple
- Variety of input and output options
- 2 XLR/TRS combo jacks with premium phantom power mike preamps
- Mac OS X CoreAudio and Windows XP WDM ASIO 2.0 support
- Zero-latency, direct monitoring

In Figure 6-7 you can see how this unit is connected to multiple devices.

This list covers only a small portion of the features this product offers. Please visit the manu-facturer's website for full product specifications.

 Note Given that this product does offer phantom power, you should be able to produce a high-quality podcast with three components: a laptop, an FA-66, and either a dynamic or condenser microphone.

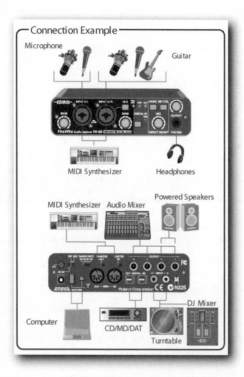

FIGURE 6-7: Edirol FA-66 diversified component connections.

Mixers

We have all seen huge professional audio mixer boards with 200 knobs on them in movies or at concerts. They look pretty intimidating, but in fact, mixers are very easy to use. There is a wide difference in quality and price. The basic mixer that a podcaster needs starts at $49.95 but can top out as high as $500. The mixer you purchase will depend on how serious you are about your sound quality. Space may also be a consideration.

So, why would you want a mixer in the first place? I'll be honest: If you're doing your show from your car or on the go, a mixer is probably not what you need. Someone doing a show on the road would be better off purchasing one of the FireWire interfaces that has multiple audio inputs and is battery-powered.

Those of you who will be recording from your home or business with a mixer can take advantage of the following:

- High-quality, low-noise microphone amplifiers
- The capability to insert external audio
- Multiple microphones
- The ability to record telephone interviews
- Hand control of audio levels versus using a mouse
- The capability to patch in special effects

My goal has always been to record the podcast, encode the file, upload it to the server, and be finished. I do not want to spend two to three hours doing post-audio production processing. To do that, my audio has to be delivered to the computer in the best possible shape. What I started podcasting with is not what I have ended up with.

If you are experimenting, you will find eBay (http://ebay.com) a good source for used mixers that can be had for bargain prices. In fact, I sold most of my initial equipment on eBay after I upgraded to my current rig.

You need to think about the various audio sources you plan to record. I found that I was doing telephone interviews and mixing in audio clips that I still had on a cassette, of all things. Some of you will choose to input your background music via your media player as opposed to doing so directly from your PC.

Note I personally found it easier to turn the volume down manually on my background music via the mixer while talking as opposed to dealing with a mouse and trying to move a slide bar on a media player like Winamp with 20 different things going on within the PC.

Caution Before I get into this too deeply, I need to make sure that you do not make the same mistake I did. If you choose a microphone that requires phantom power, you will want to make sure that the mixer you buy has phantom power. I drove well over 120 miles to a store that had the mixer I wanted, only to have to drive all the way back and return it the next day because the model I purchased did not have phantom power.

When you read an advertisement that says a mixer has *12 channels*, it means you are getting 12 mono channels or 6 stereo channels. Typically, 2 to 4 of those channels will be for the microphone with phantom power, and the remaining 8 channels will allow you to input 4 stereo devices. Unless you will be recording a live band, you will probably only ever need an 8- to 12-channel mixer.

Mixer Classifications

There are definitely different classes of mixers. The quality of sound that comes out of these components has a lot to do with the preamps and electronics found inside. There are also some special features on higher-end mixers that allow you to control audio flow directly from the mixer as opposed to having units daisy-chained together. I will talk about typical configurations for wiring all of these components together in the "Mixer Wiring Setup" section later in this chapter.

Standard Features

Inexpensive mixers simply allow you to plug/mix in multiple audio sources, and provide amplification to your microphone. The vast majority of mixers on the market are configured with phantom power, but every once in a while you will find one that isn't. All mixers let you set the audio levels of each channel, and of course, there is a single master output channel for you to input into your sound card.

All mixers that I reviewed had at least three discrete equalizer frequency ranges. These equalizer settings are very helpful in removing ambient noise when you use only a computer, mixer, and microphone. You can get a good mixer for under $100 with the following features:

- Multiple audio inputs
- Three- to four-band equalizer
- Audio levels that can be set per channel
- 10 channels
- One master output
- One headset output

My first mixer was a Behringer Eurorack UB802 mixer (`http://behringer.com`) that cost around $50 new. I used this mixer for a long time and still take it with me when I travel. You can find this mixer at almost all audio shops and on the Internet.

Advanced Features

If you decide that you want to start adding some additional audio-processing components to your recording process — let's say a compressor or an audio processor, which I cover in detail in the "Audio Processing" section in this chapter — you need a better mixer. Mixers that have channel inserts give you a great deal of control over how audio is routed within the mixer.

A mixer equipped with channel inserts does automatic routing of the audio signal when plugged in. A typical scenario is this: Your microphone audio input is plugged into the mixer; then the input audio from your microphone is immediately diverted and sent out to the channel insert connection point. Then the audio signal is routed by a cable into another piece of equipment, typically an audio compressor. Once the signal is processed by that external piece of equipment, the audio is routed back and inserted into the mixer through the same specially configured channel insert jack. The processed signal can then be equalized, and have other audio inputs mixed with it, and finally be routed out to your PC.

What is even more cool is that you can take the audio output from your PC and connect it into a port on the mixer. This gives you the ability to listen to the input and output audio with a flick of a switch and without moving wires.

You may say, "That sounds like more than I will ever need." But if you are having noise issues or your signal from your microphone is low, read the rest of this chapter carefully to understand why you need one of these high-end mixers.

Note You must mute the return audio during recording to keep from creating a loop. Typically, I take the return channel off mute only when I am playing back recorded audio. Some of you may not choose to do this and instead move your headset from mixer to PC output.

For these types of added features, you will pay more. Typically, these mixers have better audio amplifiers, give you more control over audio settings, and have more dynamic equalizers. Luckily, there are enough choices of mixers on the market today to meet the budget of the most shoppers. Table 6-3 lists mixers within a variety of price ranges.

Table 6-3   Mixer Resources

Manufacturer	Model	URL	Estimated Price	Features	Editor Rating
Behringer	UB802	http://behringer.com	$49.95	Standard	**
Yamaha	MG10/2	http://yamaha.com	$96	Advanced	***
Mackie	1202-VLZ Pro	http://mackie.com	$450	Advanced	*****

Mixer Reviews

I have personal experience with two mixers on the resource list. I based my decisions on what equipment to purchase by reading the Podcast Rigs website at http://podcastrigs.com.

Behringer EURORACK UB802

This is a great mixer for those podcasters who do not wish to spend a lot of money, but who are in need of a standard featured mixer. Having used this mixer for four-plus months, I have nothing bad to say about it. You might see mixed reviews, but for the price you get a lot of features. It is very quiet. The only complaint I have with it is that the microphone amplifiers get very noisy if I turn them up too high. I have used a variety of microphones with it, including a MXL-990 and a MXL-V69, all of which sounded great. If it had the channel inserts, as discussed in the "Advanced Features" section, I probably would never have upgraded. Figure 6-8 shows a Behringer UB802.

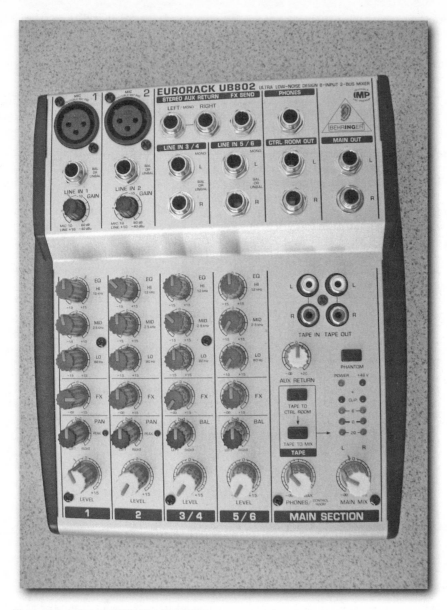

Figure 6-8: Behringer EURORACK UB802.

Behringer does make a 12-channel mixer with channel inserts at a reasonable price. I have no experience with that mixer.

Mackie 1202-VLZ Pro

Mackie is a name that you can absolutely trust. The workmanship that goes into building superior products is simply amazing. You can feel the difference. The audio amplifiers that are built into the VLZ line are amazing and world recognized.

There is a significant difference in sound quality and amplifier capabilities as compared to any standard model mixer I have experimented with.

Some of you may consider the mixer overkill because you probably won't use all of its functions. I found that, even though I fill only half of the available channels, the purchase was worth it just for the amplifiers in the unit. Figure 6-9 shows a Mackie 1202-VLZ Pro.

FIGURE 6-9: Mackie 1202-VLZ Pro.

Mixer Wiring Setup

As always, you will want to review the documentation that comes with your mixer. The drawings shown here portray only a typical setup.

Prior to hooking up your mixer's main out to your PC or recording device, turn on your mixer and turn your main mix all the way down. Then plug in the mains to your PC. If you do not do this, you can cause damage to your audio input.

Standard Block Diagram

The following diagram shows a basic layout of a mixer like the Behringer UB802. It is not at all complicated. In Chapter 8, we will discuss in detail the process of setting up your recording levels. Figure 6-10 shows a basic block diagram of how to hook up a standard mixer.

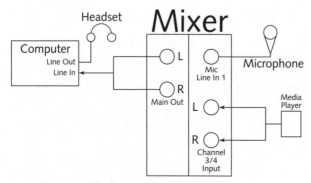

FIGURE 6-10: Standard mixer block diagram.

You should always consult your owner's manual for connection procedures. All mixers come with detailed instructions and if you purchase one used, you will want to go online and download a manual from the manufacturer's website.

The main thing to remember is this: A standard mixer will give you control over audio levels going to your computer. The mixer will provide amplification of your microphone audio through the amplifiers in the mixer. You can control noise by finding a happy balance between the line and microphone input settings on your PC.

Advanced Block Diagram

The main difference between a standard mixer and an advanced mixer is the ability to add additional audio processing components. Advanced mixers also enable you to monitor the audio coming out of your sound card by wiring the audio output to a channel so that you can monitor what you have just recorded without moving headsets around. Figure 6-11 shows an advanced mixer block diagram configuration.

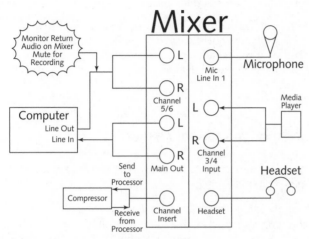

FIGURE 6-11: Advanced mixer block diagram.

What I like about the advanced mixers is fairly straightforward: The channel insert allows me to process the audio before it is sent through the equalization stage on the mixer. If I have some audio that I want to insert into the mixer that has already been processed, I can route that audio so that it is mixed in cleanly and not sent to the extra processor.

Note The computer audio feedback connection is for playback only. You should select mute on the input channel during recording. Not doing so causes a feedback loop. If your mixer does not have a mute switch, you will want to listen to the recorded audio directly on your PC as opposed to relying on wiring as displayed.

Audio Processing

If you walk through a music store or look at the various types of audio-processing equipment available today, you probably would not know where to start. I sure didn't. I had some DBX processing components that I used 20 years ago, but a lot has changed. My need to look for some audio-processing solutions resulted from the fact that I am recording my podcast in my home. We all know that homes have a lot of background noise.

During one podcast, my wife was in the garage arranging some of the holiday boxes. I could not hear her banging around down there while I was sitting in the office with my headset off, but my condenser microphone picked up that thumping sound very clearly. I also have four computers in my office, and even though I have reduced my noise levels by nearly 35 dB by buying new ultra-quiet fans and the like, there was still some background noise getting through.

Call me a perfectionist for wanting studio conditions in a non-studio location. I have come very close to achieving that with a small investment. I can only speak of my personal experiences, so if you have an audio issue that you cannot overcome yourself, drop me an e-mail at podcastbook@gmail.com and I will do everything I can to get you hooked up with the best resources.

Solutions to Typical Audio Issues

I want to explain the process I went through to improve my show. This will help you understand the importance of some of the audio-processing equipment I review in this chapter.

Most podcasters experience some of the same issues, so hopefully, understanding the process I went through and the audio solutions I discovered by trial and error will help you out. I had several issues to contend with: I had noise issues, low microphone amplification, uneven frequency response when I was recording, and harmonic degradation. I went after these issues one by one.

1. I purchased a good microphone to flatten the frequency response, making it pretty even across the board. Even prior to throwing the other equipment at the problem, I realized that the new microphone made a world of difference.

2. Next, I purchased a good mixer. This connected my great microphone to a great pre-amplifier that did not introduce any noise that wasn't already in the environment.

3. I purchased a DBX 266XL, which contained an expander gate and compressor. The expander gate is used to remove noise, and the compressor is used to smooth out the dynamic range of the signal and increase frequency response.

4. Finally I added an Aphex 204, better known as the aural exciter. It re-creates and restores missing harmonics at both the low and high end of the sonic spectrum.

Using these items resulted in audio quality that I have been extremely happy with and has amazed the listeners. Typically, no one component can create perfect audio. The thing to remember is that I am using the same equipment I am writing about, so this is not a theoretical solution. It is a real solution in use, today.

We have talked about everything in this list except for the last two items, so let me cover gate and compressors and an audio processor that I fell in love with. I will also give those of you on a budget an all-in-one solution.

Here are two more great resources for help:

- **Podcast Rigs (http://podcastrigs.com):** This site is dedicated to audio quality.
- **Podcast Alley (http://podcastalley.com):** Forums of podcasters helping podcasters.

Compressors/Gates

One of the most important audio processors you can buy is a compressor. A compressor is a device that smooths out the dynamic range of a signal. If you have a noise issue, you will want a compressor that has an expander gate. The gate will not let sound that is below the level you set get through.

In my case, I was fighting fan noise. The expander gate was able to block the majority of the fan noise and allowed only the sound of my voice through, which is at a louder level than the fan noise. The compressor works in relation to the expander gate setting, and you can set reaction times that determine how fast the compressor reacts to a signal that breaks the expander gate threshold. For a very detailed explanation of what a compressor is, visit `http://music-and-technology.com/compression.html`.

There is a lot of gear on the market today, and the choices you make will depend on your situation. If you have a low-noise environment, you may be able to get away with just a compressor like the DBX 160A. In my case, since I had the noise issue, I went with the DBX 266XL that had the combo compressor and gate. You can find these components at `http://dbxpro.com`.

APHEX 204 Aural Exciter and Optical Big Bottom

What I found was that after my shows were compressed into MP3 format, I sounded like I was talking in a room that had no furniture. (My office has no carpet and a wooden desk). The audio tone also sounded (what I call) sharp and had no depth. I wanted to spice up the sound, and I added an aural exciter.

The Aphex Aural Exciter is a processor that recreates and restores missing harmonics at both the low and high end of the sonic spectrum. Aphex products are known for their superior sound reproduction, and the Aphex 204 is an industry leader. I love the sound that comes out of this processor. There has even been a scientific study done on the Aphex 204; you can find detailed information at `http://aphex.com`. The Aphex 204 can be found online for as low as $199.

There are a number of audio processors on the market today, and sadly I can only talk about equipment that I have used. Podcasters helping podcasters has allowed me to learn a great deal in a short period.

I highly recommend that you visit `http://podcastrigs.com` because this site is updated on a regular basis and has suggestions for podcasting equipment.

An All-in-One Audio Processing Solution

Many of you will not have the budget to go out and purchase the boxes I have outlined. When I was just getting started, I used a standard mixer and struggled to get the audio to sound good. I was on a budget, and the wife was giving me the evil eye when I started asking to add components. However, through a recommendation at Podcast Rigs, I was able to pick up a box that is an all-in-one solution. My listeners noticed the difference the very first show. I consider it the best $100 I have spent in a long time. This box makes the sound through that $49 standard mixer come alive.

The Behringer UltraVoice VX2000, which can be found at `http://behringer.com`, retails for $105. It is a multifunction device that has a microphone-amplifier, discrete vintage input, expander, tube emulation, compressor, equalizer, and de-esser all built into one box. This is the perfect piece of equipment for those of you running a standard mixer. You need to visit the Behringer website (`http://behringer.com`) and read about what this box can do.

I used the microphone amplifier. To reduce noise, I used Behringer's version of a gate, called *discrete vintage input.* I used the expander, the equalizer, and the de-esser.

You can connect your microphone to the VX2000 processor. It has phantom power. Then you can route the audio directly into your computer or connect it through the microphone input of your standard mixer. You can also use this with mixers that are equipped with channel inserts, because it has special jacks for channel insert use only.

The Behringer UltraVoice by itself solved many of my issues, but you get what you pay for — I did a good 20 shows with that box before I upgraded to the equipment I reviewed previously.

You may say, "This is a lot of equipment." My response is that I have done my best to find you both economical and high-end solutions to the most common issues podcasters are experiencing to date.

Digital Device Recording Considerations

The majority of podcasters, including me, record their podcasts on their computers. There are also a lot of podcasters recording their podcasts to a variety of different types of devices, including:

- Cell phones
- PDAs
- iPod with iMic
- Pocket PCs
- Digital MP3 recorders
- Professional digital recorders

The list is endless. Many of you will want to record podcasts while traveling or on the way to and from work. In Chapter 7, I will talk about different recording scenarios, but there are some lessons that we all can learn from the experiences podcasters have already had.

Why Computers Are Not the Best Audio Recorders

Case in point: I was very late one night getting ready to do my show. I had researched all the online articles, laid out all my show notes, and was ready to start. I loaded my recording software, did my sound checks, and proceeded to record the show. Approximately 35 minutes into a 40-minute show, my computer froze. I literally screamed because I had already spent an hour getting ready for the show and finding all the news articles I wanted to talk about. I was left with nothing but my computer show notes. Of the 50+ shows I have created, I have had technical difficulties with the computer twice.

I was smart though: After my first incident, I purchased a mini-MP3 recorder to use as a backup recording device. (I will talk about various MP3 recording devices later in this section.) So now, when I record a show, not only is it being recorded to my computer, but I also run a separate line from my mixer to the line in on the MP3 player. In recent weeks, I have been using my Mac Mini as my secondary recording device as a way to learn how to process audio on a Mac.

Computers are weird sometimes and will cause you a lot of grief. These incidents are not limited to Windows users. They happen to Mac users as well. So, this is one of the considerations you may want to take into account when deciding what type of device on which to record your shows.

Environment and Noise

Some people have found that their computers create noise and strange sound artifacts. I know that before I purchased a better sound card, I spent several days trying to isolate a sound that was actually being generated by my computer. I also found that a device in my home was not being grounded properly, and every time it ran I could hear a slight hum in my headset. Homes are not designed to be audio studios, but with a little work, they can be made into very good podcasting studios.

Some of you may simply decide to buy a digital recording device so that you can record in any location at any time without having to worry about your computer locking up or giving you the ill fated Blue Screen of Death.

Digital Recording Device Considerations

After my first computer lockup, I was determined to record all of my shows to my external digital recording device. I found that the streamlined process I had used when recording to my PC was hindered. I had to do extra processing with the external media device, primarily because audio clips that I would normally have played on my PC had to be spliced into the recording.

So, what was happening was basically this: I would finish recording and then transfer the recording from the digital media recorder to my PC. I would then have to import it into my audio-editing software, Adobe Audition, and then find the areas in the recording into which I wanted to insert my audio clips. I would have to cut the show into chunks, insert the clips, and then create the final MP3.

As you can see, this was not the best solution. So, I then routed audio out of my computer into the mixer and routed all of the combined data onto the digital recorder. This saved me a lot of time because I was able to insert the clips on queue and did not have to reedit the final saved file.

These are considerations for recording on a digital device:

- Time
- Editing
- Quality of the digital media recording
- Audio feedback—can you listen to what is being recorded?

Some of you will choose to record on a digital device. My recommendation is to record to a PC as the primary device and use the digital recorder as a backup. If you decide to use a digital recorder as your primary device, make sure that you develop a production plan that will make it easy for you to produce the program with the least amount of pain. I will say this: The second time my PC crashed I was very happy that my digital recording device was running because it saved me from having to create the whole show over again.

Selecting the Best Digital Recorder

When I first thought about buying a digital recorder, I broke out in a cold sweat. I went looking at some of the various music store sites to see how much those devices cost; I was shocked. I was relieved when I found out that I could get a decent recording from the same device I was using to listen to MP3s.

Many of you have portable media devices that have a recording option, and if you're lucky enough to have one of those already, you only need to check a few things out to make sure you have a device that is going to give you the quality your listeners deserve.

Most of the MP3 player/recorder models on the market today have menu options that allow you to set the bit and sample rates. Professional standalone digital recorders that are designed to be used in small home studios and portable sets are packed with many more features.

I will discuss two categories of digital recorders:

- The MP3 player/digital recorder solutions
- Professional digital recorder solutions

MP3 Player/Digital Recorder Features

Pay attention to bit rate. You want a recorder that is capable of recording at a high bit rate— 64 Kbps or higher. Some of the MP3 players on the market today record only at very low bit rates. Luckily, many support bit rates that are much higher than those you would normally want to record at.

Some of the recorders on the market today record in a proprietary format. Until recently, the iRIVER MP3 player/recorders recorded only in a proprietary format, and the included interface software would convert the audio to a non-MP3 format, requiring the file to be converted one additional time. It is best if the player can record in native MP3 format.

Many of the MP3 player/recorders have Automatic Gain Control (AGC), but some of the AGC circuits are not the best, so you will need to make sure that the AGC can be turned off. This way you can set the gain level of the microphone to a pre-determined level.

It is best if the unit supports USB 2.0, because you will be creating large files, and it is discouraging to have to wait for the file to be transferred to your PC.

It is essential that you be able to plug a set of headphones into the headphone jack and be able to hear what you are recording. I learned in my DJ days that being able to listen to that feedback was essential to developing good recording skills.

Finally, there is nothing more discouraging then having to have a stack of AA batteries that you have to feed to the recorder the way you put money in a juke box. Make sure that your unit has a long battery life.

MP3 Player/Digital Recorder Reviews

Every electronics company in the country seems to be getting into the MP3 player business, and many of them use some of the same internal chip sets. The only difference is the code that the manufacturer has written to support them. Luckily for podcasters, most manufacturers enable all of the chip set's features. They know very well that the majority of consumers are going to purchase the device to listen to music only, but they add recording to their feature list to push the fence sitter into buying the product with the rationalization that he or she can use it as a dictating device. Little did manufacturers realize that their desire to have a long list of features played right into the hands of the exploding podcasting revolution.

 Note One disappointing thing is that Apple did not anticipate this. Of all the MP3 player/recorder devices on the market, the Apple iPod has no native support. You can buy the add-on microphone from Griffin Technologies (`http://griffintechnology.com`), but the bit rate is so low that you will want to publish your podcast at lower than AM quality.

iRIVER IFP-790

iRIVER (`http://iriver.com`) is one of the premier portable media device manufacturers. iRIVER makes a wide variety of MP3 player/recorder devices that are almost all podcast-friendly. The IFP-790 retails for $139. I personally own this MP3 player/recorder. It packs a powerful punch, considering that it's only a little bigger than a cigarette lighter. Figure 6-12 shows how small this device is.

The IFP-790 has the following recording features:

- It supports MPEG 1/2/2.5 Layer 3, WMA, and ASF file types.
- It supports from 8 Kbps to about 320 Kbps (OGG: 44.1 kHz, 96.1 Kbps to 225 Kbps) bit rates.
- The battery life is 10 hours.
- It is AGC-configurable.
- It enables audio feedback.

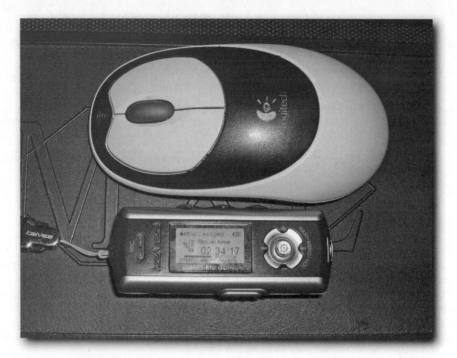

FIGURE 6-12: iRIVER IFP-790.

The majority of units in the iRIVER family of media devices have sufficient storage and positive features to make them nice digital recorders. The newest models have firmware upgrades that make them look like USB devices when plugged into your computer, and you can access the device with a regular drive letter.

Note You must use the included software package to pull audio files off the device and convert them into a useful format.

Samsung Yepp YP-MT6

The Samsung Yepp is known for exceptional battery life and is almost the same sized form factor as the iRIVER. It is another exceptional portable digital recorder. You can find more info about the Samsung line of portable media players/recorders at http://samsungyepp.com. The YP-MT6 retails for $119.

It has the following recording features:

- It supports MPEG 1/2/2.5 Layer 3 file types.

- It allows for bit/sample rates of WMA, ASF (8 Kbps to 320 Kbps)/(8 kHz to 48 kHz).

- It allows for bit/sample rates of OGG (8 Kbps to 192 Kbps bit rate)/(8 kHz to 48 kHz).

- It has a 42-hour battery life.

- It allows for audio feedback.

 Note Because manufacturers are introducing new player/recorder combinations all the time, you will want to make sure that the player has a line in connector. Some of the players have only a microphone built into the unit.

Pocket PC

Pocket PCs can be used to record podcasts. Although they run an actual operating system onto which you can load software, you will find that various audio recording programs on the market today do not support very high bit rates. Regardless, you can use the Pocket PC and be up and recording in a few minutes.

Professional Digital Recorders

This products are in a class all their own. Unlike the inexpensive portable digital recorders we just talked about, these products were designed to record very high-quality music. The majority of these professional digital recorders record in the WAV format. This will require you to move the media to your PC and compress the recording into the publishing format of your choice. Luckily, the price difference between these units and the portable units is not as great as you would expect. You will pay a minimum of around $400 dollars for one of these units.

The majority of the digital recorders on the market today are targeted toward multitrack recording, so many of the recorders are capable of receiving multiple inputs; thus, they are multichannel. In fact, some of the digital recorders can double as a mixer and a recorder, with some of the features of standard and professional mixers.

I really like the units that use SmartMedia cards as the storage medium. This makes it very easy to transfer the data to your computer after you have completed recording. Many are also self-contained and will run on battery power. These digital recorders are packed with so many features that it is impossible to list them all. But I will highlight a few characteristics that I like in professional digital recorders:

- Portable

- Battery-powered

- Four track minimum

- Media storage card capable

- Internal hard drive

- FireWire/USB 2.0 PC interface

- Sampling frequency of 44 kHz minimum

- Audio monitoring

Having never owned one of these units, I did a lot of asking around and reading online reviews. I am always very cautious of online reviews, because I do not know how many times the manufacturer has had an employee put in a review for the benefit of the company. I decided to call five leading audio equipment sales companies and ask them quite bluntly which professional digital recorder they recommended to new customers and what their most popular selling items were. I also called several of these same companies and asked for a demo unit to try for four to five days so that I could write a review from something that I had physically touched. All of those companies refused, which made me wonder what it takes to get on the demo list.

In Table 6-4, I list companies and models that I recommend you check out.

Table 6-4   Professional Digital Recorder Resources

Manufacturer	URL	Model	Price	Editor's Rank
Edirol	www.edirol.com	R-1	$550	*****
Fostex	www.fostex.com	MR-8	$299	***
TASCAM	www.tascam.com	DP-01	$399	****
ToneWorks by Korg	www.korg.com	PXR4 Pandora	$299	***

Telephone Interview Equipment

Many of you will want to do telephone interviews, and I found out the hard way that recording telephone conversations is not as easy as it sounds. When I used some rigged wiring that I had at home to record interviews, I found that my voice came in very loud, and the person I was speaking to came in very weakly. This made for a very unbalanced recording, which I spent a great deal of time fixing.

If you plan on doing a telephone recording only once in a while and don't mind the editing, there are some very inexpensive solutions. Those of you wanting to do call-in shows will need an interface box that is specifically designed for on-air or almost live to hard drive recording.

There are vendors who have telephone interface equipment for standard phones along with interfaces for PBX-type phone systems you may have at your office.

As with everything else in this chapter, you get what you pay for. For those willing to do a little editing of the recorded interview, a simple line interface from Radio Shack (http://radioshack.com) will work. The "Smart" Phone Recorder, control stock number 43-2208, priced at $29.95, is an inexpensive solution. But this interface will create highly unbalanced audio.

Note   When doing an interview, you always need to ask if the party you are speaking to if it is okay to record the interview. You do not want a surprise later when you get a callback saying that you did not have permission to record and podcast the interview live.

One of the industry leaders is JK Audio (`http://jkaudio.com`). They have a nice selection of telephone interface equipment. I do only a couple of interviews a month and went with what I call an in-between solution, their Inline Patch (`http://jkaudio.com/inline-patch.htm`). It is perfect for conducting interviews at home, and it does a great job of leveling the recorded signal. This unit retails for $270. Figure 6-13 shows the Inline Patch.

For those of you who will be doing telephone interviews more often, I recommend that you upgrade to JK Audio's Broadcast Host (`http://jkaudio.com/broadcast-host.htm`). This unit retails for $495, but is worth every penny.

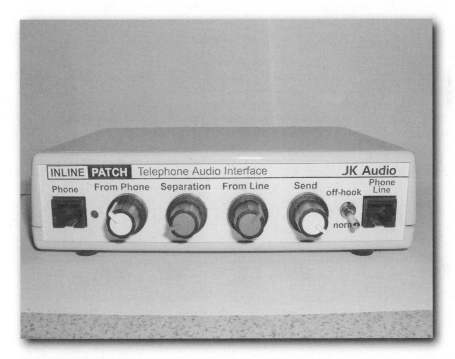

FIGURE 6-13: Inline Patch.

Cell Phone Recordings

Recording audio comments to your cell phone and having them published on the Internet has been going on for a long time, with companies like `http://audioblog.com` having put together a subscriber's network, where people can send audio comments to their weblogs from their cell phones, using the service as a conduit.

In the past, those have been 2- to 5-minute posts. Now that cell phones have more storage, it only makes sense that people are going to want to record podcasts on their cell phones. A few podcasts are being done on cell phones, but the podcasters are typically transferring that data to PCs after recording due to insanely high prices on sending files that large to their web servers.

Summary

I have discussed a great deal of equipment to help you nail down what you need when creating a professional studio. Here's a check list for you:

- Microphone: dynamic or condenser
- Mixer: standard or advanced
- Computer sound card, fans, and cases
- Audio interfaces
- Digital recorders: MP3 or professional digital recorder
- Audio processors

I have provided you with some direction in case you decide to take your podcast to the next level. Many podcasters continue today with the basic setup of a microphone and a computer. That's all you really need to create a fun and enjoyable podcast. You create the content, and they will listen. In Chapter 7, I will talk about all sorts of fun places for recording your podcasts.

Recording Your Podcast and Performing Postproduction Tasks

part

Recording Locations

You have assembled all the tools you need to record a podcast. The question you have to ask yourself now is, where do I record my shows? I decided from the very beginning that I would record whenever and wherever the opportunity presented itself. You don't have to record in your studio. You can create your podcast while driving to work, making dinner, or taking a walk.

You can create a podcast from almost anywhere. You can podcast live events of interest to you and your listeners. You can podcast from restaurants and coffee shops. I have heard podcasts that were recorded on international flights, in cars on bumpy roads, or by people on nature walks.

We begin looking at podcasting from your home and then veer away from the norm to cover aspects of podcasting in less normal places. This chapter is full of helpful hints to make your podcasts run smoothly, no matter what venue you choose.

Podcasting in Your Home

Most podcasters record their shows from their homes, apartments, condos, and lofts. Some have been banned to the garage with the typical roll of the eyes that nongeek wives give their geek husbands. Now don't get me wrong; podcasting isn't relegated to the guys. The ladies are getting in on the action, too.

There are a few female personalities out there who blow the stereotypical ladies-are-nice theory. Some women talk trash like adolescent boys in a high-school locker room. You have women giving women advice, and women giving men advice. They provide lots of material that you wouldn't find in a *Dear Abby* column. It seems that some of the ladies are more over the top than the guys.

There are even husband-and-wife teams putting out shows. Some podcasters, barely into their teen years, are putting together tech shows.

When podcasting from your home, the main thing to remember is that this is your home; don't turn it into a broadcast studio. A few simple things you can do when you are preparing to record your show will help your production value.

I have a rule: I start recording, and I don't stop even if one of the kids comes in needing a drink of water. This is podcasting after all; it's live to hard drive. We aren't sitting in a radio station in a completely sterile environment. My suggestions in Chapter 6 gave you the tools to improve the quality of your recording and your environment, but, hey, life is life.

Simple suggestions to make podcasting at home a more rewarding experience:

- Give your dog a bone so he doesn't bark.
- Stop all major construction work.
- Turn off the A/C to reduce vent noise.
- Close the door to the room in which you are recording.
- Get the room lighting in the mood your show requires.
- Turn off unneeded computers.
- Unplug the office phone.

Control your environment at the level you want. It's as simple as that!

Now that I've done over 50 shows, I have a ritual I go through. For some reason, I feel the need to brush my teeth before I record my podcast. I guess it's a psychological thing — like not wanting to have smelly breath when speaking to people. I usually pound an energy drink 30 minutes prior to recording to get pumped up. Just prior to show time, I turn down the lights. The glow of the two monitors gives me that control-room feel and puts me in the tech-talk mood.

With a full-time job, kids, wife, pet, house, and so on, I typically don't get to record my shows until around 10 p.m. So, after putting in a full day at work and dealing with things at home, my body is saying *go to bed*, but my brain is saying *podcast*. This recording ritual works for me. Each person is different, so you have to experiment to find your own.

Creating Podcasts Outside the Studio

There's nothing wrong with creating your podcasts in a controlled environment. Broadcasters have been doing it for years. But working from unlikely places can breathe new life into your podcasts and add spontaneity. In this section, I discuss podcasting sites you may not have thought of.

The Walking Podcast

Some of us can do two or three things at the same time. My wife is famous for making dinner, talking on the phone, and orchestrating through hand gestures exactly what chores she needs me to take care of. So I figured if my wife could act like a traffic director, I should be able to talk and walk at the same time. My problem is that I have a tendency to stop walking and start expressing myself to the audience that isn't there.

Can you imagine the kids in my neighborhood? They must holler at their moms and say, "Hey, there's that strange guy walking and talking to himself again." But with technology the way it is and headsets quite small, I figure that a lot of people just think I'm talking on my mobile phone.

One of the new types of podcast starting to show up is the *sound scene tour*. In a sound scene tour, you give listeners a tour of an area via the podcast. When I go home to Michigan, I love to visit my grandfather's farm, with its 40 acres of woods. It was a great place to explore when I was little and a great place to think. I would often see deer and other animals. When I was older, I hunted in those same woods.

So, you can be guaranteed that the next time I go back to Michigan, I'll take the whole world for a sound seeing tour. Maybe you have a special place and would like to share it with the rest of the world.

All you really need is a microphone headset combo and an MP3 player that is capable of recording, as I covered in Chapter 5. That's it.

Podcasting in the Car

Did you know that a car makes almost the perfect studio? It has wall-to-wall carpeting with sound barrier insulation. The closed-in space is like a recording studio. I am sure that the majority of you won't haul your computers, extension cords, microphones and so on out to the car to do a podcast. But consider using your car when you are meeting someone for an interview and the location is too noisy. Obviously, a vehicle only makes a great studio when you are sitting still with the engine off. I know that my car isn't all that quiet when I'm rolling down the road, especially when I'm trying to avoid blowing a tire from the potholes that are so prevalent on the roads in Hawaii.

Podcasting from the car requires no more equipment than a sound scene tour does: a microphone headset combo and a MP3 player capable of recording.

Here are some tips for podcasting in your car:

- Do a sound check both while sitting still and while rolling down the road.
- Use a hands-free device.
- Don't cover both ears with a headset; use a headset that covers only one ear.
- Drive the speed limit.
- Don't podcast in school zones.
- Don't read show notes while on the move.

 Some of us have a hard time chewing gum and walking at the same time, so a word of caution: As with talking on a cell phone, be it hands-free or not, you risk crashing your vehicle and killing yourself or, worse, someone else. So, please consider this before you create a podcast in your vehicle when you are driving. We don't want to lose a podcaster to a traffic accident because he or she was trying to drive and podcast at the same time.

Podcasting in Public Places

Podcasters are taking their shows to streets, bars, restaurants, clubs, and coffee shops. It takes a certain level of self-confidence to plug in your microphone and record a podcast in public. Talk about being self-conscious. Personally, I don't think I could sit down in a coffee shop full of customers and start recording a show. But it definitely could make for a fun time. I was talking to a podcaster, and he said that creating his podcast in public has been a form of therapy in which he is forced to go out and interact with the public and build self-confidence.

Typically, people are pretty shy about microphones, but put one in someone's face and ask a question, and watch out. There is always something in the national news or happening in the local community that can get people pretty passionate. Plus, they will have something to talk about in the next week.

One idea I had was to leave the person with information about where your show is. Word of mouth will build listeners faster than advertising.

 You will want to take a few things into consideration if you record in an establishment that has customers at tables. You want to make sure that you are seated in an area where you are least liable to bother other customers. So, be aware of your environment. The last thing you want is someone in your face because you're disturbing his or her study time — or date.

It probably isn't a good idea to roll in with your studio gear and set up like a radio station, so try to minimize your recording rig. Take as little gear as you can: a laptop or portable digital recorder, a headset microphone, and possibly a battery-powered FireWire audio interface. Because my laptop is a power pig, I always try to sit near a power socket.

Additionally, in restaurants or places where servers live on tips, be sure to tip according to the amount of time you tie up a table! If you just buy a coffee at a busy restaurant and then sit for 45 minutes podcasting, your server loses money!

If there's a live performance going on, you need to ask permission first. Not doing so could cause some major embarrassment when security shows you the door or tries to confiscate your recording equipment.

Background noise will be an issue, so you may have to do some postproduction processing to try and filter some of it out. I cover this in detail in Chapter 9.

Being in a public place is much different from being at someone's business, and many times business owners get very fussy if you record without permission.

- Be prepared to tell the person why you are recording at their establishment.
- Generally, you should ask permission to plug your laptop into power.
- Respect the wishes of the establishment staff.

Following these rules will ensure that you are allowed to use the premises a second time.

Podcasting Meetings and Conventions

I love being able to record the meetings and forums I go to. I have learned some valuable lessons that will help ensure the successful recording of any type of public event:

- Ask permission ahead of time.
- Bring sufficient cables and adapters to connect to the meeting's audio board.
- Bring microphone and cable if the organization doesn't have an audio board.
- Bring an extension cord and power strip.
- Bring tape to secure your cables and prevent a tripping hazard.
- Arrive early.
- Come with a release form to allow rebroadcast.
- Most important, don't be an annoyance.

Every meeting will be different. Some of the conferences I have attended had no issues with my getting an audio feed from their audio mixer. Other organizers have flat out refused, and I had to resort to polite persuasion to at least have a microphone close to an audio speaker. Some of the events required me to submit a letter requesting access on company letterhead.

You may need to get a business license and a Doing Business As (DBA) certificate. I found that some simple work by me has allowed my website to acquire press credentials. Typically, event managers love press coverage, be it Internet-based or in print. Add the dimension that you are doing an audio show, and you may find doors open to you that were closed before.

If all else fails, take lots of notes and record post-conference or post-meeting. Find some connectivity and get it online as soon as possible. I have been able to get play-by-play reports from conferences I wanted to attend but could not.

Podcasting with Your Phone or PDA

If you have a phone, like the Treo, that is capable of recording an audio file, or if you have a PDA with a built-in microphone, you can record almost any place. Heck, even the MP3 players have their own external microphones, so you never know when the opportunity will present itself to record a podcast.

Carrying your rig around isn't always convenient. Your circumstances will drive where and what you want to record. You don't have to be all that structured; podcasting has a lot of wow factor. It's life's unscripted moments that are worth recording.

Here are some recording ideas:

- Town meetings
- Festivals
- Fairs
- Airplanes
- Bus tours
- Railroad rides
- Ski trips
- Fishing (the big fish story)

The list is endless. Many of you already have the gear to do a podcast on the go or in some out-of-the ordinary location. The key is to pull out your recording device, hit Record, and get busy.

Podcasting Topic Ideas

Because we live in a digital world, I decided to make a family podcast on a regular basis that talks about life and gives family advice to those who will come after me.

Sure, this is not a traditional podcast like those I have been talking about so far, but you can see where I am going. We capture some of our lives on video, but think of the advice you can impart to future generations. Or, you can just give them something funny to listen to. I can think of nothing more satisfying than to have my great-great-great-great-grandchild listen to a podcast that I created. It's like a living genealogical record.

So, before I start throwing down the philosophy of life, let's talk about some typical scenarios for a podcast. Remember, be creative and have fun, fun, fun.

Here are some topics that I randomly thought of. Any one of these could be a great podcast. Obviously, some of these ideas are location-specific, but you never know when a traveler will be trying to find information on something in your area.

- Restaurant reviews
- Walking tours in tourist areas
- Get-around tips for your area
- Bar reviews
- Club reviews
- Park reviews
- Cruise reports

- Lessons on something in which you have expertise
- Local band interviews and music
- Plays and orchestras
- Interviews
- Interview guys about meeting girls, and vice versa
- Gym workout routines
- Cooking with the kids
- Foreign language lessons
- Talks about culture clash
- Music and video reviews
- Husband-wife conversations
- Raising kids: trials and tribulations

The list is endless. There are at least a million other topics, but I hope I have given you some ideas about creating a podcast that would be fun and a sure hit.

Summary

There is no right or wrong way to podcast, as long as you get busy and do it. The adventure is about to begin and I know that you, in your heart and soul, are ready to podcast. You have the tools needed and some ideas about where you'd like to record your podcast. I have given you some simple, straightforward tips and, hopefully, some ideas on where and what to broadcast.

Are you ready?

Flip the page, and let's get it on!

The Recording Process

The moment to turn on the microphone and record your podcast has arrived. Nearly half the battle is over. Now the fun begins, and you can join the world of podcasting by recording your own podcast. There is no need to worry, because I will teach you what to do with that recording after it is sitting smooth and polished on your hard drive. Let's get busy so you can get your voice live to hard drive.

The goal in this chapter is to get your podcast recorded. I am also going to walk you through some basic scenarios to give all the novices out there a leg up.

Even with 50 shows under my belt, there is something new I learn each and every time I hit Record.

Setting Up Your Software

Throughout this book, I have made an attempt to give you solutions that will allow you to record a podcast with gear that you own, today, and I want to focus on that first. The fancy hardware tools that I discussed in Chapter 7 will come into play later, but the software utilization portion of this book will remain the same. Some of you may choose to use alternative recording software, but the setup principles are the same.

Because Windows, Mac, and Linux users will be reading this book, I will use Audacity (http://audacity.sourceforge.net). It works on all three platforms. If you have not installed Audacity, please do so now.

You and I are podcasters, but each of us has separate goals. Luckily for you and me, there are a significant number of in-depth tutorials on the Internet on recording audio. You could spend weeks reading all the different techniques. I'm going to give you the basics. Feel free to use the various tutorials on the Audacity website to dig deeper into Audacity.

Configuring Audacity

In all the following examples, I will be using Windows screen shots. The screens have slight differences for Mac and Linux users. When you load Audacity, you are presented with the screen shown in Figure 8-1.

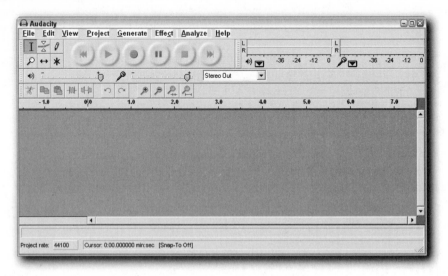

FIGURE 8-1: Main Audacity operating screen.

1. First, set all the preferences. Click File, then Preferences, to bring up the Preferences page for Audacity. You will want to take a look at the Audio I/O tab, as shown in Figure 8-2.

Upon initial setup, the Preferences page will probably display your onboard sound card. If you have purchased a secondary audio card, you will have to select the correct audio playback and recording device via the pull-down menus on the page. If you are using the audio card that came with your computer, it will likely be chosen by default.

Note

Mac users who have installed SoundFlower will want to choose SoundFlower as their primary recording device. You will find that you may have three to four recording devices to choose from. For testing purposes, you may want to choose your primary interface device, such as the iMic or the onboard microphone input on the computer, to make sure that you are getting audio in before manipulating SoundFlower. Details about the iMic can be found in Chapter 5.

Both Windows and Mac users need to take a few minutes to visit the audio sections of their computer's configuration. Windows users will find these settings in the Control Panel, Sounds and Audio Devices, and Mac users will find those settings in System Preferences. You should choose the devices you want set for default input and output.

FIGURE 8-2: Audacity Preferences Audio I/O.

Note

If you are a laptop user and use a PCMCIA audio card for recording your podcast, but remove it for everyday use, be aware that Windows will default back to the onboard sound card as the primary line in/microphone and line out settings. Thus, when you reinstall the secondary sound card, you will need to ensure that the primary recording device is correct.

2. Too often, I have been all prepared to record and then found myself without audio. Having the Audio icon available on the system tray has allowed me to enable the mike quickly, which lets me get going. There is a little trick that Windows users sometimes miss when they load their Audio control panel, as depicted in Figure 8-3.

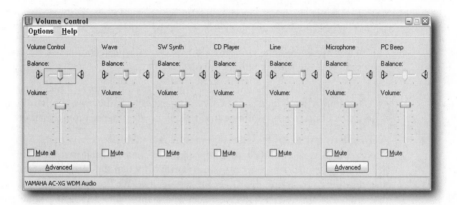

FIGURE 8-3: Windows playback volume control.

Most users don't realize that there is a separate recording control. You can control audio playback levels from this panel, but if you click Options and then the Recording button, you get the window shown in Figure 8-4.

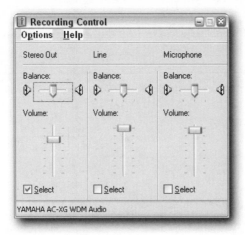

FIGURE 8-4: Recording input levels.

You will want to use this Recording Control window to control your default recording device. If you find that your line in is excessively noisy, you can lower the input level settings. Having it turned all the way up is usually not the best setting for Windows users. I will talk more about setting audio levels later in this chapter.

Note

Having the Windows Audio icon on the system tray allows me to open it up quickly to make changes if I need to, because some audio-recording programs may need a higher level. If yours is not there by default, you can enable it via Control Panel, Sounds and Audio Devices. The only equivalent in the Mac is the audio input control add-on called SoundFlowerBed.

3. Next, I want to talk about recording quality settings, so click the Quality tab in the Audio Preferences window. Figure 8-5 shows the Quality tab.

The choice you make here will impact the quality of your recording. It is going to boil down to how picky you are with audio quality.

Don't stress over this too much, because you will find that you will make changes after you have done a few podcasts. It is a learning experience that you can have fun with. When you get proficient, you may find that you start to record more than podcasts.

I currently record all my podcasts at a sample rate of 44,100 Hz with a 32-bit float rate. This 32-bit float rate will take up more space, but I have found that recording with a 16-bit float rate does not meet my audio standards when the recording is encoded after post-recording processing. Don't get me wrong, a 16-bit float rate is sufficient and will give you radio-like quality. This is an area where you can experiment and determine where you want to set your Default Sample Rate and Default Sample Format options.

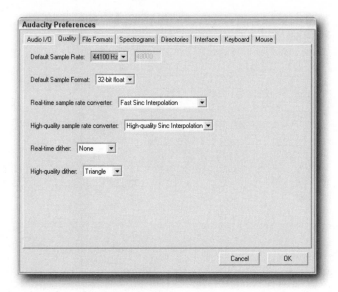

FIGURE 8-5: Audacity Quality tab.

Note

Remember, you will not know the true quality of your recording until you encode the file. When you play it back after being recorded, you'll hear the raw recording file, which is a high-quality audio file. Only after you compress the file will you know what your end sound will be.

4. Next, click the File Formats tab. Figure 8-6 shows the Preferences window File Formats tab.

There are some very important settings that you need to pay attention to here. Once you have completed the recording of a podcast, you have put down what I refer to as the "raw track." At this point, no file exists to send to a web server.

When you choose the Save function in Audacity, it will save the file in the Audacity Project format on your hard drive. The preference menu sets only the defaults that will be used if you choose to export your Audacity project to WAV, MP3, or OGG.

In Figure 8-4, I have chosen to save the MP3 Export Rate at 48; this is, in fact, a 48,000-bit rate. In Chapter 4, I gave you a table of sample MP3-encoded file sizes in comparison to different bit-rate settings.

Note

The majority of podcasters encode their files at a 48,000-bit rate. After my experimentation, I decided that I like a 64,000-bit rate. I end up with a larger file, but that's the way I want it. You will have to make that choice.

Note

As described in Chapter 5, you will need LAME to encode MP3 files with Audacity.

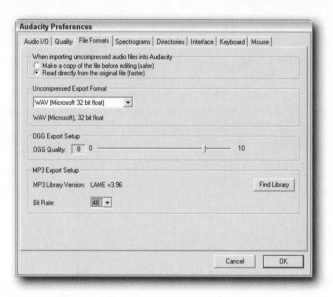

FIGURE 8-6: Audacity File Formats tab.

Figure 8-7 shows the Audacity Directories tab.

5. In the Location section of this tab, designate the storage location for project files as the drive that has the most space.

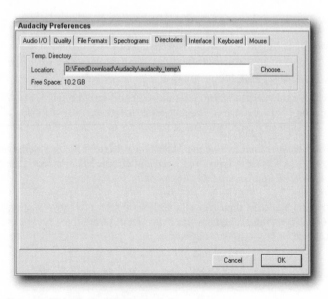

FIGURE 8-7: Audacity Directories tab.

The rest of the preference selections are very straightforward; be sure to refer to Audacity's website for answers to additional questions you may have on preference settings.

Understanding Audacity's Interface

I want to direct your attention back to the main program interface. Figure 8-8 shows the main page of the Audacity interface, with the Audio Source option expanded. Some of you will have a What U Hear option. If not, everyone should have a Stereo Out option. A lot depends on the type of audio card and interface software you have.

Many of you will want to record audio clips to Audacity that you play from a media player. Audacity allows you to isolate what it records. Figure 8-8 shows that you have a variety of options. The What U Hear and Stereo In options record every ping and pong that the computer makes and that you would normally hear in your headset along with audio from other programs.

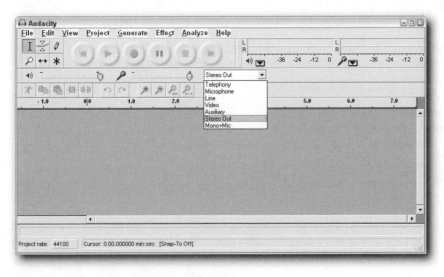

FIGURE 8-8: Audio Source options in Audacity.

The interface has the typical Stop, Play, FFWD, RWD, Record, and Play buttons, much like a standard cassette deck. The important section to pay attention to is the project rate at the bottom-left portion of the screen. The project rate is the same as the sample rate that you chose in the Preferences setting. You can easily change your default sample rate prior to making a recording. Near the center of the screen, you will see a microphone with a slide bar above it. Adjusting this setting will make a corresponding change to the device selected in Figure 8-5. This is a time-saver in that you can make changes to input levels on the fly.

Setting Your Recording Levels

Setting your recording levels is one of the most important things you will need to accomplish. It is also very difficult to explain in terms that won't cause your eyes to fog over. I am not going to give you a 1,000-word explanation, but it will be close.

Professional studios have professional soundboard people whose life revolves around getting audio levels perfect. The majority of us are amateurs, and we need to have an uncomplicated way to set input audio levels to make sure that the recording sounds good at all volume levels.

The Science of Audio Leveling

To get studio quality sound is tough for most amateurs. Most podcasters thus far have had little experience in setting audio production, so this topic can be very difficult. I am going to cover the basics and go through a setup scenario that takes several things into consideration:

- The majority of podcasters may only be using what they own today.

- The majority of podcasters will be using audio tools that are free and do not contain some of the enhanced audio processing algorithms.

- Some podcasters will be buying advanced audio electronics for the first time.

To get the best quality audio production, you could spend hours from the time you start recording to when you are ready to publish on the Net. My goal is to enable you to produce a podcast with the minimal amount of postproduction. Podcasting should be fun and not a chore.

I must emphasize *fun,* as fun for me is recording for 45 minutes, encoding the file, and publishing it. What is not fun is spending two hours editing what I just spent 45 minutes recording. Most of us do not have that kind of free time.

Some of you will want to dig much deeper into this topic, and I encourage you to do so. I recommend learning from people who do audio mastering for a living; thus, I am recommending several books: *Mastering Audio* by Bob Katz, and *Audio in Media* by Stanley Alten.

Hard-core audios buffs need to realize that the information I am about to impart is for a user getting started. I could do a hundred pages on audio processing alone, but guess what? It would make something hard that does not need to be.

I have done my best to suggest recording levels that will satisfy the majority of people reading this book. Initial audio recording levels are driven by the level of postproduction processing anyone creating audio will be doing. The postproduction tips I lay down in Chapter 9 will complement the following discussion.

The bottom line: A couple hours of experimentation will go a long way in helping you fine-tune the quality of your first podcast.

I will be the first to admit that getting my arms around the proper recording levels has been one of the most challenging things in this book. These first four steps are for those of you who are plugging a microphone directly into your computer. We will incorporate some more advanced recording level settings for those using mixers later in this chapter.

I am going to give you Todd's quick-and-dirty guide to recording levels for good sound:

1. First, you must do a half-dozen test recordings. You want to try to replicate the conditions you will have when you actually record your podcast. Find a good passage in a book or magazine that you will not mind reading a half-dozen times.

2. Read that passage aloud for at least two minutes each time. Start by adjusting the microphone levels on Audacity so that the meter is peaking between −12 dB and −6 dB. The meters on Audacity scale are in dB. You will be able to see the meter deflecting as you speak.

3. Read your passage in a normal tone of voice while recording; then save the file you have created. Adjust the microphone input slide bar, increasing the level in six incremental steps or until you get to a point where the peaks are as close to −1 dB as you can get them. Keep track of the changes you make to the slide bar so you know which recording belongs to which setting. With Audacity, it is very difficult to accurately read the meters on the software package. In the end, your ears will be able to pick the sample that sounds the best.

4. After you have created those samples, encode them all to MP3 with the bit rate you chose in Figure 8-6. Play those six samples on a variety of devices — MP3 player, car radio, home stereo — and listen to each of the clips at various volume levels. Be sure to see how the audio from each of the clips sounds with the volume turned way up and also way down.

I have found that recordings approaching −1dB that I have simply saved and published to the Internet have significant distortion on various devices when the volume is turned up very high. As many of you will want to record and publish without doing a lot of postproduction processing, these settings have proven to be safe choices for me.

As you read articles on the Internet about audio levels, you will find that they go into mind-numbing detail about audio setting levels for analog-to-digital recording. I am no audio engineer, but I do have a pretty good set of ears, and I think your ears will be able to tell you when you have found the right level.

I try to keep my audio reference level between −12 dB and −6 dB. I then try to keep my peaks between −6 dB to −3 dB. This, in turn, gives me some additional headroom so that I never exceed −.1 dB. In Audacity, you will need to eyeball the meters closely. This is one of the reasons I chose a more professional software recording package, as it has a very good audio level meter and superior postprocessing tools.

Using the levels I just outlined will result in your recordings sounding quieter than other podcasts, but you will not clip people's speakers or headsets when you vocalize something.

When you go to a movie theater, you will hear explosive sounds that have a large dynamic range. Typically, a person sitting in a Dolby-enhanced movie theater will experience as much as 20 dB of change in the audio that he or she is hearing. If you are playing that movie in your home on a modern surround sound system, you will typically experience 12 dB of dynamic range. The dynamic range coming out of your TV is typically 6 dB. So, that said, do you need or want 20 dB of dynamic range on your podcast? The answer is no, because most manufacturers do not even allow it in the design of their audio playback circuitry. So long as you can keep your short peaks to –3 dB to –.1 dB, your sound should come out sounding terrific.

Try my test; it should not take more than an hour, and you should be able to determine what sounds best for you with your setup.

In addition, I ask my listeners for feedback. That feedback has been worth its weight in gold.

Getting Ready to Record

You now have a basic understanding how to use the software and set your audio levels. Many of you will want to record your podcast and get on with it. In this next session, I am going to cover how to use other programs on your PC to add audio clips. I will also discuss the integration of a mixer and other components that you may have to contend with when getting ready to record. Finally, I will talk about the actual production of the show, and in Chapter 9, I talk about postproduction of your podcast.

Incorporating Audio Clips

Those of you running a very basic setup will want to be able to play audio clips and maybe even background music. I do this today on my Windows machine with Winamp (http://winamp.com) and on my Mac Mini with QuickTime (http://apple.com). QuickTime is versatile in that I can open up more than one instance of the program on my desktop to create a queuing system. Figure 8-9 shows multiple instances of QuickTime and Winamp loaded on my desktop.

So, what happens is this: While I am recording my show, I keep these windows open so that I can play my intro, which is queued, and when needed, I can play a couple of segment fillers. Here is my typical setup:

1. I have my show set up in a play list, so I load Winamp and load the play list with the intro. I play the clip and make sure that the audio will not be about the same level as my voice.

2. If I have received promotional clips or have an advertiser spot, I load those in QuickTime, as I can very quickly open multiple instances of QuickTime by selecting New Player in the QuickTime menu.

3. I then make sure that Audacity has Stereo or What U Hear? selected prior to starting the show.

4. When I'm ready, I can start Audacity recording and play the intro to start the show. As I progress in my show notes, I then play the audio clips I have loaded in QuickTime.

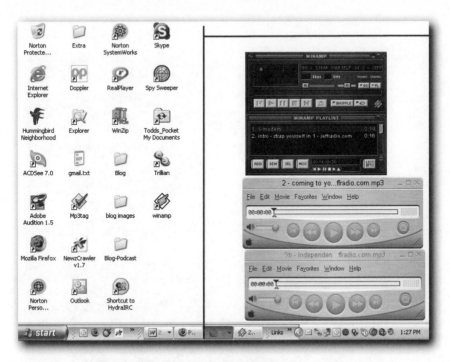

FIGURE 8-9: QuickTime and Winamp with queued music.

Not only that, but I can queue up sound effects and so on. This saves me from needing to cut and paste the audio clips into the recording in postproduction.

Incorporating and Setting Up the Mixer

If you have purchased a mixer, there are some important setup items to address. Do not rush to plug the mixer into your computer. You need to set the mixer output levels before you plug it into your PC. Connecting it too early could cause damage to your sound card, or worse. Figure 8-10 shows a mixer with the specific areas that I will be discussing highlighted.

When I received my Mackie mixer, it came with a mini-tutorial that I used to set the gain settings. Not all manufacturers are so kind. If you have a Mackie mixer, I strongly recommend that you follow the manufacturer's instructions. They are the experts, so use their tutorials if they provide them. The first mixer that I purchased did not have a way to truly isolate the channels like the Mackie mixer does. Information and instructions for the Mackie 1202-VLZ Pro can be found http://mackie.com/products/1202vlzpro.

I want to talk a little about amplifiers. This info applies to any electronics device. In any electronics system, the first amplifier or pre-amplifier in the path is one that you hope the manufacturer has invested the most money in. Given the standard electronics theory that the noise floor is set by the first amplifier, you want high gain, low noise. The first pre-amplifier in the Mackie has exceptional gain and low noise.

Trim or mic pre-amp

Channel gain   Main mix

FIGURE **8-10:** Mixer level settings.

Caution

Plugging or unplugging the microphone while phantom power is turned on could damage your microphone.

Mixer Leveling

In the following set of instructions, I walk you through the leveling procedures for a mixer: Plug your microphone into the mixer and hook up a pair of headsets to the mixers' headphone jack. Please read each of these steps before performing them, as some of you will want different settings.

You are going to level each of the channels that you have audio components plugged into. These leveling rules apply to speaking into a microphone and an external audio device to the system. The key to leveling is isolating every channel from every other channel while performing the procedure, so that when they are used together, they all have the same output level.

Some mixers have solo buttons. The solo buttons allow you to isolate a channel from other channels. This is so you can effectively level the mixer one channel at a time without interference from other channels.

Those of you with mixers that do not have solo channels will need to disconnect all other inputs from the mixer with the exception of the channel being leveled.

Tip

Prior to disconnecting a microphone, turn phantom power off or remove power to the mixer.

1. Mixers commonly refer to the main output as the mains. Do not plug the mains into your computer yet. Turn the headphone volume control to between one-quarter and one-half way up, basically loud enough so you can hear something.

2. If you have a solo button on your mixer, follow procedure A. If you do not, follow procedure B where broken out.

Note

The mixer's microphone pre-amplifier is controlled by the trim setting or trim control knob. Not every channel on a mixer is capable of plugging a microphone into those that will have a trim setting. The trim setting controls the gain of the pre-amplifier that I have been talking about.

3A. Adjust the pre-amplifier trim setting on the channel your microphone is plugged into. Start with it fully counterclockwise. Zero out the equalizer settings. Engage the solo button. Turn the channel gain knob fully counterclockwise.

3B. Adjust the pre-amplifier trim setting on the channel your microphone is plugged into. Start with it fully counterclockwise. Zero out the equalizer settings, disconnect all other input components, and turn the channel gain knob to Unity.

Note

On all mixers, there will be a mark on the scale next to a knob or slide control that says "U" or "Unity."

4. The Main Mix setting should be set at Unity.

5. Most mixers have a level meter that may display –20 dB, –10 dB, –6 dB, 0 dB. High-end mixers have much better meters. If your meter has fewer indicators, you will have to watch the meter carefully. You should now speak into the microphone and normally adjust your trim setting until you have a steady –12 dB to –6 dB, with peaks hitting between –3 dB and 0 dB on the mixer's meter.

6. Adjust the equalizer on the channel to your taste, check your levels again by speaking into the mike, and adjust your trim or channel gain as necessary to compensate for any loss by adjusting the equalizer settings.

Note

If your mixer has cheap pre-amplifiers, you should be able to hear quite clearly when you have reached a point where you are starting to introduce too much noise. You may have to reduce the trim setting below Unity and increase channel gain. This should only be done by those with starter mixers.

7A. The end goal is to be able to use the trim knob to set your channel output level on those channels with microphones. After you have set the level with the trim, disengage the solo button, and turn the channel gain to Unity. Record your trim setting on a piece of paper. To level another channel, simply engage the solo button on the next microphone channel and repeat the previous steps.

7B. For those without a solo button: After you have the levels where you want them, mark the positions of all the knobs. After you have the positions marked, turn trim fully counterclockwise and channel gain fully counterclockwise, remove power, and disconnect the microphone. You can then go back and repeat the steps for each additional microphone channels that you want to use.

8. If the audio device does not have a trim knob, for example, an MP3 player or audio input from a phone line, you will need to use the volume knob on the device in the place of the trim setting. Any device that has its own volume control or gain control should be hooked up to a channel that does not have a trim knob. Connecting an audio component to a microphone channel is not advised.

If you have a compressor or voice processor, skip to "Incorporating Audio Processors" before performing step 10.

9A. All solo buttons should be disengaged, and the channel gain should be set to Unity across all channels.

9B. When you have all channels leveled individually, you can restore all knob positions to their marked positions and reconnect all gear with the mixer power turned off.

Having the mains hooked up to your computer when you first turn your mixer on could cause damage to your line in connection. You should always connect the mains last and disconnect first.

10. Turn the Main Mix knob fully counterclockwise. Then plug the main outs into the line in on your computer or digital recorder. Then return the main's setting to Unity. (See "Refining Audio Settings with Your Mixer" for more information.)

Some of you may wonder what the difference is between main mix gain and channel gain. Each of the channels has independent channel gain controls that feed audio to the main mix, which in turn controls the main's signal level output.

Incorporating Audio Processors

After you finish your channel leveling, you should be able to enable the compressors or other audio-processing devices one device at a time and set those individual components up according to the manufacturer. By enabling these devices, you will see some loss of audio gain. That is the primary reason all these devices have their own gain control. Use the gain controls on the audio processors to recover only the signal lost through the processor.

Refining Audio Settings with Your Mixer

Most high-end audio cards in computers today come with their own audio-setting tools. If you have such a tool, you may find that it actually tells you in decibels where your input level on your computer's line in is set. Figure 8-11 shows the Sound Blaster audio control panel in Windows.

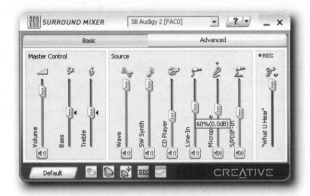

FIGURE 8-11: Creative Labs Audio input control.

Most of the settings you see here duplicate what you find on the Windows audio control settings. But what I like about Creative is that it tells me that I have my line in setting set to 60 percent, or 0.0 dB. This means that those of you who have mixers and have completed the leveling procedure outlined earlier should not have to make any changes to your PC setup to have perfect levels for your digital recording. All audio cards in computers have amplifiers, whether the card is built into your PC main circuit board or is an external card that you have installed yourself.

Note There has been some discussion in news groups as well as in conversations I have had with microphone manufacturers that those using Macs may not be able to use all of my input level guidelines, and, in fact, may have to input your audio signal at a higher level than those that are required by a Windows-based PC because you can't fully control the amplifiers that are on the sound cards that come with the Mac.

If your PC only allows you to adjust your line in setting through the Windows interface, my suggestion is to run the same leveling procedures I outlined in the beginning of the chapter. This will allow you to achieve the same results without a fancy sound card. That said, expect higher noise levels, and you may have to lower the line in setting in Windows and increase the main mix out level. It's a balancing act.

If you have a high-end card, setting the input level to 0 dB should be all you need to do. Feel free to do a sound test while the recording software is running to verify.

Using the Mixer

At this point, you are all plugged in and ready to go. I have found that because I took the time to really get my system dialed in, I rarely have to touch any of the gain controls on the mixer. The only thing I may have to adjust is the gain on an audio device that is plugged into a channel.

I have to be careful when I play audio clips through my MP3 because some can be at a different level. We have all played music on our MP3 players and have had to adjust the volume from song to song due to the way the music was mastered initially or the way in which it was encoded from the CDs into MP3 format with different programs. You should try to use the device's audio control to make those changes. But many times, it is just as easy to turn down the channel gain.

I encourage you to mute channels that are not hooked up to anything.

Real-Time Queuing

We have all heard DJs make mistakes on the radio. They queue up the wrong song or commercial or even have dead air. I've found that I sometimes fumble and have a big dead air space in my recording. Because I've vowed to not edit my shows, I live with it. But what I have done is map a function key on my computer to the Pause button within the recording software that I use. So, if I begin to fumble while trying to get an audio clip played on the computer or set up on my portable media player, I can quickly hit the Pause key. This is not a perfect solution because the Pause key works only when I have the recording software in the foreground on my Windows machine.

I solved this by hooking up a second monitor to the same computer. If you do not have that luxury, you need to orchestrate how your show is going to go down and put queues in your show notes so you can scan ahead while talking. This goes back to the chew-gum-and-walk-at-the-same-time theory. Some people are better at it than others.

Monitoring Audio Levels

During the recording, I keep an eye on the recording levels going into Audacity. Call it not trusting my instincts. We can all get wrapped up in a subject and start to get loud. I call it my soap-box rant time. When that happens, the audio levels rise higher than I want them to.

I have actually been recording my sister's children and ours singing songs. It seems that when they get in the car, they always sing. So, we thought it would be fun to put some of the equipment to use and record some music tracks to put on a CD to send to the grandparents.

I learned a lot during that two-hour recording session. I learned that what you are recording will dictate how much you need to monitor the mixer and recording levels. I had always wondered why sound guys at concerts were huddled over the mixer console. There is no such thing as the perfect setup. The kids sang some of the songs at the top of their lungs, and others they sang very quietly, so it made me constantly monitor the recording levels.

Obviously, if you are a one-person podcasting show, this may not be an issue, but if you are doing a roundtable discussion, you will want to keep an eye on your recording levels and adjust the channels as necessary.

Setting Up a Back-Up Recorder

I have already discussed how computers will crash on you at the most inopportune times and make you so mad that you want to smash them into a million pieces. This will only happen to you once before you come back to this book and say, "Yep, he told me so," and then decide to put a permanent back-up solution in place.

If you are recording to your PC, put in place some form of back-up recording at all costs. If you do not trust your computer, invest some money and do all of your recording directly to a digital recorder. I have used two solutions in the short time I've been podcasting:

The first was my iRiver IFP-790 MP3 player/recorder. It presented its own minor challenge. I knew how to set the input level of the computer, but I had to experiment with the player to find the best audio input level. Luckily, the device has its own Line Input Level selection. It can be changed by adjusting the setting via a digital slide bar. I figured that setting the input level to 10 was probably not a good idea and that 50 percent would probably be too low, so using my electronics experience, I set it at 7. Knowing a little bit about how most engineers figure things, I guessed that this would be the best setting.

It turned out that this was a pretty good guess because the levels that were recording to my PC and the iRiver were nearly identical. No matter what mixer you are using today, there is always a headphone output that you can run a line out of to your backup recording device while still listening to everything via your headphone out on your PC.

Note

Using an MP3 player/recorder is great for events where you need to be mobile, but for long-term digital recording, I recommend one of the digital recorders I described in Chapter 6. I used mine strictly for back-up purposes.

The second solution was using my Mac Mini as a secondary recording device, and I basically set it up the same way I did my windows PC. However, I found, as I have indicated in this chapter, that I had to boost the input level nearly 20 dB to get the recording level correct on the Mac Mini using the Griffin iMic interface.

The solution that I eventually want to use is a real professional digital recorder. People who have used them have said that the sound level meters on the digital recorders very closely match what is being displayed on their mixer, which has allowed them to set their input gain at Unity.

Ready, Set, Record

You have everything dialed in, and now it's time to record. You have your glass of water, and you're ready to hit the Record button on Audacity. Because many of you will be recording with equipment that you have on hand, you may have already realized that you will have some background noise. So what should you do?

The 10-Second Environmental Sample

When you hit the Record button on Audacity, the first thing you need to do is be quiet. I want you to keep your mouth shut and not move around for the first 10 seconds. Use the time to do your final mental prep. You want to collect an environmental sample, which you will use in Chapter 9 during postproduction to get rid of some noise. Figure 8-12 shows a 10-second environmental sample.

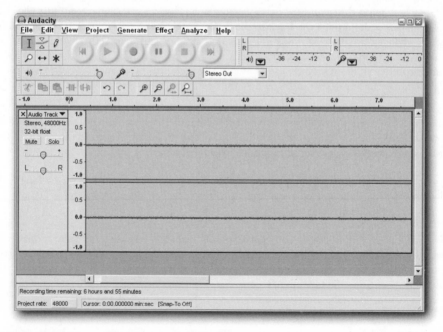

FIGURE 8-12: 10-second environmental sample.

After you have completed your environmental sample, kick off the show. Those of you who use factory-delivered sound cards will see a level of noise on your baseline similar to that shown in Figure 8-12. In Chapter 9, I will show you how to remove most of that noise with some software processing. In Figure 8-13, you can see the noise baseline from a professional audio card.

The difference is an amazing 24 dBs! The preceding two samples were obtained from the same computer. In the first example in Figure 8-12, the main in from my mixer was plugged into the factory audio in line, and in the second example, Figure 8-13, the main in from my mixer was plugged into the professional audio card.

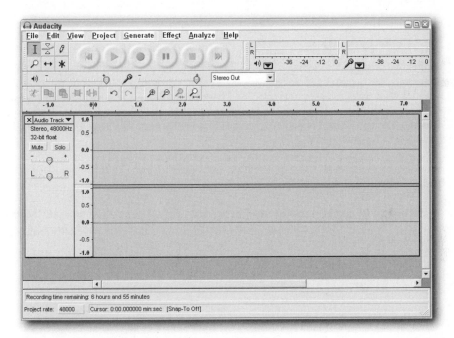

FIGURE 8-13: Professional audio card with no noise present.

The Introduction

It is important to remember that 10, 20, 50, or 100 shows down the road, you will have picked up new listeners. Some will have found your podcast from sites other than your home page. So, it is important to welcome new listeners and let them know where they can find your show directly. I do not go into a personal biography every show, but at least once every two weeks I give a standard 30-second quick-and-dirty bio. It is probably a good idea to put a link to your bio on your home page.

This is my typical introduction: "The *Geek News Central* podcast *day* and *date*." I play my intro music and then say, "Welcome to the *Geek News Central* podcast. I am Todd the Geek at *Geek News Central*. We are recording today from Honolulu. Hawaii. Welcome to the podcast. For first-time listeners, we want to welcome you to the show; we are glad you found us. If you haven't visited our website, please do so by going to www.geeknewscentral.com, where you will find links to all our shows and links to great play lists of shows I listen to. We are a proud member of the Tech Podcast Network. Make sure you check out Tech Podcasts at www.techpodcasts.com."

Note You will notice that I said both the show name and date. This is so people driving down the road know what show is starting and what date it was recorded.

The Show Lineup

I usually do a very quick rundown of what I have planned to go over, and I always include a few teasers in the beginning. This is a typical ploy to get people to listen to the whole show. After all, I want them to listen to everything I have to say. Being a podcaster means that you probably have a message you want people to listen to — so, put in a few teasers. I also put teasers in for other podcasters that I support. If I know that they have something coming up, I'll add that to my commentary.

Tip A teaser can be as simple as "Later in the show, we're going to give you some exclusive info on why such and such happened."

A teaser could be for another show you are helping to promote. "Hey did you hear that the guys over at Show X will be talking about this tomorrow?" I love using teasers during promotions; it is just another traditional way to try and keep your audience engaged.

Contact Information

I always try to give contact information a couple of times during a show. This way, by the time your listeners have heard your show four or five times, they'll be able to send you e-mail without having to hunt for the contact information — they'll know it by heart. Sometimes, I only put the information out once a show because it may not fit. I always include my e-mail, skype, and voice mail number.

Administrative Information

I call this my personal time with the listeners. I'm human, and I talk about things that are happening with me, the show, changes, or anything else that does not fit into the regular show content. Typically, I go on for five to seven minutes. This content is important because your listeners want to connect with you!

The Meat

I have already found all the articles I want to talk about. I have trained myself to read those articles completely so that I know what I am talking about, even though I may have a full understanding of the issue. The reason for this is that reporters love to throw an angle on their stories. So, you could very well rant and rave about something only to find out later that you were wrong, when a listener sends you an e-mail asking, "What's the matter with you? The writer of the article was of the same opinion as you, so why were you dumping on the guy?" Those pesky reporters have gotten me into trouble on more than one occasion, when they have been playing devil's advocate right up to the last sentence in their articles.

Make sure that you don't rush; cover the topic completely. My personality is such that my brain is already on the next subject when I am still mid-sentence. If you love to talk like I do, then you will have to find a fair balance.

Closing

I always thank listeners for taking the time to listen to the program. I am thrilled to have a large audience and I want to make sure that they know I appreciate them listening to the show. I also give them contact info and encourage them to provide feedback on content and delivery. In addition, I remind them when the next show is going to be on the air.

Special Segments

Special segments are sections of the show that depart from your ordinary format. I typically don't do a lot of interviews, but when I do, it's usually a big name. The interviews are all pre-planned, so I will publicize the interview prior to its happening. Talking up something is a great way to build your audience.

Telephone/Skype Interviews

You may find that you are able to do an interview on a nonpodcast release day. Because I only release shows Tuesdays and Fridays, I may have to splice in an interview or something that I captured earlier in the week. You need a plan to work the interview into your regular recording. I typically leave myself two to three seconds of dead air. Here's an example: I recorded an interview with Mr. Important yesterday. So, while I record the show, I will say something like, "Yesterday I had the great pleasure of interviewing Mr. Important or Important Company (as a side note, no questions were provided to the guest prior to the interview). Here's the interview." (I insert the interview into the two to three seconds of dead air I left here. "Okay, wasn't that interesting? I particularly like the following point," and so on.

So, what you have done is made it very easy to splice in that special segment in postproduction. This can also apply to skype interviews and telephone interviews.

Advertisements

If you decide to take on advertisers, you want to make sure they get their money's worth. Obviously, the listener can fast-forward through the ad, but for your advertiser's sake, you really don't want them to. The key is to keep the advertisements short, sweet, and to the point.

Make sure you work with your advertiser to provide some added value for listeners—discounts, free trials, and the like—which can preface the ad. I try to insert the ad in random places on my podcast.

Recording Pitfalls

We all stammer and say "uh" and "hmm" and a variety of other empty words. You will find that if you are prepared and you know your material, you won't stammer as much. My favorite word is "uh," so as time goes on, I have tried to reduce the number of stammers I make. This will also help you in public speaking gigs. Here's a list of other concerns:

- **Background music:** I would caution you about playing background music: If you have a heavy metal song playing in the background, what will your listeners be paying attention to? Probably not you. So, whenever you play music, play it softly. Be careful of your music selection: nonvocal pieces are best.

- **Dead air:** Dead air is going to happen, so the only real advice I can give you is to note the time and if you have decided to edit, you can go back and cut the dead air out in postproduction processing.

- **Starting and stopping:** You will find that you need to pause the recording sometimes: the phone rings, the baby cries, the wife comes up with a new chore. You get the idea. Before you hit Pause, note the time and make a note of what you were talking about and what you plan to cover next. This will let you start up again easily after that crisis is over. I do my best never to hit Pause. After all, you're podcasting, and life is full of real and unplanned moments.

Telephone Interviews

We have all seen interviews on TV; the process always looks so slick. What most people don't know is that usually, but not always, the person being interviewed has had a list of questions from which to prepare. I like to do interviews raw and uncut, without providing advance questions. But that doesn't mean I don't need to be prepared.

If you have never met your interviewee, it would be wise to do some research and get some background information—that way, when they say "I used to do this or that," you're not scratching your head feeling like an idiot.

Finding detailed information may be difficult, and I will usually ask the person coordinating the interview if he or she has a biographical sheet on the person for use in preparing my interview.

I try to plan my interview well in advance and work through the flow of questions. You may already have an idea how the questions will be answered. Be prepared if the person says that he or she is not at liberty to talk about something. You must be prepared to ask the same question a different way.

Conducting the Interview

Before starting the interview, I spend two to three minutes explaining how it will work. First I thank my interviewee for taking time out of his or her busy schedule, and then I explain the following:

- That the recording is not live but is being prerecorded.
- That I will not edit the interview once it is completed.

After that, I:

- Perform a sound check to make sure the audio levels are good.
- Let the interviewee know that we're going to start.

As soon as I hit Record, I tell listeners that this is an interview recorded between Todd Cochrane and (the name of the person I am interviewing). I then pause for a few seconds and start my introduction.

I cut the month and year out but leave it in the master file for historical purposes. Once the interview is finished, be sure to thank the interviewee again. I usually tell him or her that I will give a report on how many people downloaded the show and general comments that I received on the show. With permission from listeners, I forward questions they may have directly to the person I interviewed or his or her designated representative.

Using Skype: One-on-One or Multiple Party

Recording conversations in skype can be a real challenge because audio has a tendency to drop out sometimes. I always find it best to do one-on-one interviews or conversations via land line. That way I can control the content.

A number of people are using skype with limited success, but if you want to do a multiparty interview, this is one of the few inexpensive solutions. Recording is no different from recording with any other device on your PC. You just fire up Audacity, select Stereo out for the source, and hit Record.

Using the Double Ender Setup

I hate to produce a podcast with poor audio quality, so I use what is termed the *double ender*. You are connected via skype or a phone line, and both of you have Audacity running with mirrored setups. So, preplanning is critical. What happens is that each of you gets ready to record, and you do a countdown. The goal is for both of you to hit Record at the same time. When you are finished, the other person sends his or her high-quality MP3, and you combine them to make a single high-quality recording from two tracks recorded in separate locations.

In Figure 8-14, you see two separate tracks of audio that will be combined into a single track of audio.

You can see two separate audio recordings. This is only a sample file, but I have done double enders with four separate parties all recording on their end. We have everyone encode the MP3 at a 128-bit rate so that we don't have too much audio quality loss when we mix all the streams together and publish at a lower bit rate.

It is important that the person doing the mastering of these files listen to the whole show to ensure that there is no overlap. On rare occasions, you may have to split an audio file and move it a fraction of a second left or right to keep from having people step on each other.

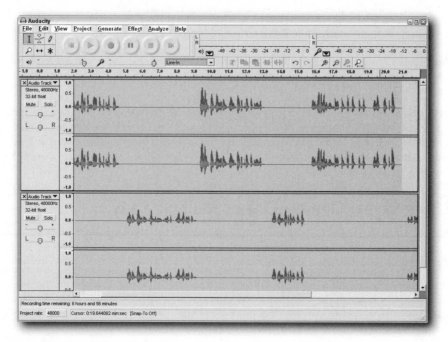

FIGURE **8-14: The double ender.**

Summary

Congratulations, you have recorded your first podcast!

I have provided the essential elements needed to set up Audacity. The software works almost identically across the three operating systems: Windows, Mac, and Linux. It is important to remember to record your podcast at a sample rate of 44,100 Hz.

I have given you the basics on setting up your audio and encouraged you to do some testing to make sure your audio levels are good.

I have also given you some very detailed insights on how to set up your mixer and provided my leveling procedures. Be sure to always refer to your owner's manual to ensure that your mixer is set up according to the manufacturer's recommendations.

I talked about ways you can use your mixer in the production of a podcast from patching in audio segments to telephone interviews.

You now have the information you need to put together a game plan in producing a structured podcast. But remember to have fun. Use my process to spawn your own ideas and show structure.

Preparing and knowing your topic is important when getting ready to do a special segment, such as an interview. I have provided you with the tools to integrate interviews into your shows.

This toolbox of knowledge, along with tips and tricks, will set your podcast apart from others and allow you to quickly build an audience.

Recording Postproduction

Those of you who are just starting out and using equipment that you own today will likely need to do some postproduction audio processing. For example, you may have too much background noise, or you may be using an inexpensive $7.95 headset from a local retailer that makes your audio level sound weak.

You may also be conscious of the number of "umms," "ahhs," and "hmms" that populate your show. You may want to cut those out of your recording so listeners, at least in theory, think you have polished speaking skills.

As I have said all along in this book, the amount of postproduction processing you do has a lot to do with your personality, the time you have, and so on. I don't do any postproduction processing because the recording is what it is. I do get a certain amount of feedback on this and have probably lost a few listeners, but I simply don't have time for lots of editing.

Have I ever done postproduction processing? Absolutely, but the mistake has to be huge. On my 44th show, I was talking about a subject and I went overboard on it. When I reviewed the recording while uploading it, I listened to the passage that would have more than likely caused some major issues. The topic was such that I weighed the potential legal issues and decided to cut the comment. I had to cut 32 seconds of audio out of the recording—better to cut 32 seconds than have a legal issue. So, even if you adopt my strategy of not doing any postproduction processing, don't rule it out.

I'm going to cover the top postproduction processes that have been beneficial to me through my 50+ shows. With that said, let's get your show produced.

Understanding the Postproduction Process

It's important to clean up your audio in a methodical way to ensure that you have the very best product in the end. As an example, you always want to do noise reduction first. It does not make logical sense to amplify your audio signal with the noise still in the recording. By following these steps, you will have a much cleaner recording in the end.

1. Reduce noise

2. Adjust audio levels

3. Normalize

4. Splice content

Reducing Noise

In Chapter 8, I had you collect an environmental sample. This is where we are going to use that environmental sample to capture a noise baseline that will be used to get rid of or process out most of the noise throughout your podcast. It should be noted that anytime you remove noise from a recording, you will also be removing, to some extent, parts of the audio that you just recorded and this could change the tone of your recorded voice.

You have to be very careful in determining the amount of noise to remove before it starts impacting the sound of your voice or other elements. Audacity and other audio-processing programs have an Undo feature that you will want to employ if any procedure that you run does not turn out the best.

To follow these steps, you should have Audacity loaded and be seeing something similar to what's shown in Figure 9-1.

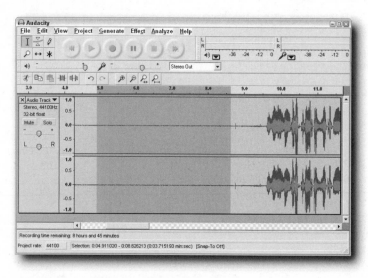

FIGURE 9-1: Audacity with noise sample selected.

1. Using my mouse, I selected a segment of the environmental sample. You need to grab 3 to 8 seconds of a sample. Leaving that sample selected on Audacity, click Effect and then Noise Removal.

Note

It is critical that you never sample a modulated section of noise, and by *modulated,* I'm referring to the section of audio that is displayed starting at approximately 10 seconds. It is critical that you use unmodulated noise.

Figure 9-2 shows the noise removal screen that pops up.

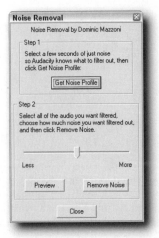

FIGURE 9-2: The Audacity Noise Removal window.

For Audacity to remove noise, it has to sample the noise floor in your recording. The window has a note that instructs you to "select a few seconds of just noise." Clicking the Get Noise Profile button initiates that collection. You will notice that the window disappears after clicking Get Noise Profile. This is okay, because the makers of Audacity realized that you would next be selecting a portion of your audio track that contains noise.

To determine how much noise reduction to apply, do not select the whole segment. Highlight a minute's worth of audio so that you can preview a section of your recording to ensure you have the slide bar settings where you want them.

In Figure 9-3, I selected a portion of audio to be sampled.

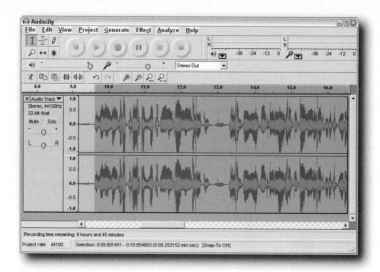

FIGURE 9-3: Audacity recorded segment slated for noise removal sampling.

2. Now that you have selected a sample section of audio, open the Noise Reduction popup window again. You will want to pay particular attention to the next session. In Figure 9-2 there is a slide bar in the Step 2 portion of the window. Initially, you can go with the default slide bar setting and right-click the Preview button. The small segment of audio that you have chosen will be played for you with the noise removed. I recommend listening to this on a pair of headphones. I would also recommend that you try changing the slide bar to see what the differences are from one extreme to the other. Adjust the slide bar as necessary until you find the best trade-off between noise reduction and the quality of the audio the noise reduction process leaves.

3. When you have found that sweet spot, close the Noise Removal window and go back and highlight the entire audio area from which you want noise removed. Open up the Noise Removal window again. Make sure the slider is where you left it and select Remove Noise.

Your processor speed and the size of your audio file will determine how long this process takes. On most audio files under 45 minutes, it will probably take 5 to 10 minutes to perform this task.

Figure 9-4 shows most of the noise removed from the original audio clip.

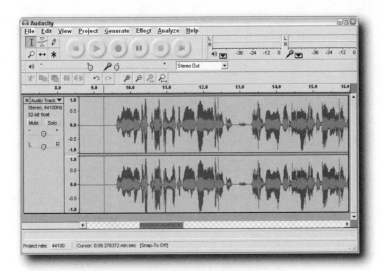

FIGURE 9-4: Noise is removed from the audio sample.

You can see on the audio track window how much noise has been removed in and around the 0.0 line on the above scale. If you do a comparison with Figures 9-1 and 9-3, you will see how much cleaner the audio looks.

Note It is important to remember that the audio you have recorded has not been encoded, so you will lose some additional audio quality when you convert to MP3. This is important to remember when using any of these filters. The only way to get a real feeling for what is happening during the various postproduction tasks is to experiment. If you understand that there is a trade-off to every process, you will be better prepared to compromise. You may want to leave a little more noise in the audio so that the final encoding sounds a little better.

You can now select and cut that environmental sample from the audio file.

Adjusting Audio Levels

You will notice that in Audacity's Recording window it is almost impossible to tell exactly what the audio levels are for your recorded podcast. It is imperative that you work very hard to get your audio levels at the right amplitude and the same level. Figure 9-5 shows the Audacity Audio Track amplitude scale.

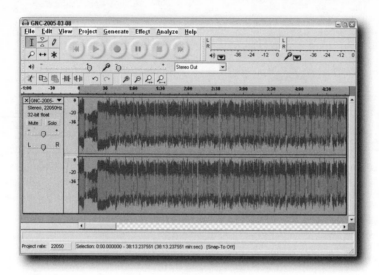

FIGURE 9-5: Audacity Audio Track amplitude scale.

In Figure 9-5, the scale display differs from that shown in Figure 9-4. You change the display by selecting the down arrow opposite the X on the audio track. A menu there allows you to change the way the scale is represented. In this screen shot, I have switched to a dB scale, which gives you a better representation of what your recorded audio levels actually are.

If you have not taken the time to set your audio levels as I told you to in Chapter 8, you may get done recording and ask, "Are my levels good?" I know from experience that you can look across the spectrum and almost immediately determine where you may need some more amplification or even where you need to lower an audio level.

The marker below 0 is −6, and you can see that this recording had levels pretty much between −6 and −3, with a few peaks at 0. I would fix only the very beginning of the track, where the audio level is low. I know from the timing that is actually my intro; thus, its levels need to be raised.

Figure 9-6 shows the same recording in Adobe Audition.

Professional tools such as Adobe Audition will give you a more detailed look up and down the scale at exactly what you have recorded. In Figure 9-5, you do not have as dynamic a scale. The point I want to make here is that you will need to eyeball it somewhat with Audacity, whereas in Adobe Audition you will be able to see scale with greater clarity. My personal opinion is that Audacity makes up for that because it implements some auto level tools in its amplification section.

FIGURE 9-6: Audio levels displayed in Adobe Audition.

Figure 9-7 shows a portion of an audio clip that was obviously recorded with levels that are too low.

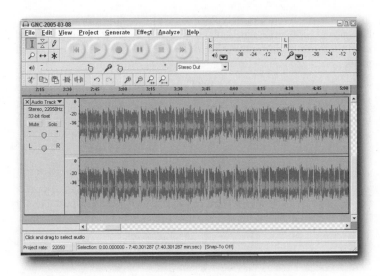

FIGURE 9-7: Portion of an audio clip that has been recorded too low.

I will amplify only that section of the audio clip to demonstrate the difference in levels.

1. To make a change, select the section of the audio that you want to amplify with your mouse, the same way you would select an area of text in a Word document, and then choose Effect ⇨ Amplify from the menu.

Note When you open Amplify in Audacity effects, it automatically figures the maximum amount by which you can amplify the segment you have selected without clipping.

Figure 9-8 shows the Amplify window.

FIGURE **9-8: Amplify window.**

2. If you do not trust Audacity to automatically choose the amplification amount, then you will want to estimate how many decibels of amplification you want to apply to the selected audio segment. I allowed Audacity to pick the amplification level. On all the tests I ran, it did a great job.

In Figure 9-9, I amplified the lower audio level segment of the recording.

You can see that between the 7-second and 22-second marker, the signal has now been amplified 6 dB. I personally have a very hard time telling the difference between 6 dB and, say, 10 dB, but you have to trust the tool.

Note If you choose to enter a level increase or decrease manually, eyeballing it is not always good enough, and you end up amplifying a signal too much or too little. Don't fret; just select Edit ⇨ Undo. You should always undo a section of audio that you have amplified incorrectly and then try a new setting. Never double-amplify a signal.

As you may have realized, the Amplify window in Figure 9-7 can also be used to reduce the amplification of a recorded signal by inserting a negative number (−3, −4, and so on).

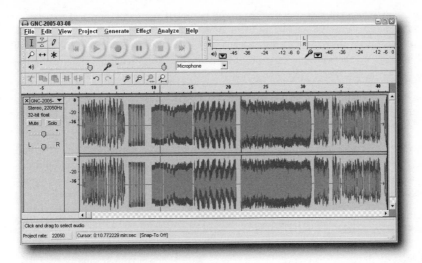

FIGURE 9-9: Section of amplified audio.

Normalizing

Because Audacity only comes preconfigured with certain audio processing tools, I am giving you examples of things you can do with the audio levels that are already built into Audacity. Audacity enables you to use plug-ins and commercial audio processing tools (that can be bought separately) if you so desire.

But before I dig into normalizing, I want to cover something that not many podcasters know. There is one audio processing tool that Audacity does not have, and it is commonly referred to as *Root-Mean Square (RMS)*. RMS is a math formula used to find the average amplitude of an audio selection. RMS amplitude reflects perceived loudness better than peak amplitude.

The key to its success is its ability (through a process similar to normalization that I will talk about next) to raise those audio passages that are low to an acceptable level while at the same time preventing the highs from getting too high. Those of you who use an application that has RMS should read up on how to use that tool. The improvements to my audio have been so remarkable that I no longer normalize. Those using Adobe Audition should refer to the Group Waveform Normalize.

Note It is critical that any audio file processed with RMS have some headroom, meaning the peaks of your audio file need to be between –6 dB and –3 dB.

Many podcasters still use the Normalize feature because it is a quick way to raise audio levels across the board as long as the entire clip is at relatively the same level.

I did use Normalize a great deal in the beginning but was confused about the proper way to use it. It always helps to read the manual, but you know us geeks. . . It's like asking for directions — we think we can find our own way. Because I lacked a clear understanding of the Normalize effect, I used it incorrectly for a couple of shows and was doing myself more harm than good.

The mistake most people make is to think they can level all the audio in a single shot using Normalize. This is not the case. The normalize effect amplifies the entire audio file equally; if the original audio reaches a loud peak of –2 dB and a low of –8 dB, normalizing to 0 dB amplifies the loud peak to 0 dB with the low peak only moving to –4 dB.

So, don't fall into the trap of trying to normalize an entire audio file, unless the entire audio clip is at relatively the same level. If you have audio levels that are uneven, you should only normalize the audio after you have done your best to get all audio segments as close as possible to equal levels. This requires you to amplify different audio level segments separately.

I am going to walk you through the process of normalizing a section of audio based on a real-world podcasting scenario.

1. Let's say that during a recording you play an audio clip on your computer that you have Audacity record. When you are finished recording, you end up with a recording that has the audio clip's audio level much weaker than your spoken voice actually was. Figure 9-10 shows a clip of audio that had mismatched audio levels.

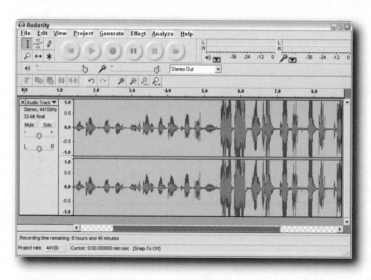

FIGURE 9-10: Audacity audio clip with unequal levels.

2. You may think that this is extreme, but I guarantee it will happen to you. Select the portion of audio that is low, and using the procedures I outlined earlier in this chapter, amplify it to a level so that the whole file is nearly equal.

Figure 9-11 shows the equalized audio levels.

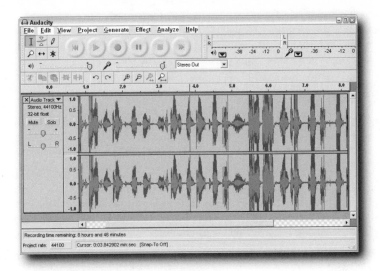

FIGURE 9-11: Equalized audio levels.

3. After amplification, the audio levels are very close to being equalized. But it is also obvious that you are now going to clip some electronic components when the audio is played back because some peaks in the clip are too high. Highlight the entire audio clip and select Effects ⇨ Normalize. In Figure 9-12, the audio is normalized.

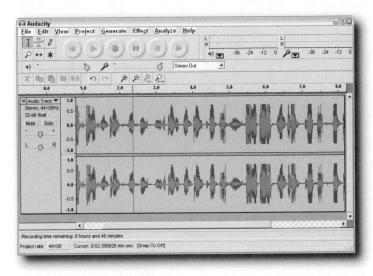

FIGURE 9-12: Normalized audio.

You know that the audio levels from the two segments are nearly the same level; this will allow your listeners to maintain a constant volume on their listening devices. If you aren't happy with your results, use Undo and try different settings. Audacity normalizes to a set value. On Adobe Audition, you can set the level of the normalization manually.

Splicing Content

You will find that sooner or later, you will need to splice in audio, be it an advertisement or an interview. This will require that you cut or copy audio from one file and paste it into another.

Sometimes, if you did not pause at the area where the segment is going to be spliced, you will find it tough to paste in the clip cleanly. Luckily, when you have enough space, doing so is very simple and sometimes a lot of fun. If you are really good, the audience probably will never be able to tell that you spliced in a clip. If you mess up or don't have room to splice in some audio, find some dead air in your recording and copy and paste in a small segment.

Remember the technique I taught you when preparing your audio clip for an interview insert in Chapter 8? I will use an interview as the scenario in the following example.

Assume that you have recorded your podcast and now want to splice in an interview from a previous recording session. Figure 9-13 shows Audacity with two tracks of audio.

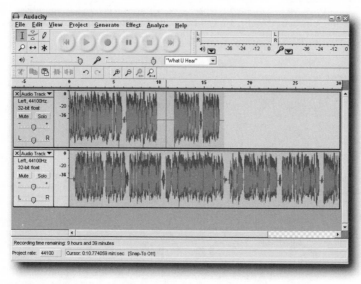

FIGURE 9-13: Audacity with two channels of audio.

The top track contains the regular show content, and the bottom track contains the interview. You have already prepared your podcast for the insertion of that interview and know where you have to splice it in because you left a big space at the 10 to 11 minute spot on the top track.

1. Using your mouse, highlight the entire interview, which is on the bottom track, and select Cut from the menu. Now place your mouse on the point in the first channel where you want your interview to be spliced in. A marker will appear on the channel, as indicated in Figure 9-13.

2. You can move that marker with the right and left arrows on your keyboard to get it in the exact spot. You can also click Play at this point, and Audacity will play the audio at the marker point. When you are happy with the placement, select Paste from the menu and the Audio clip will be spliced in.

Figure 9-14 shows where the audio clip has been spliced and where you have inserted your interview into your recording.

So, as you can see, the interview is in there very cleanly with lots of dead air in front of the clip and after it. You can then focus in on the area that you spliced and cut any excess dead air by highlighting the area and selecting File⇨Cut from the menu to cut it out.

Note Editing Audacity audio clips is as easy as using a word processor.

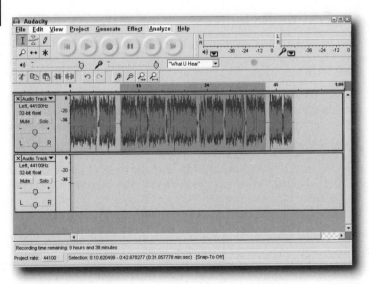

FIGURE 9-14: Audio from bottom track spliced into top track.

General Postproduction Tips

Don't get wrapped around the axle; these tips will put you well on your way to getting your first podcast ready for encoding. I encourage you to experiment, but the tips I give you here will cover the majority of the effects you will ever use. I have played with the reverb and other effects but generally was not happy with the outcome and ended up undoing what I had processed. I would be very careful about using other effects on unsaved Audacity projects.

Adding Real-Time Effects

I have done minor experimentation with the real-time effects. You apply these effects as you record; thus, you are stuck with the effects if they did not turn out the way you planned. So, if you use any of the real-time effects, such as hard limiting and filters, be sure you do some test recordings and encode the files to see what they will sound like to your listeners.

You may ask what hard limiting does; well, it is simply a software setting that ensures that your audio does not spike above a preset level. Filters can be used to reject specific frequencies or add effects such as reverb or more base.

Note   When you are in a high-noise environment, the hard limiting feature comes in handy, so don't discount the appropriate use of these real-time effects.

Finding Audio-Editing Resources

There are literally hundreds of tools for audio — so many, in fact, that it will make your brain hurt. If you're like me, the fewer programs loaded on your PC, the better. There are a great number of tools that are free or low cost, in keeping with the theme of producing a podcast with what you have today.

Audacity will be more than adequate for creating your podcast. I do not recommend any third-party tools. But I will point you to some resources in case you want to create something outside the scope of this book.

- Tucows (`http://tucows.com`) has one of the best resources for shareware audio programs on the Net. They rank the applications using their famous cow ranking system. What I really like about Tucows is that they have applications for all operating systems (`http://tucows.com/top_section_1570.html`).

- Those of you looking to make promo spots, intros, or special effects for your podcast can't go wrong with Sony Acid Music Studio 5.0 (`http://mediasoftware.sonypictures.com`). This version is under $100 — affordable for almost everyone.

Everyone has heard a radio show's theme songs or some audio segment played as an intro. Lots of podcasters are putting together intros and even short show promos that they can share with other podcasters.

Figure 9-15 shows the Sony Acid Music Studio 5.0 interface.

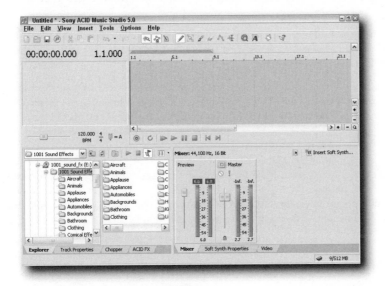

FIGURE 9-15: Sony Acid Music Studio 5.0.

This is the best program for creating intros and show promos. Additionally, you can purchase literally thousands of sound effects that have been professionally mastered, which you can use to create great promos and sound effects for use in your podcast. The software comes stand-alone without audio clips, but you can find tons of royalty-free sound effects on the Internet or purchase them through Sony. Depending on how you want to spice up your show, you may consider using Sony Acid Music Studio 5.0.

Saving Your Recording

I am bouncing up and down in anticipation because we are on the second leg of the process and one step away from making you a bona fide podcaster. You have the audio clip edited to your satisfaction, the audio levels look good, and you have removed the noise.

Some people will suggest that you save the Audacity project often while you are editing. Your mileage will vary, but I have rolled the dice a lot and opted not to because, typically, saving the file every time you make a change increases postproduction time to unacceptable lengths. Saving a project in Audacity is different than actually exporting and encoding the file. A saved Audacity project will take several hundred megabytes of storage space, depending on your show's length. Encoding is the physical process of converting that project from Audacity format to MP3 format.

You have decided in the Audacity preferences at what bit rate you will encode the file. You are definitely going to want to save the file in MP3 format. But are you also going to take the time to produce the file in alternative formats?

MP3 is universal, and you will be safe with this single file format, but what if your show is about Linux? The Linux crowd really loves the OGG format, and some Windows users prefer WMA; we can't discount the Mac folks who like AAC. It's up to you to choose the number or formats.

Note It's a lot less of a headache to just produce MP3.

Audacity will allow you to export in MP3 format, as long as LAME is loaded. OGG encoding is built in, as is WAV. Because WAV files are so big, producing a podcast in WAV is not a consideration. But if you want to create AAC and WMA format podcasts, you will need to export your audio in WAV format and then find a third-party program to convert that file to ACC and WMA formats.

File-Naming Conventions

Be smart when deciding on your naming format. This is the progression in file naming formats that I went through:

- GeekNewsCentralPodcast-20041012.mp3
- GeekNewsCentral-2004-12-1.mp3
- GeekNewsCentral-2005-2-3-mp3
- GNC-2005-04-04.mp3

Why do you think it took me that long to get to the format I use today? Listener feedback directed all of these changes. Listeners wanted to be able to easily read the filename in their media players. They also wanted the files to be listed sequentially on their computers.

Creating the MP3

Okay, go ahead — pull the trigger!

1. In Audacity, select File, then Export as MP3.

2. Choose the directory to save to. (I create new folders for each show.)

3. Enter the filename of the file.

4. Click Save and sit back.

In most cases, exporting to MP3 should take a few minutes. You will find that creating files in OGG format will take considerably longer, but the process is no different with the exception that you choose Export as OGG vorbis in Step 1.

In Step 2, by creating a fresh directory with the show date as the folder name, you keep your shows organized. By keeping each show's files in an individual folder, you avoid confusion when you add the ID3 tags, which you'll do next. By the way, congratulations for getting the MP3 file live to hard drive.

Adding an ID3 Tag to Your File

Adding an ID3 tag to your audio file is very important. It will ensure that your program gets played and that it is tagged correctly so that listeners can easily organize your show and other shows they listen to into the play list. Not having an ID3 tag is the kiss of death, and shows will end up falling into an abyss on someone's iPod or other MP3 player.

Note   An ID3 tag is a file that is attached to an audio file. It contains album, artist, track, and other machine-readable information.

Podcasts do not fit perfectly into all the standard music categories, so I have made a few improvisations. Windows or Mac users have what they need to add the ID3 tags with the software that comes with their computers — they can use iTunes or Windows Media Player.

You need to edit the following tags:

- **Name or Title:** I use the same name as my filename — GNC-2005-04-04
- **Genre:** Podcast
- **Track Number:** This is the sequential number of the show.
- **Album:** I enter the podcast website address.
- **Music Category:** Podcast (Windows Media Player)
- **Artist:** I enter my name.
- **Grouping:** Podcast.
- **Composer:** I enter the podcast website address (iTunes).
- **Comments:** I include contact information and my voice mail number and anything else that I think is important.

Editing ID3 Tags with Windows Media Player

Editing the MP3 tag is a relatively easy process:

1. Open the freshly created audio file in Windows Media Player. Right-click the audio file and select Advanced Tag Editor. Figure 9-16 shows the Advanced Tag Editor window with the Track Info tab opened up.

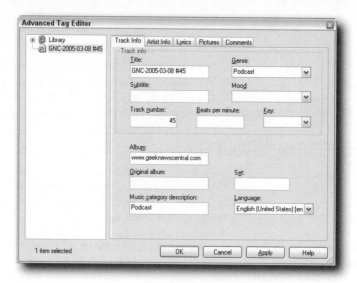

FIGURE 9-16: Windows Media Player track info.

2. There is some flexibility in what you enter, but I've found that the information I inserted into these ID3 tag entries is in line with the majority of podcasters. Fill out the tab with your show information, and then click the Artist Info tab.

3. In the Artist Info tab, enter your name under the artist. Filling out the rest of the fields is up to you; I have found that most players use only the categories I recommend be filled out. Next, click the Pictures tab.

4. On the Pictures tab, most podcasters have a small graphic from their website that they insert into the MP3; this is the same as album art. Next, click the Comments tab.

5. On the Comments tab, I put e-mail contact information, my skype name, and also the show's voice mail line and any other content I feel is pertinent.

Editing ID3 Tags with Apple iTunes

If Apple iTunes is your default media player, double-click your audio file. Once Apple iTunes is loaded, right-click the file and select Get Info. Figure 9-17 shows the ID3 Tag Editor opened in Apple iTunes.

Apple iTunes includes the same basic information as the Windows Media Player, and almost everything is contained on this tab. I find editing ID3 tags in iTunes easier than in Windows Media Player, because everything is pretty much on one screen. You can add your artwork (a.k.a., a picture) in the Artwork tab and click OK.

Using ID3 Tag Software Tools

Alternative software tools are available to help you edit your ID3 tags, and I use a program specifically designed to modify ID3 tags. I do this because I have more than one file format; thus, it is a pain to edit each file separately. Being able to enter the data once saves me a lot of time.

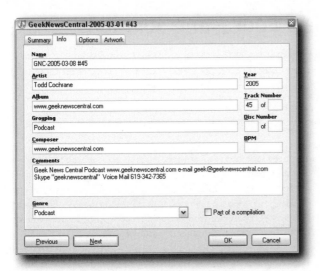

FIGURE 9-17: ID3 Tag Editor in Apple iTunes.

Again, literally hundreds of these applications are available. I like Mp3Tag. It is donation ware, which you can find at http://mp3tag.de/en/index.html. The beauty of this program is that you can populate your default information in the settings. Then, editing takes only 60 seconds because you do all the files at one time. Figure 9-18 is a screen shot of Mp3Tag.

In this screen shot, all these entries are populated based on what I inserted during the configuration. During the setup, I leave the title and the track number info blank, so those are the only two entries I have to input.

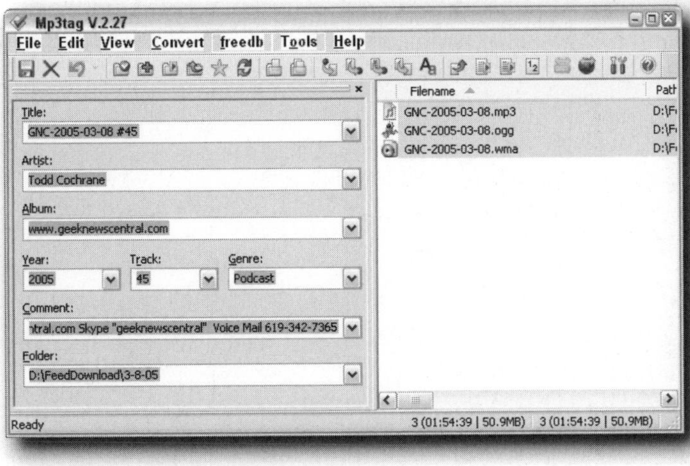

FIGURE 9-18: Mp3Tag v. 2.27.

Alternative Immediate Podcasting Solutions

Your podcast is created, and you want to get this thing published immediately. If you have gotten this far, I'm sure you have thought about hosting, which we will cover in Chapter 11. Chapter 12 covers publishing.

If you just realized that you have to put this podcast someplace on the Net, I obviously haven't done my job here. Regardless, there is a solution for everyone, although this solution is very limiting.

If your podcast is less than 5 minutes long, you can submit it via e-mail to `http://open podcast.org`. The type of material you are allowed to submit is very specific, so please visit the website and read the publishing guidelines. Do not abuse this service, because you are using someone else's bandwidth; it is being provided as a service to the podcasting community at large. A call-in line is also provided, which you can call to leave up to a two-minute message that will automatically be published. A lot of podcasters e-mail mini site-promos or announcements to the site.

A new service was launched in March 2005 by `http://Audioblog.com` that takes care of all the publishing; all you have to do is e-mail in your podcast. Details were still not fully published when this book went to press.

Summary

Your podcast is in the can, as the industry slang says. But I like to say, "It's live to hard drive." You now have a piece of showmanship and one of the cleanest and best produced podcasts today. If you followed all the steps I gave you, then you are quite literally four to five months ahead of the bell curve compared to those who have not purchased this book. This is, of course, assuming that you had zero experience with the process of getting an audio file ready to be put on the Internet.

Turn the page, and I will help you find a hosting service that can keep up with the growth demands of your podcast.

Hosting and Preparing to Publish Your Podcast

part

IV

Finding a Web Host for Your Podcast

You have your podcast produced, and it is now sitting on your hard drive. Some of you already have hosting plans and will be ready to publish almost immediately. But there are certain issues you should be aware of before you upload your podcast to your web hosting provider — ones that could cause your wallet to become significantly lighter.

Some of you will need a hosting account for the first time, and I understand the trepidation you must be feeling. I remember shopping for my first hosting provider four years ago and knowing absolutely nothing on the subject. I learned the hard way that if something sounds too good to be true, it probably is.

The last thing you want to do is end up on a host that is run by a teenager to support his online gaming habit, only to find out that a hundred of his buddies are accessing the machine you are on and have it loaded with all kinds of external processes that cause your podcast to be downloaded at the speed of a snail crawl.

Choosing a Hosting Provider Wisely

Literally thousands of web-hosting providers exist; many of these are large, professional companies dedicated to providing hosting services. What some-times happens is that a geek like me needs a dedicated server to run some special applications and finds out that the dedicated box that he or she is on has a lot of spare bandwidth and hard drive space. So he tries to cover some expenses by opening a little hosting company. You will see people advertis-ing $2.95 specials that give people a little storage and a little bandwidth. Those types of accounts are probably fine for people who want to put up a little family website with some pictures, or for someone who would like to host his or her own domain someplace. Such folks are not concerned with uptimes and overall server speed. Typically, these super inexpensive plans are good for setting up a site that serves static web pages, some pictures, and maybe even a weblog. These are not processor- or bandwidth-intensive applications.

Along with that cheap site comes very little support, and sometimes the live body you get on the phone is the server's owner; he probably is the one solely responsible for the box. So, if he's on vacation, your response time to a down website may not be as fast. Then there are the professional hosting companies, but sometimes being able to tell the difference between a professional and someone trying to cover expenses can be tough.

When I was searching for a host for *Geek News Central* three years ago, I knew what my goal for that site was. I figured that eventually we would reach a readership level that would require a robust hosting service. I knew that I wanted real 24/7 technical support, where I could reach a live body on the phone to help fix problems that might crop up. I also wanted a server that had enough storage to handle the website along with four of my other not-so-well-known domains. Knowing that *Geek News Central* would account for the bulk of that traffic, I planned that the server could be upgraded as time went on and that it could handle up to 100 GB a month in regular website traffic.

Most hosts will sell you a plan like that knowing full well that very few sites will ever hit 100 GB a month. They actually gamble that you will not have that much traffic.

I had great intentions, but when it came time to execute those decisions, I chose poorly. It took me about an hour of shopping to settle on a host. I also foolishly signed up for a whole year of hosting. Signing up and giving my credit card info was easy. Getting started was tougher. I found that my request for installation of certain modules my weblog software needed took two to three days, and many times I would never get a response from the provider to a trouble ticket. I did not press very hard because I was just getting started. Eventually, I got everything up and running. But the experience taught me to be more selective during future purchases.

Luckily, I did not lose my mind or have a heart attack when the service went offline from time to time. Despite the rough spots, I was generally satisfied until my account was sold to another hosting company. I found that the new company had more server issues and that things weren't firing on all cylinders.

I also found that the higher my bandwidth usage each month, the worse the service seemed to get. I believe this was deliberate, because the host probably did not expect me to come close to using 100 GB each month and when I did, it was cheaper for them to lose me as a customer than to keep me happy.

My choice was to change hosts and ask some very hard questions of the host to which I was moving. I will provide you with those hard questions and a shopping list of features that you should look for, including real-world examples of bandwidth considerations.

What a Good Host Will Provide

It's important to get a live body on the phone when you are deciding on a hosting provider. Tell that person up front that you will be serving legal audio content from the account and see what kind of reaction you get. See if he or she tries to sell you a higher-service package than what you think you will need when getting started. Here is a short laundry list of items that a good host will provide on their website and on the phone. I will discuss each of these points in detail:

- **Clear and precise explanations of the customer service hours and support provided:** You will find that hosts with exceptional customer service also brag about this the most, and they very clearly state their hours of operation. You need to ask very pointedly when they have techs in the office who can work on problems that the phone support reps cannot. Also ask what the normal response time is for trouble tickets.

  You may find that a host claims to have customer support 24 hours, 7 days a week, only to find out later that they actually have Monday through Saturday, 9 to 5, along with deferred support by way of trouble tickets.

Case in point: My initial provider stated that it had 24/7 live technical support, but I found that if I called on a Saturday, I was lucky to get someone on the phone. Often, I was asked to leave a message because all technicians were busy (yeah, right), and mysteriously nothing would get done to the trouble ticket until 8:00 A.M. PST the following Monday. Because the provider gave the impression that someone was working, I could not prove that it did not have true 24/7 tech support.

- **Clear bandwidth limits and overage charges:** You will see a lot of hosting providers advertising that they allow 65 GB of transfer per month. However, some providers divide that number by the number of days in a month, and you will, in fact, get a maximum of 2.2 GB of traffic per day. This does not fit well with doing a podcast once a week when you know that your traffic will spike over a 6- to 12-hour period. The quickest way to lose listeners is giving them a message that you are over your bandwidth limitation when they try to access your site. So, you will want to ask if there is a daily limit.

- **Clear information about bandwidth usage overage charges:** The next thing you need to clarify is what happens when you hit your bandwidth limit. Does the provider shut down your feed, or do you get charged for the overages? I have seen providers charge as much as $1 to $3 per gigabyte when you go over your bandwidth limit. The penalty for going over can be expensive. Unless you are willing to incur that cost, I would advise you to get an account that simply shuts down when you hit your limit.

- **User agreements:** You must take the time to read the entire user agreement; web hosts are always very specific about what you can and cannot do with the account. It is imperative that you read the user agreements, because oftentimes, you will find clarifications to their front-page advertisements.

I print the user agreement and highlight areas that I have questions about before I call to find out more about service plans.

- **Clear explanation of the type of backbone your host is on:** You will find that most of the hosting companies have their servers in protected facilities that typically contain hundreds, if not thousands, of computers all running in highly secure buildings. Hosting companies typically rent rack space for their machines or they rent machines from a much larger company. But it is important to know what type of Internet backbone the facility is connected to and if they have redundant connections with multiple providers.

■ **Public discussion forums:** One of the first things I look for is an open discussion forum hosted by the provider. If it has its act together, it will provide a section for new customers as well as existing customers. Take some time and read through these forums to see how well the company reacts to problems. Look for customer praise, and on the opposite end look for disgruntled customers to see whether they were ignored or handled professionally by the support staff.

■ **Clear upgrade path:** I have had hosting accounts and have been very pleased with the service, only to find that as my needs grew, their basic plans did not. Typically, hosting companies offer two or three hosting plans and that's it. So, you need to plan for the time when you need more bandwidth or storage capability. Make sure that you ask the provider for a detailed breakdown of the costs associated with upgrading the hosting plan beyond their basic plans. Many times, you will find that there is no upward flexibility. If that is the case, you will have to weigh your options.

■ **Service-level guarantee:** This is one of those areas in which you are usually at the mercy of the hosting provider to give you a credit if a problem arises. I once had a host go offline for 72 hours straight, and then they tried to fight giving me a credit on my account for not meeting their service-level guarantee. I have found that most hosting companies say they will honor their service-level guarantee and ensure a 99 percent uptime. You have to do a little math to see what that really means. Assuming a 30-day month, that gives you a total of 720 hours in a month; to stay within their 99 percent guarantee, they have to be online only 712.8 hours a month. But the real difference comes in when a host guarantees 99.9 percent uptime; then hey have to be online 719 hours.

Tip

Many times, the only way I am alerted to a site being down is when a reader lets me know. I could employ a tracking service, but those tracking services cost nearly as much as the hosting service does. So, unless you really scour your logs, there may be times that you cannot prove you were offline for a given period. My conclusion is that very few providers can meet the 99 percent service guarantee, and most hosting clients will never offer a credit and may fight you when you try to get one.

■ **Great user tools and host features:** Hosting providers will typically provide a built-in interface tool like Cpanel or Plesk, which you, as the owner of the account, can use to get your host up and running. Cpanel and Plesk are web-based interfaces that allow the novice a clear and easy way to add e-mail accounts and mailing lists, set up databases, and manage files, along with a significant number of other tools to manage your website.

■ **Domain registration:** Many hosts offer free domain registrations, but you need to be sure that the domain is in your name and not in the name of the company with which you are hosting. So, if they offer a free domain registration, be sure that they register it in your name; then if you decide to move to another host, you will have no trouble taking the domain with you. This is absolutely critical.

Finally, advice abounds out on the Net. Don't let someone talk you into hosting with a company before you read the fine print and ask the questions I've provided. I found an article that covers some of the same material. Please review the seven independent suggestions from `http://webhostingtutorial.com/articles/choosing_a_webhost.html`. The site also has some good tutorials for the novice.

Understanding Unmetered Bandwidth Usage

Some hosting providers will say they give you *unmetered bandwidth*. Typically, unmetered bandwidth means that a host claims in front-page advertising to offer unlimited bandwidth. This is where you really need to dig into the user agreement and get someone on the phone to answer some serious questions. Few, if any, hosting providers actually provide true unmetered bandwidth. Many times, there is a limitation to what you can do with the account and still qualify for unmetered bandwidth, so be very careful.

Some hosts are not very up front about what they allow, and the limitation is buried in line 500 of the user agreement.

Most of the unmetered bandwidth deals come packaged like this: They say that as long as you are hosting content on the website that is being updated and you have steady traffic to the website itself, and as long as the file download requests originate from a link on your website, they will honor the unmetered bandwidth. Some are more limited in that they allow unlimited web page hits but count any files being downloaded under a separate data bandwidth classification.

I am not a fan of these so-called unmetered hosting plans. Your mileage will vary and buyer beware. Again, if it sounds like it is too good of a deal, it probably is.

But the catch is that these hosts usually give you a limit to the number of gigabytes up front, and then, when you are getting close to your limit, you have to call and ask for some more. This is their way of protecting their service so that a rogue person does not abuse the hosting plan. Regardless, you must always read your user agreement and understand the limitations on the account.

Now, let's talk about the different types of hosting accounts.

Shared Hosting

The vast majority of hosting accounts you see advertised are known as *shared hosts*. In a sense, this is like living in an apartment building with 100 or 1,000 residents. All the residents share the incoming water connection, use the same trash, and rely on a company to manage the external building, including cutting the grass, and so on.

You will see hosting plans that range in price from $2.95 all the way up to a $100 or more per month. If you are a new podcaster, a shared hosting plan that fits your budget will likely be all that you need until your show grows.

The list of features that each host offers will vary and is oftentimes directly related to what type of server it is. You will have a choice of Windows or Linux. I prefer the Linux boxes because some of the applications I use do not run well on a Windows machine.

Note With shared hosts, you will not have access to the physical computer; your only access to that computer will be through a web-based interface such as CPanel or Plesk.

The following list recounts the baseline features you should require of a shared host:

- Disk space under 5 GB.
- Bandwidth up to 100 GB.
- FTP accounts (1 to unlimited).
- E-mail accounts (10 to unlimited).
- MySql databases (1 to 10). If the provider does not provide 10 databases, go someplace else.
- Subdomains (1 to 10). You should be able to host more than one domain on the account.
- Domain registration and renewal (1).
- Free website plug-ins (10 to 25). These are applications that will install automatically.

The list of features can be extensive, and since you can shop around, look for a host that offers the most features, along with all the other items we have already talked about. I recommend that everyone producing a podcast do their posting with a weblog, because it is the easiest methodology to implement. Some of you will choose not to do it that way, but those of you who do will want to make sure that your host is weblog-friendly because many weblog packages require additional Perl modules.

Understanding Backbone Technologies

Internet backbones are run by companies such as MCI, AT&T, and other mainstream network services companies. There are a dozen or so major networks that are all interlinked; the fiber and wires that connect them are literally spread nationwide.

Hawaii, for example, is a major tie point for data communications going to Japan, Australia, Guam, and other locations. These major tie points have cables, or, in this day and age, fiber optics, connecting the countries.

These tie points exist in various major cities worldwide. Server farms are built in and around these major tie points, the goal being that they are close to a major network hub. Hosting companies that have their act together buy data lines to tie into these hubs from more than one provider, which gives them redundancy, traffic flexibility, and speed. If there is a technical problem on a specific network, most of these server farms where your website information physically resides are self-healing: if a line goes down from one, data provider traffic is simply rerouted to another.

Your host must physically plug a network cable into the server that you are hosted on just like your home Internet connection. Thus, it is important that the host you go with has some redundant backbones.

Obviously, you will want to get the most bang for your buck, so be picky and shop around. Subscribing to a shared host that doesn't offer the recommendations listed here is putting yourself at risk of not being able to grow a little bit within the hosting account.

Typically, hosts will not reveal the kind of hardware they are running, nor will they mention the speed of the processor or amount of RAM. Obviously, you hope that the machine they are running on has a lot of horsepower under the hood. If the host is proud of the hardware their shared hosts are running under, they will advertise it on their websites.

Note I have not found a shared host yet that was not capable of running a weblog.

Here are some other typical features that come standard on hosting accounts:

- **CGI-BIN:** All servers have a CGI directory that allows the execution of certain web applications. Most hosts allow CGI files to reside almost anyplace on a server.

- **CGI-Library:** Some hosts will provide a library of CGI scripts so you can install everything from page counters to form submission tools.

- **PHP support:** All hosts support PHP scripts that are found in a large majority of web applications today.

- **Perl support:** Perl is an open source CGI scripting programming language.

- **Server-side includes:** Allows web pages with scripts built-in to access the web server for the requested information before displaying it on the web page.

- **FrontPage support:** Support to use Microsoft FrontPage–designed websites.

- **FTP/shell access:** FTP access allows you to upload/download data to your website. Shell access on shared accounts allows you to access the UNIX command prompt.

- **Webmail:** Allows you to read your e-mail online.

- **Log reports and files:** It is highly critical that you have access to your weblog files so that you can analyze web traffic.

Note At the end of this chapter, I give you a list of resources you can use to find hosting accounts with reviews and a list of podcast-friendly hosts.

Virtual Dedicated Servers

Virtual dedicated servers are considerably different from shared hosts, yet in some ways they are almost the same. Imagine that a virtual dedicated server is a complex that you live in with five other families, and you all have to do your own yard work and clean up outside, yet the water coming into the facility and the trash removal is shared.

Signing Up For a Service

Here is a recommendation that will save you some heartache down the road. When you decide on a provider, sign up initially with a month-to-month plan. This way, you can try the service for several months, and after the third month, if you like your service, you can sign up for a whole year.

Virtual hosts require a certain level of expertise to set up, and I do not recommend this for the novice. When I upgraded to a virtual dedicated server, I essentially got a machine that could host web pages; I could set up e-mail accounts, but none of the services or Perl modules I needed were preloaded. This meant that a system administrator had to go in and set up the machine. Most hosting companies simply sell you a box and expect you to maintain it. Virtual dedicated servers typically give you more flexibility in storage and bandwidth. But you manage everything, and you set up and configure everything. If you don't have a clue what I'm talking about in this section, then a virtual dedicated server is not for you—unless you are willing to pay someone to set it up.

Note

Virtual dedicated servers are a minor step up in performance as compared to a shared host and, typically, have very low amounts of RAM. They can become overloaded if your traffic levels get too high. Luckily for me, I have a good friend who is a Linux administrator, and he set up my box. I did pay him for his work. If you have no geek friends that can handle this, setting up one of these boxes can be expensive.

When the setup was done, things were good to go. The server I went with has 20 GB of storage, 500 GB of allowable traffic with the option to buy more if I go over that; plus, the price wasn't bad. My yearly hosting fee is approximately $500, but I did find out that these virtual dedicated servers are usually a little underpowered, and because you are still sharing bandwidth with others, you can experience serious slowdowns in server performance during the first 24 hours after a podcast release.

You will find price ranges for virtual dedicated servers between $35 and $135 per month. I am sure this price range is starting to scare some of you. Well, I haven't revealed my secret weapon yet, so keep reading.

Dedicated Servers

At some point as my show continues to grow, I will have to move to a dedicated server. It's like buying your own home—but in a way, that's a good thing. You can add options to the box, such as more drive space and RAM, and even decide what type of processor you want to run. A dedicated server does come with a very steep price tag. Typically, dedicated servers start on the very low end at $75 per month and increase to $400 to $500 per month. Obviously, if you have a podcast that needs to be served by a machine such as this, you will need a sponsor for your show or a permanent advertiser.

Tip   It is cheaper to buy a year's worth of hosting.

Podcast-Hosting Scenarios

We talked a little in Chapter 4 about considerations for your hosting plans. In this section, I am going to explain what you can expect based on raw listeners and typical site traffic totals.

Running a static website where you have a few pictures and some text and conservative graphic sizes will stretch your allowable bandwidth a very long way. Throw a podcast on that server and watch your bandwidth meter steadily climb towards the moon.

In all the following examples, I will assume that you are creating a 20-minute podcast and that you produce two shows a week for a total of eight per month. I will also assume that some of your listeners are downloading the show more than once.

Note   Based on tests I have run, the number of listeners who download a show more than once could be as high as 10 percent. The reason for this is that some of the podcatcher clients are a little buggy and can download the show twice by mistake.

I will also assume that you have encoded your podcast at a bit rate of 44,100 and a sample rate of 22.050 kHz, making your average MP3 file 7.1 MB.

Scenario 1: A Small Audience of 1,000 Listeners

Let's do the math:

- 1,000 listeners × 8 podcasts a month = 8,000 total downloads
- 8,000 downloads × 7.1 MB = 55.46 GB
- Adding the 10 percent duplicate traffic puts you at 61 GB of traffic per month.

Considering growth factors, it would be unwise to even consider having an account with less than 100 GB, even for podcasts with small audiences.

Scenario 2: A Medium Audience with 5,000 Listeners

Again, do your math:

- 5,000 listeners × 8 podcasts a month = 40,000 total downloads
- 40,000 downloads × 7.1 MB = 277.34 GB
- Adding the 10 percent duplicate traffic puts you at 305 GB of traffic per month.

This is why, when my audience reached a certain level, I moved to a virtual dedicated server, and even that box is showing serious strain under the load of 8,000+ listeners. My personal hosting cost at this point in the equation is approximately $50 per month.

Scenario 3: A Large Audience of 15,000 Listeners

Use the same equations:

- 15,000 listeners × 8 shows per month = 120,000 total downloads
- 120,000 downloads × 7.1 MB = 832 GB
- Adding the 10 percent duplicate traffic puts you at 915 GB of traffic per month.

This is easily the dedicated-server level. Some will say that even those reaching medium audiences will want a dedicated box.

Are you starting to see why underwriters and advertisers may become critical when you reach the medium audience size? I will go into advertising in detail in Chapter 14.

Podcasting on a Tight Budget

You will need to make some decisions in order to podcast on a small budget. The following are tips you can take to the bank. You will be able to podcast, but you will need to make some trade-offs.

- Produce short shows.
- Encode at a 32,000 bit rate rather than at 44,100, which will reduce your file size by a third.
- Do only one high-quality show a week.
- Produce a region-specific podcast and find local sponsors.
- Host your shows on http://Libsyn.org.
- Host your shows on http://Podlot.com.
- Use the free service at http://openpodcast.org. (Do not abuse it! Follow the rules.)
- Put a tip jar on your site and ask for a monthly donation.

There may even be more options in the coming months, and I will cover some emerging commercial options in Chapter 15.

I know that the numbers I have stated here can be intimidating. The last thing you want to do is have your website go dark after five shows because you ran out of bandwidth.

An alternative is to have your audience help you distribute your shows with BitTorrent.

The Secret Weapon

Before I upgraded to a virtual dedicated server, my hosting requirements were growing on a daily basis. Luckily, a hosting provider came on the scene that charged not for bandwidth but for storage.

So, what I did was this: I ran my website on the shared host that I was on, and my monthly hosting price fell in the lower-midrange price monthly fee. I then used a company called Libsyn (www.libsyn.org) to store my files and from which to distribute them. For a flat fee of $5 per month, they allow me to store and distribute up to 100 MB of data. When my plan rolls over on its anniversary, I get a fresh 100 MB of storage. They also offer several other plans, with 250 MB of storage for $10 per month, 500 MB of storage for $20, and so on.

So, before I rented the virtual dedicated server, my hosting cost for my show was approximately $25 per month. I moved to a virtual dedicated server to have more control over my content. As it turned out, the virtual dedicated server started having problems handling the load. So I moved my MP3 back to Libsyn and have been a happy camper ever since. The folks at Libsyn continue to serve up my files, handling the hosting and distribution beautifully.

Libsyn is building slowly and purposefully to ensure that their service stays top-notch.

They have a distributed backbone. When new shows come in, they are put on their fastest servers, and as the demand slows down, they are automatically shifted to secondary servers. Their service is not unlike others in that they depend on the fact that some shows will be more popular than others and, hopefully, through a law of averages, they will make enough money to pay the bills and stay in business. Thus far, they have been doing a magnificent job. If you want to help me out, click the referral icon on my podcast page (www.geeknewscentral.com/podcasts). You can help this dad cover his hosting costs.

You can host with Libsyn exclusively, but at this time, you have to use their posting interface. And if you're serious about podcasting, you can't really define your brand in a way that I would recommend by using their interface. But they do have a complete package that is ready to go today; you can sign up and upload your file and be live in about 15 minutes. So, for those of you who do not want to deal with setting up a separate hosting service, this may be the best option. I will discuss building your brand in Chapter 14.

Alternative File Distribution Methods

Because your files are distributed as direct downloads, there is no way to reduce bandwidth costs unless you spread file distribution among your listeners using peer-to-peer (P2P) technology.

Peer-to-peer is a wonderful tool for distributing files; sadly, it has gotten a very bad rap due to illegal file sharing. Slowly, though, podcasters are starting to implement BitTorrent as an alternative way to distribute their shows. Some of the podcatcher applications have BitTorrent built in. Some of the bigger shows that did not have the resources to buy bigger servers forced their listeners to the BitTorrent distribution method.

This method comes with challenges because some people do not understand the technology, and while they may be happy to download the file from your website, they may not be at all happy helping distribute it via their upload path. Generally, those who understand the technology will gladly help out. I describe the BitTorrent P2P process that podcasters are using in the next section.

BitTorrent

BitTorrent is a great weapon to cut down on your bandwidth usage, but it comes with unique challenges. Until your show reaches about 1,000 listeners, the BitTorrent distribution technologies may not help you. The key to BitTorrent is known as *seeding*.

To understand what seeding is, you need to understand how BitTorrent works, and then you will understand the positives and negatives of the technology.

There are two sides to the process: downloading and tracking. The people downloading are called *seeders*, or *leachers*, and the tracking is done by a server-side component that monitors who is downloading. Typically, an MP3 distributed by BitTorrent must have at least one person continuously seeding the file. This is necessary so the site acting as the tracker can route download requests to the seed, which then starts sending the file to the party that requested it.

If no one is seeding the file, it will be impossible to download it. The technology works extremely well when you have multiple people seeding a single file. When a request for a download comes in, all of those who are seeding start sending portions of the file to the person requesting the download. This creates a torrent of data being pushed at the person.

In turn, as soon as the person downloading the files gets a few segments of file, the software turns that data around and helps push or seed that file back to others who are downloading.

When BitTorrent is used to distribute video content, it is not uncommon to be able to download an entire DVD in a very short period of time, even though the file may be extremely large. This is because a lot of people are helping distribute the file.

Typically, Internet service providers (ISPs) limit upload speed. If you have ever uploaded a file, you will notice that it takes longer to upload than to download. The reason for this is that the majority of people are downloading on the network, so the ISP assigns 90 percent of its available bandwidth to downloading and 10 percent to uploading.

With that understanding, you may only be contributing 40 kilobits per second to seeding, but if 50 people are contributing 40 kilobits per second and only a few people receive the file, the person on the receiving end is benefiting from his or her ISP having devoted 90 percent of its bandwidth to downloads because the person could potentially receive the file at 2,000 kilobits per second. (This is hypothetical.) I have personally never seen a BitTorrent file download any faster than 980 kilobits per second.

The challenge comes when you are the sole initial seeder, and to really make it work, those who have completed downloading the file need to leave their clients running to help in the distribution. So, if you can get your listeners to help you seed the file, you can offload a great deal of your traffic. Of course, this requires cooperation.

Server-Side BitTorrent-Seeding

There is movement underway to develop what is called *server-side seeding*. You upload the original file on your website and then, using a specially installed utility, run the actual server-side tracker on your website or go with the solution I lay out in the next section.

Server-side seeding allows the first wave of downloads to happen quickly, which results in fast seeding of the file. The traditional seeding method is very slow in the beginning and becomes faster over time. Server-side seeding uses your website's high-speed capability to eliminate that bottleneck, and as soon as a preset number of seeders are available, your web host quits seeding and lets the BitTorrent clients running on your listeners' computers do the work; you do not incur any more bandwidth charges. When the seeders drop below the preset level, it picks up the load again.

This technology is for early adopters and is not widely supported. But you can find a recently released Server-Side BitTorrent client at www.blogtorrent.com.

Using BitTorrent Hosting Services

I have found one very unique service and I use it personally because I didn't want to try to set up a BitTorrent tracker or use one of the public trackers where my legal download would have been intermixed with questionable material.

When I found the Prodigem Hosting Service (www.prodigem.com), I was able to get an account with a maximum of 250 MB of storage, which allowed me to upload my MP3 files and, through Prodigem's automated system, create a BitTorrent file. They provide the server-side tracker and the perma-seed. Figure 10-1 shows the Prodigem Hosting Service's home page.

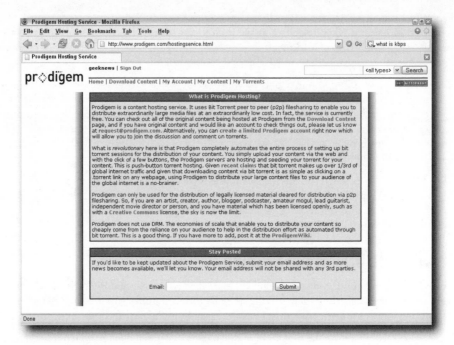

FIGURE 10-1: Prodigem file-hosting service.

This home page shows some of Prodigem's terms of service. Some of you may need to use this service, and have I worked out a deal for you. I talked with the website's owner, and those of you who have this book can request an account on their service.

Note There is no guarantee that you will get an account. This service is free and subject to change at any time. I do not guarantee their service or have financial ties with the provider. I have simply found the service to be exceptional and am personally recommending it.

You will need to send an e-mail to request@prodigem.com. In the e-mail, mention that you read about Prodigem's service in Todd Cochrane's *Podcasting* book and would like an account. You will have to agree to the terms of service. In Chapter 11, I tell you how to link your weblog entry to the Prodigem file that is created. This will initiate a BitTorrent download.

Some of you may be intimidated with the service, so I will provide you a mini-tutorial on using it. Once you are logged into the Prodigem service, you will find yourself on the page displayed in Figure 10-2.

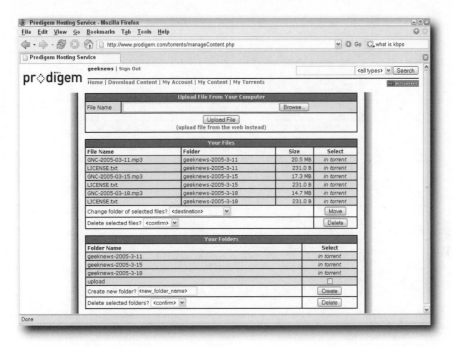

FIGURE 10-2: Prodigem: My Content window.

Note   As you can see, I have a URL typed in for a location of a file that will be uploaded to the service. I have found it much easier to upload my MP3 to my hosting account and then have Prodigem download from my website.

1. Click Upload Web File. The service will upload the file. When it is completed, Prodigem will notify you by e-mail. Come back to this page and scroll to the bottom.

2. Figure 10-2 shows the Create new folder option. You will need to create a folder on the service, just as you would on your PC, so you have a place to store the file you just uploaded. To keep everything organized, I use YYYY-MM-DD. Click Create and a new folder will be added in the Your Folders list.

3. Scroll to the top of the page and select the file you have just uploaded. Using the push-down button on the destination window, choose the directory that you have just created and then click Move. This moves the file you have just uploaded into the directory you have just created. The file is now in the proper place, and you are ready to create a BitTorrent file. Select My Torrents from the top of the page. Figure 10-3 shows the My Torrents page.

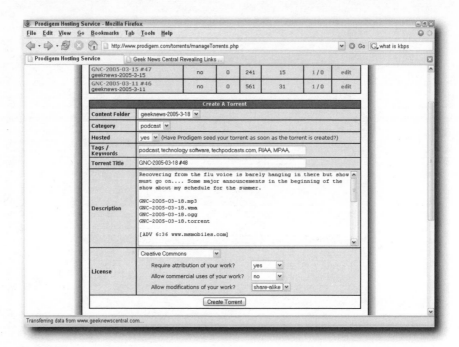

FIGURE 10-3: My Torrents page.

4. With the My Torrents page loaded, the form in Figure 10-3 will not be filled out. Follow the example in the figure to fill out the page. (Notice that I have selected the geeknews-2005-3-18 folder.) After you get everything set the way you want, press Create Torrent. It will take you to a verification page, and you will have to confirm the selection. Once that is done, the torrent is created. You can reload the My Torrents page and you will see that the file is all set.

5. Prodigem has thought this through quite well; they also created that special RSS feed for you with the enclosure information we talked about in Chapter 1. When you click the My Account button, it loads an account information page. Figure 10-4 shows this page.

You can see that they provided a variety of info and the link to the RSS feed. I will cover RSS in detail in Chapter 11. But you can see the link that Prodigem has created for you. You will be able to create a link on your website pointing to that URL, and those listeners who understand and are willing to use BitTorrent feeds can enter that URL into their podcatcher application.

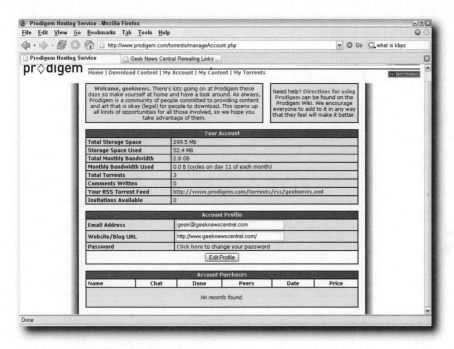

FIGURE 10-4: My Torrent page RSS feed link.

Using Internet Archive

At some point, say, after you've done around 50 podcasts, you may want to think about archiving them. Setting up an archive at `http://archive.org` is the best way to ensure that your podcasts will be saved permanently. Be sure to read through their FAQ and get familiar with the archiving process. The Internet archive is not to be abused by using it as a hosting service; that is not their charter.

Podcast-Friendly Hosts

We have talked about what you should look for in a good host. I have had my share of good ones and bad ones. I can speak only from personal experience and have had very good success with a handful of companies.

Because I want all of you to have a wonderful podcasting experience, I am going to point you at several hosts that have good reviews from podcasters and that I personally have had exceptional service from.

Note Of course, I can't guarantee levels of service with these hosting providers. I only know that my experience to date has been positive. These hosting providers provide adequate bandwidth for beginning podcasters. I use them in conjunction with Libsyn.org and Prodigem.com.

Table 10-1 lists my personally recommended hosting providers.

Table 10-1   Podcast-Hosting Recommendations

Company Ranking	Domain	Cost	Storage	Bandwidth	Editor's Ranking
BlueHost	bluehost.com	$6.95 monthly	2 GB	75 GB	*****
midPhase	midphase.com	$7.95 monthly	3 GB	Unmetered. (See details on host website.)	****
GoDaddy	godaddy.com	$19.95 monthly	4 GB	200 GB	*****
.Mac	mac.com	$49.95 yearly	1 GB	Unknown	****

Note Some podcasters have been using their .Mac accounts to share their podcasts. To date, Apple has not cut off any of their users. But I am concerned that it could only be a matter of time before Apple reacts. I have a .Mac account but have never used it to distribute my podcast. Some of the top names in podcasting continue to do so. My personal recommendation is that if you do use your .Mac account, do so only if you know your podcast will not have a large audience. I believe in paying my way, and my personal opinion is that hosting on .Mac is an abuse.

Resources for Finding a Host

If you do a search on the Internet for web hosting, you will find thousands of links to hosting companies. As I sorted through dozens of websites, I found it very difficult to find objective sites that did hosting reviews because many were just fronts for their own brands.

So, be careful when you search the Internet for web hosting companies. I have come up with a short list of resources that I feel are pretty good starting points:

- WEBHOST Magazine (www.webhostmagazine.com)
- WEBHOST Directory (www.webhostdir.com)
- TopHosts (http://tophosts.com)
- List of Webhosts (http://webhosts.thelist.com)

Summary

Setting up a new web host service is pretty fun stuff for a geek but can be intimidating to the uninitiated. You may need to seek help, but if you take your time and continue to use the resources that I recommend, you should be able to get your website up and running very quickly. I have given you advice on what to look out for when you go shopping for a host and some of the realities of producing a podcast. Most importantly, remember the following:

- Read the user agreement.
- Sign up for a monthly plan until you are comfortable with the host.
- Understand all the facets of your bandwidth caps and overage charges.
- Don't be afraid to ask for help. Geeks love to help!

Podcast Publishing and Distribution Methods

I t is time to establish your online presence. It is important that you take as much care in getting your website ready as you have taken in creating your podcast. The simple fact is that now as you prepare to upload and publish your show notes on your website, along with getting your website fully capable of supporting the podcatcher clients, you must remember that your website is a reflection of your podcast. Your site says a lot about you and needs to stand out so that it leaves a lasting impression.

I am not a web designer. I employed a graphic artist to design my site and believe that, in the long run, it will pay off because my listeners recognize my branding.

Setting up a weblog or launching a standard website is part of the podcasting process. Some of you may have to ask for help to get your podcast ready for public distribution, but I hope that I give you enough solutions to satisfy even novices. I will discuss readily available commercial solutions and online resources you can use to set up your site yourself or to have someone set up a site for you.

Podcasting with a Weblog

I am hoping that by now you have been exposed to weblogs. The term *weblog* is a combination of the words "web" and "log." A weblog, better known as a *blog*, is usually a web-based application that contains journal entries usually time-stamped in reverse chronological order.

My website at www.geeknewscentral.com is a weblog. I manage its content with a web-based application known as MovableType (www.sixapart.com). The MovableType application was installed and configured by me; luckily, it had great instructions because — like some of you — I was faced with setting up my first weblog some time ago.

I did not start out using MovableType; instead, I chose a free service called Blogger (`www.blogger.com`). What was great about Blogger was that they made it as easy as shopping online. I clicked and chose how I wanted the site to look, and everything was automated and very simple. When I was ready to post an entry, it was as simple as typing in a Word document. At the time, I was just writing a weblog; this was before podcasting.

There are several types of weblog applications: web-based applications that you install, host and manage, web-based applications that another company hosts and manages, and desktop-based applications that automatically upload configurations and changes you make to your site. An example of this last one is Radio Userland (`www.userland.com`).

My personal feeling is that the easiest way to publish your podcast is to use a weblog. Most of the weblog tools are as simple to use as a word processor. Publishing your show notes and the links to your MP3 on a weblog is very easy, and the majority of you will find that it feels natural.

If you have a weblog today, you may be a few steps away from making your podcast available. For those of you who do not, a lot of the information I gave you in Chapter 10 about things you need to pay attention to when picking a hosting provider will come into play right now.

 Note Keep in mind that even if you choose to use one of the free fully-hosted services like Blogger, you are still going to need a hosting provider to host your files.

First and foremost, you will have to decide which weblog application you want to work with. I will break weblogs down into two categories. One will be the type you have to install and configure yourself. The second will be free, and all you have to do is make some minor changes to be ready to podcast.

You will find that you have more flexibility if you choose to install and configure things yourself. The reason for this is that you can have multiple sections to your website with one dedicated to your weblog. You will also be able to offer a variety of feeds, and if you choose, you can set up one of those BlogTorrent server seeders. It may not be the easiest way initially, but in the long run, the choice could have huge benefits.

It is also rumored that all-in-one solutions are about to be made public from websites, such as Odeo (`www.odeo.com`), but up to this point there has been a lot of talk and little action. Another possible solution might be coming from Adam Curry and his new website, at `www.podshow.com`.

Self-Hosting Weblogs

In this section, I review three popular self-hosted weblog applications. Two of them are podcast-ready upon installation, and one needs minor configuration updates.

These weblog applications are popular for good reason: they are easy to set up. This is not to say that other content-publishing systems are not podcast-ready, but I feel that these three are the most popular and the easiest for you to get started with.

These applications support Real Simple Syndication (RSS) enclosures. Remember, way back in Chapter 1, when I talked a little about enclosures? Well, after reading Chapters 12 and 13, you will know everything I know about enclosures.

Let me be honest here: this is a general statement that applies across the board, and you need to pay attention. If the software you use to publish your website cannot produce an RSS file with enclosure support, then you will be creating more work for yourself, and producing your show will require more time. I do not recommend website publishing platforms such as Adobe GoLive or FrontPage. If your site is already designed around these infrastructures, I will give you ways to make them podcast-friendly in the next chapter.

I want you to have fun. Getting you set up is a necessary evil, but once this is completed, you will be much farther ahead than the person who does not take my advice.

My goal here is to make sure that you don't get that "oh, no" feeling in the pit of your stomach. This is going to be a walk in the park, and if it becomes too hard, then I offer some alternative solutions later in the chapter.

We will get into RSS and enclosures hot and heavy in a few minutes, but first let's get you some information on the weblog applications that I recommend. Table 11-1 lists resources for self-hosted weblog applications.

Table 11-1   Self-Hosted Weblogs

Application	Website	Price	Desktop/ Web-Based	Install Required	Editor's Rank
MovableType	http://sixapart.com	$69.95-$99.95	Web-based	Yes	****
Radio Userland	http://userland.com	$39.95 annually	Desktop-based	Yes	*****
WordPress	http://wordpress.org	Free	Web-based	Yes	*****

Note   An unsupported version of MovableType is available for non-commercial use . It is limited to one author and three weblogs. If you are computer-savvy, you may get away with this version, but I prefer to have a supported product and I also can commercialize my site with the right license from Six Apart (`http://sixapart.com`).

These applications will require installation; each of the specific applications has great installation instructions. The installation is straightforward, and the degree of support for the applications is pretty close across the board. I won't go into how to install these applications. You can use each of their respective support forums. All the vendor sites have active support forums, and you will find help if you need it when installing the application.

You may ask what the major differences are among these weblogs. The following sections discuss the various types of weblogs.

Understanding Web-Based Weblog Applications

With the web-based weblog, the weblog application, content, and database reside completely on your website. You must have Internet connectivity to write articles and have access to old posts. So, once you are all set up, you will publish everything through your web browser or through software tools like BlogJet (www.blogjet.com) that can run stand-alone but still require connectivity to publish. The installed applications have editing tools that you access from within your browser.

I like the flexibility of web-based weblogs. I can be anywhere in the world, and as long as I have Internet access, I can post articles and information to my weblog.

This does mean, though, that when new software updates become available for the application, it has to be manually installed, and you need a little more technical knowledge to upgrade the applications and manage the site's weblog database.

Overall, though, the flexibility of being able to post whenever I have access is great.

Understanding Desktop Weblog Applications

Radio Userland is the only weblog package I am aware of in which the core software editing and configuration package resides on your computer.

What I like about Radio Userland is that you can edit a post on your PC anytime, even when you are not connected to the Internet. If you do this, the next time you have connectivity, the application will upload the new post to your website. The drawback is that you must designate a single computer to do all your posting because the archive and configurations are on the same computer.

One unique feature with Radio Userland is that the installed software runs a mini, internal web server on your PC. The application then uploads changes to your website automatically as you make changes. Use your interface to the application with your browser primarily to make changes to configuration and to do editing. The master database resides on your PC.

Note   Radio Userland provides hosting for your website for $39.95 a year. You get only 40 MB of storage on their site, and their maximum upload is 1 MB. This is great for hosting a weblog and a launching point for your podcast, but you will still need to find a hosting provider like Libsyn (http://Libsyn.org) to take care of the podcast files, which will generally be larger than 1 MB. It is rumored that they are working on a podcaster-specific package.

MovableType

I am a bit prejudiced in selecting MovableType. Part of that stems from my having used it for three years and understanding the power of the application; still, it is my choice in self-hosted weblog applications. It is not the easiest of the weblogs to configure for podcasting, but I do feel that it offers the most flexibility, especially for those of you who decide to offer more than one audio format and want to separate your podcast post from the other content you may want to put on the site.

Note Those considering using MovableType may want to consider purchasing the *MovableType 3 Bible Desktop Edition*, by Rogers Cadenhead, published by Wiley (ISBN 0-7645-7388-8). This book contains everything you need to know to prepare and set up the software and customize templates, in addition to presenting information on how plug-ins work.

The great thing about MovableType is that they have developed the application so that third-party programmers can build programs and tools that will plug in to the application to give it more functionality. Figure 11-1 shows the main menu screen for MovableType.

As you can see, I have three weblogs set up. The first is my main weblog, where all my daily non-podcast content is entered. The second is the actual weblog where I post my podcast information, and the third is my Link Blog, where I throw articles that were not worthy of main page publishing. Each of these three configurations points to a different location on my website:

- geeknewscentral.com
- geeknewscentral.com/podcasts
- geeknewscentral.com/linkblog

I found it easier to set up multiple weblogs to handle separate functions than to use categories, which I will be recommending in the other reviews.

At the bottom of the page is an entry that says "MT-Enclosure v1.4.1.2." This application is a third-party plug-in that extracts media links from blog entries and creates enclosures in RSS 2.0 feeds.

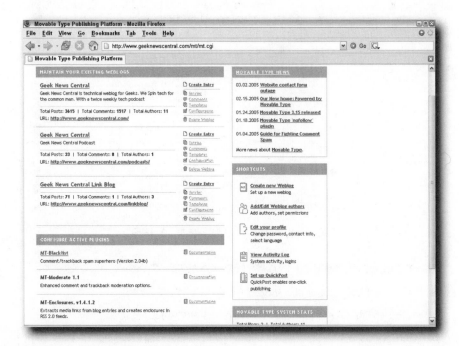

FIGURE 11-1: MovableType main interface.

Note A *plug-in* is an add-on software element that adds functions or features to the application. There are literally hundreds of possible plug-ins for use with this application (see http://sixapart.com/pronet/plugins).

As with everything else in the industry, podcasting caught fire so quickly that many weblog applications were not "enclosure-ready." Using the flexible architecture of MovableType, a programmer by the name of Brandon Fuller created a little utility that inserts the enclosure information into the RSS 2.0 feed that MovableType automatically creates.

Adding Enclosure Support to MovableType

After you've installed MovableType and created a test post, you will want to download the MT-Enclosure plug-in (http://brandon.fuller.name/archives/hacks/mt enclosures) and install as it per the instructions included in the downloaded zip file. It is very simple to install. You will be required to upload a file to the website and make the changes outlined in the install document.

To summarize that document, which should not be substituted for the actual instructions, you download the plug-in and unzip the contents into a directory on your PC. Using your FTP program, log into your server and navigate to the location where you installed MovableType. This will be the base directory, and the directory structure will look similar to that shown in Figure 11-2.

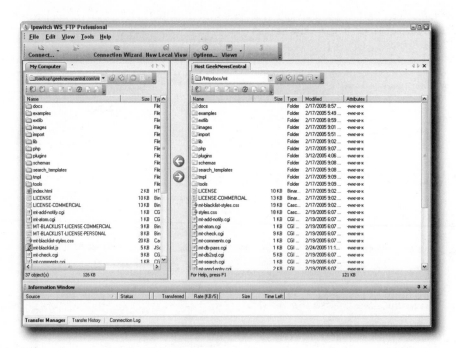

Figure 11-2: MovableType base directory.

If you look at the list of files and directories, you will see one that says `plugins`. If you have yet to install a plug-in in your installation of MovableType, create the directory, because it is not created by default. Name the directory **plugins**. After it is created, navigate to that directory and transfer the file named `Enclosures.pl` that you unzipped to a location on your computer. Figure 11-3 shows the transferred `Enclosures.pl` file in the plugins directory.

You will notice that there are other items in the directory, because I have other applications installed, so don't be worried if your directory has only one file. The next step will require you to make a minor change to the default RSS 2.0 template.

Templates in MovableType are important text files, with a great deal of text that will not make a lot of sense to you. I am going to show you the before and after examples so that you can be assured that you have edited the template correctly.

On the main page of your website, you will see the word Template. Click that, and you will see the Template menu, as shown in Figure 11-4.

In this menu, you see an entry that says RSS 2.0 Index. Click that, and you will be shown text in a window that should look like what's shown in Listing 11-1.

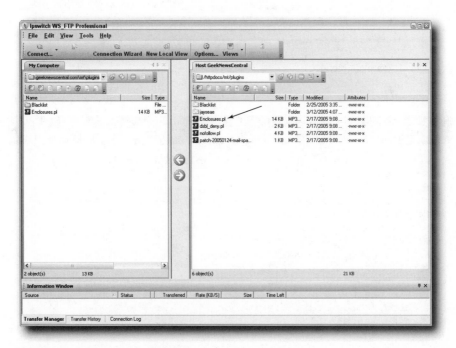

FIGURE 11-3: Enclosures.pl transferred to the plugins directory.

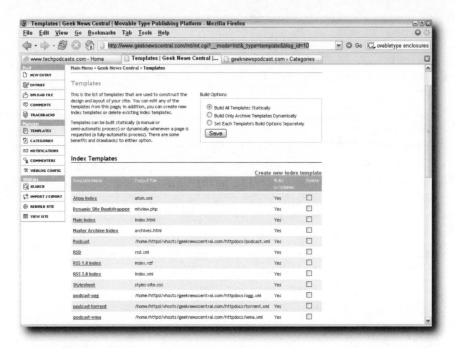

FIGURE 11-4: Template menu.

Listing 11-1: RSS 2.0 index contents — original

```
<?xml version="1.0" encoding="<$MTPublishCharset$>"?>
<rss version="2.0">
<channel>
<title><$MTBlogName remove_html="1" encode_xml="1"$></title>
<link><$MTBlogURL$></link>
<description><$MTBlogDescription remove_html="1"
encode_xml="1"$></description>
<copyright>Copyright <$MTDate format="%Y"$></copyright>
<lastBuildDate><MTEntries lastn="1"><$MTEntryDate
format_name="rfc822"$></MTEntries></lastBuildDate>
<generator>http://www.movabletype.org/?v=<$MTVersion$></generator>
<docs>http://blogs.law.harvard.edu/tech/rss</docs>
<MTEntries lastn="15">
<item>
<title><$MTEntryTitle remove_html="1" encode_xml="1"$></title>
<description><$MTEntryBody encode_xml="1"$></description>
```

```
<link><$MTEntryPermalink encode_xml="1"$></link>
<guid><$MTEntryPermalink encode_xml="1"$></guid>
<category><$MTEntryCategory remove_html="1"
encode_xml="1"$></category>
<pubDate><$MTEntryDate format_name="rfc822"$></pubDate>
</item>
</MTEntries>
</channel>
</rss>
```

All this information looks pretty geeky, doesn't it? Well, what you are going to do is insert the piece of text <$MTEntryEnclosures$> near the end of this file. If you look at Listing 11-2, you will see where I inserted the text.

Listing 11-2: RSS 2.0 Index Contents — modified

```
<?xml version="1.0" encoding="<$MTPublishCharset$>"?>
<rss version="2.0">
<channel>
<title><$MTBlogName remove_html="1" encode_xml="1"$></title>
<link><$MTBlogURL$></link>
<description><$MTBlogDescription remove_html="1"
encode_xml="1"$></description>
<copyright>Copyright <$MTDate format="%Y"$></copyright>
<lastBuildDate><MTEntries lastn="1"><$MTEntryDate
format_name="rfc822"$></MTEntries></lastBuildDate>
<generator>http://www.movabletype.org/?v=<$MTVersion$></generator>
<docs>http://blogs.law.harvard.edu/tech/rss</docs>
<MTEntries lastn="15">
<item>
<title><$MTEntryTitle remove_html="1" encode_xml="1"$></title>
<description><$MTEntryBody encode_xml="1"$></description>
<link><$MTEntryPermalink encode_xml="1"$></link>
<guid><$MTEntryPermalink encode_xml="1"$></guid>
<category><$MTEntryCategory remove_html="1"
encode_xml="1"$></category>
<pubDate><$MTEntryDate format_name="rfc822"$></pubDate>
<$MTEntryEnclosures$>
</item>
</MTEntries>
</channel>
</rss>
```

After you have added that text, as indicated in the example, you should save and rebuild the template.

From now on, anytime you provide a URL link to a media file in a weblog entry, the MT-Enclosures plug-in will read the link to that media file and create the proper enclosure tag in your RSS file.

Supporting Multiple File Formats with MovableType

I am going to throw you a curve ball here. Many of you will want to produce a show in more than one audio format. As I said earlier, I create audio files in MP3, WMA, and OGG format. Luckily, Brandon Fuller, when he created this plug-in, thought about that too and designed a way in which we could designate a specific extension to be included in the RSS 2.0 output file.

For a podcatcher to work properly, you should never have more than one enclosure element in the RSS 2.0 file per weblog post. Listing 11-3 shows an actual RSS 2.0 file with an enclosure element. I will break this down a little further so you understand.

Listing 11-3: Actual RSS 2.0 file with enclosure tag

```
- <rss version="2.0">
- <channel>
<title>Geek News Central</title>
<link>http://www.geeknewscentral.com/podcasts/</link>
<description>Geek News Central Podcast</description>
<language>en-us</language>
<copyright>Copyright 2005</copyright>
- <image>
<title> The Geek News Central Podcast!</title>
<url>http://www.geeknewscentral.com/gnc-link.jpg</url>
<link>http://www.geeknewscentral.com/podcasts/</link>
- <description>
We talk tech for the common man. With a twice weekly tech podcast
</description>
</image>
<lastBuildDate>Fri, 18 Mar 2005 04:04:58 -0600</lastBuildDate>
<pubDate>Sun, 20 Mar 2005 05:19:11 -0600</pubDate>
<generator>http://www.movabletype.org/?v=3.15</generator>
<docs>http://blogs.law.harvard.edu/tech/rss</docs>
- <item>
<title>Geek News Central Podcast #48 2005-03-18</title>
- <description>
<p>Recovering from the flu voice is barely hanging in there but
show must go on.... Some major announcements in the beginning of
the show about my schedule for the summer.</p>
<p><a href="http://libsyn.com/media/geeknews/GNC-
2005-03-18.mp3">GNC-2005-03-18.mp3</a><br />
<a href="http://www.geeknewscentral.com/podcast/GNC-
2005-03-18.wma">GNC-2005-03-18.wma</a><br />
```

```
<a href="http://www.geeknewscentral.com/podcast/GNC-
2005-03-18.ogg">GNC-2005-03-18.ogg</a><br />
<a
href="http://www.geeknewscentral.com/torrent/btdownload.php?type=t
orrent&file=GNC-2005-03-18.mp3.torrent">GNC-
2005-03-18.torrent</a></p>
<a href="http://www.gizmodo.com/gadgets//glow-brick-night-light-
036322.php">Glow Brick Light</a></p>
</description>
- <link>
http://www.geeknewscentral.com/podcasts/archives/2005/03/geek_news
_centr_29.html
</link>
- <guid>
http://www.geeknewscentral.com/podcasts/archives/2005/03/geek_news
_centr_29.html
</guid>
<category>Podcast</category>
<pubDate>Fri, 18 Mar 2005 04:04:58 -0600</pubDate>
<enclosure url="http://libsyn.com/media/geeknews/GNC-
2005-03-18.mp3" length="15372416" type="audio/mpeg"/>
</item> </channel>
</rss>
```

As you look closely at the text after `<item>` in the raw file that is formatted as RSS 2.0 in XML format, you will see in the HTML text that I have physically linked to four separate media files:

- GNC-2005-03-18.mp3 (`http://libsyn.com/media/geeknews/GNC-2005-03-18.mp3`)

- GNC-2005-03-18.wma (`http://www.geeknewscentral.com/podcast/GNC-2005-03-18.wma`)

- GNC-2005-03-18.ogg (`http://www.geeknewscentral.com/podcast/GNC-2005-03-18.ogg`)

- GNC-2005-03-18.torrent (`http://www.geeknewscentral.com/torrent/btdownload.php?type=torrent&file=GNC-2005-03-18.mp3.torrent`)

Yet, when you look at the bottom of the file, you will see the enclosure entry:

<enclosure url="http://libsyn.com/media/geeknews/GNC-2005-03-18.mp3" length="15372416" type="audio/mpeg"/>

You may ask why there is only one enclosure entry. There is only one because you actually have all four media files linked in the item.

Important Weblog Podcast Posting Considerations

Many people ask me why I have a weblog for my regular content and a weblog for my podcast even though, on show nights, I put a post on the main page as well as the podcast-only page.

The reason for that is simple: If you look at the template for the RSS 2.0 Index file, you will see an entry that says `<MTEntries lastn="15">`. This tag tells the MovableType software engine to put only the last 15 entries in the RSS 2.0 XML output file.

I write three to four non-podcast articles every day on my weblog; thus, I do not want new subscribers getting information that is a month old, and generally hope they will get info that is less that a week old.

So, by creating a separate weblog that has only podcast posts, I guarantee that people have access to the number of shows I configure using the preceding tag. If your shows will have relevant information in three months, then you want that number to be high. In recent weeks, I have been lowering that number.

My podcasts are about tech news happening this week, so I do not want people to download more than the past eight shows.

This is where the power of MovableType shines through. Let's go back and discuss additional features that were built into the MT-Enclosure plug-in. The author allows some rules to be added to the template file. When I had you put the `<$MTEntryEnclosures$>` tag in the RSS 2.0 Index file, I did not tell you about these optional rules.

Note These optional rules are needed only if you are producing more than one media type for downloading.

To separate media feeds and maintain the one enclosure per item rule in the RSS 2.0 file, I used the following tag instead: `<$MTEntryEnclosures include="mp3"$>`. This forces the plug-in to create only an enclosure tag for an MP3 file.

The trick I have used at Geek News Central is to provide multiple listener RSS feeds that are each branded for a specific file type. If you look at the file at `http://www.geeknews central.com/wma.xml`, you will find only the WMA extension media files listed in this separate RSS 2.0 file.

The way I created these separate feeds was simple. If you go to Templates in MovableType and select Create new index file, you can then create a secondary index file by cutting the modified RSS 2.0 index template entry you edited earlier and pasting it into the new template. Change the enclosure entry to the file extension of your choice — for example, `<$MTEntryEnclosures include="wma"$>` — then name the template whatever you desire.

Caution The filename that you enter needs to be different from `index.xml`. I kept it simple: `wma.xml`, `ogg.xml`, `torrent.xml`.

Setting up MovableType should take less than an hour, including getting the tag information set up. You can always request installation help from MovableType's professional support network. Podcast-specific setups can be forwarded to me at podcastbook@gmail.com, and I will do my best to get you connected with someone who understands the process.

WordPress

A growing number of people are using WordPress. In fact, many hosting providers provide automatic installation of the application through what is commonly referred to as a "Fantastico." The hosts that I have recommended all have this service. As long as they have version 1.5 or greater, you will get enclosure capability immediately. There is no modifying of templates. So, from an installation perspective, Fantastico makes it easier for those who are not as technically inclined.

WordPress configuration management is very different from MovableType's, because it does not lend itself easily to creating multiple weblogs. This is not to say that it cannot create multiple weblogs, just that it isn't as apparent how to do so.

Instead, most podcasters are simply setting up dedicated categories to create separate listings of podcasts.

Figure 11-5 shows the default install page of WordPress.

FIGURE 11-5: Default startup page after WordPress install.

Here's how you do it. Once you have WordPress installed, you will need to set up a category. Name it **podcasts** and don't put anything in that category unless it is an actual podcast post. This way, you can offer your listeners a separate link to your RSS feed. Figure 11-6 shows the categories page.

Having this separate category will allow your listeners to subscribe to your podcast-only feed. This is what the URL will look like for the RSS 2.0 subscription feed location for your podcast: `http://www.anydomain.com/wp-rss2.php?category_name=podcasts`.

Then you will want to add an RSS 2.0 link on your main page pointing at that same URL (`http://www.anydomain.com/wp-rss2.php?category_name=podcasts`). This will be for your independent podcast feed link.

You can add this link by selecting Presentation ➪ Theme Editor ➪ Sidebar Template and looking through the HTML to determine placement.

WordPress has a number of default templates to choose from, and their support forums at `http://wordpress.org/support` have a lot of very helpful people.

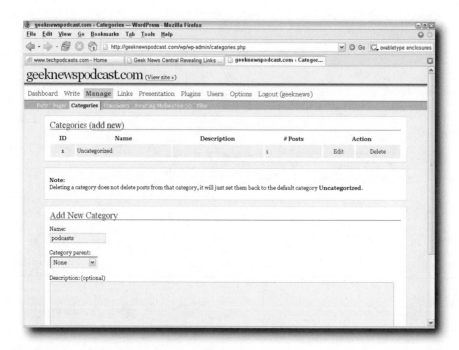

FIGURE **11-6:** WordPress category setup page

The preceding steps should be all you need to make your WordPress installation good to go for podcasting. I am unaware of a way to support multiple file formats from within the current WordPress setup. Those of you planning to offer multiple audio file formats will probably want to consider MovableType as the platform of choice.

Radio Userland

I used Radio Userland as my first weblog program and liked its ease of use. It has podcasting support built in. Radio Userland looks no different from other weblog clients, except that you will notice that when you are using your browser, it will be connecting to a mini web server running on your PC.

Prior to writing this book, I had not used Radio Userland to publish a podcast, so I decided to use it with a domain I needed to get busy on anyway. Figure 11-7 shows the default startup page when Radio Userland loads.

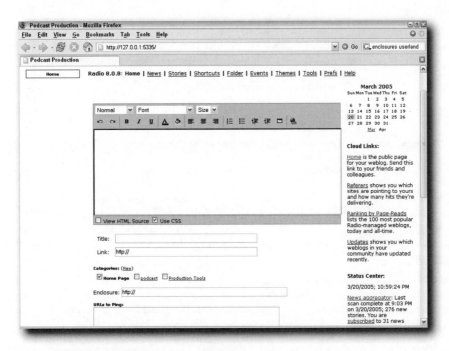

FIGURE 11-7: Radio Userland main page after setup.

You will see in this figure a box for an enclosure link. This will not show up by default; use the following steps to activate it. Figure 11-8 shows the category setup page.

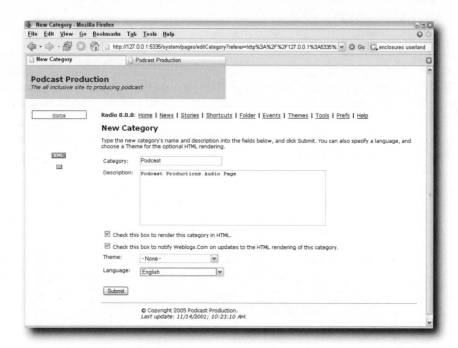

FIGURE 11-8: Category addition.

Just as with WordPress, it is critical that you add a podcast category; this will allow you to provide a separate RSS 2.0 feed that has only enclosures. This screen can be found by clicking Preferences ➪ Categories ➪ New Category Page. Once that is set up, you will need to make changes in the News Aggregator section. Figure 11-9 shows the RSS Enclosures page open.

You can reach this page by clicking Preferences ➪ RSS Enclosure. The critical element to choose is the "Check this box. . ." if you want to be able to add enclosures to your own output channels. After you have done this and submitted the changes, click the Home menu item, and you will be back to your home page. The enclosures block will be enabled.

Note   Detailed instructions to automate the delivery of your podcast with Radio Userland can be found at `http://radio.userland.com/discuss/msgReader$35098`.

You are ready to podcast. Again, using Radio Userland for hosting is fine, but they cannot accept podcasts larger than 1 MB. You will need to use a third-party hosting service for podcasts larger than that.

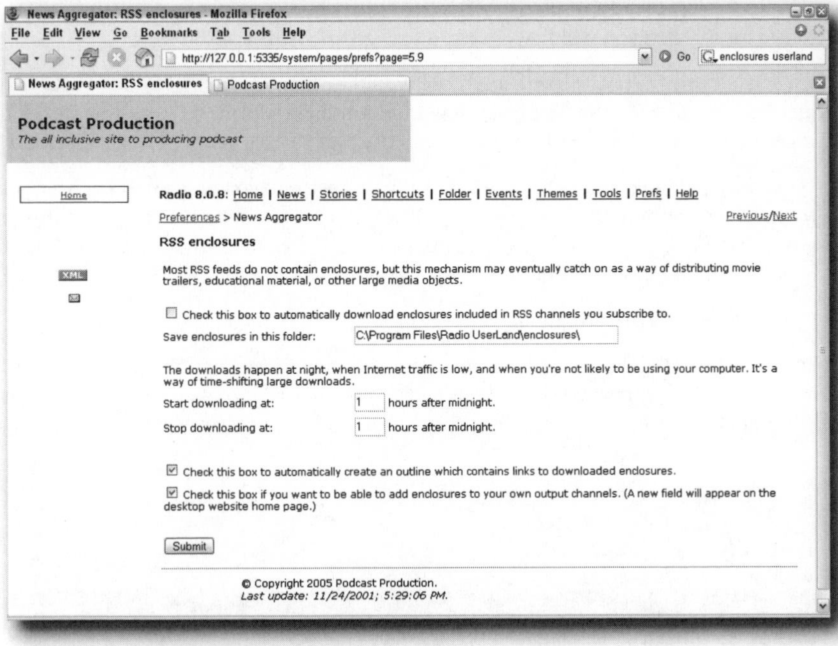

FIGURE 11-9: RSS Enclosures settings.

Using Commercial Weblog Services

Many of you will already have a weblog, be it a free account on Blogger or MSN Spaces, or you may have an account on TypePad for which you pay a monthly service fee. These are great services in that they take care of the hosting for you, along with all the infrastructure. Thus, there is nothing to install. You load your browser, log in, and set up your site. They even offer a number of easily modifiable site templates. These services typically allow you to upload only a very small audio file and come with very low bandwidth allowances. In Table 11-2, I point you to some of the commercial weblog services.

Table 11-2 Commercial Weblog Services

Application	Website	Price	Desktop/ Web-Based	Install Required	Editor's Rank
Blogger	www.blogger.com	Free	Web-based	No	***
LiveJournal	www.livejournal.com	Free to $25 per year	Web-based	No	****
MSN Spaces	http://spaces.msn.com	Free	Web-based	No	**
TypePad	www.sixapart.com	$4.95 to $14.95	Web-based	No	***

If you have a weblog already, or do not want to go through the pain of setting up one of the previous solutions, then you will have to use a service to host the audio files.

This is where a hosting service like Libsyn.org would be a good hosting choice to stash audio files. Such services provide the best of both worlds: you have a place to store your audio files that is reasonably priced, plus you can use one of the free weblog services to get started.

This comes with an issue that is easily fixed. Some of the free blogging solutions have yet to support enclosures, although, hopefully, they all will in the near future. I can only think that the reason they haven't all jumped on the bandwagon yet is the concern that people will create and host shows on a system that was not designed to host audio.

Figure 11-10 shows Blogger's main page.

Blogger (`http://blogger.com`) is a very versatile weblog application, and because it does not support enclosures with their RSS feeds, you will need to use a service known as FeedBurner. Figure 11-11 shows the front page of the FeedBurner website.

FIGURE 11-10: Blogger's main page.

FIGURE 11-11: FeedBurner's main page.

FeedBurner (http://FeedBurner.com) got lucky; the service was initially created as a service that enhanced RSS feeds. They realized that podcasters were having trouble with enclosures for RSS feeds and came to the rescue.

The service is simple to use. As long as your weblog service can create an RSS 2.0 file, which the majority do, this service can import that feed and transform it into an RSS 2.0 feed with enclosures. FeedBurner simply reads your existing RSS file and then detects the link to the media player and spits out a new feed with the enclosure information.

Tip

FeedBurner can be used with any hosting solution that produces an RSS feed. Although I like what FeedBurner is doing, you must realize that you are entrusting your entire audience to their service. If their service goes down or is not available, then your subscribers will not get your show on a timely basis. They do have great tracking tools and lots of "gee whiz" types of feed enhancements. But I, personally, am not ready to trust someone else with the "glue" that gets my audio file from my host onto my listeners' portable media devices.

Podcasting without a Weblog

I want to say up front that producing a podcast without a weblog is possible, but you will have to take some extra steps, and the process will not be automated. I understand that many of you will already have invested money in an infrastructure or publishing system. This should not dampen your spirits, because there are a number of very successful podcasters who are not using weblogs as their primary publishing tool.

Luckily, tools are available to podcast without a weblog. I will discuss and demonstrate those RSS tools in the next chapter.

Summary

You now have key information that moves you toward the final steps in publishing and in getting your podcast available to be enjoyed by your future listeners. I have given you information on:

- How to install your own weblog application
- How to create independent RSS feeds
- Options for using existing free services, such as Blogger and MSN Spaces
- Services that you can use with weblog-publishing solutions that do not create RSS 2.0 files with enclosures
- Information on producing your podcast with your existing non-RSS-compliant tools

If you have not realized how important RSS with enclosures are, in the next chapter you get to know why RSS 2.0 feeds with enclosures are the glue that holds it all together — they allow podcasters to distribute media automatically to the masses.

The Life Breath of a Podcast: RSS 2.0 with Enclosures

Y ou should understand by now that without RSS with enclosures, you will not have the mechanism to facilitate the automatic distribution of your podcast from the Internet to your listeners' portable media devices. Some companies will cry foul and say "no, we delivered audio to people's audio players." That may be true, but it wasn't free. Isn't technology awesome? The barriers are coming down in all mediums, and the people shall be heard.

But podcasting isn't just for individuals. Traditional radio, such as the BBC and National Public Radio, have adapted quickly, along with some terrestrial radio stations. The appeal of podcasting has continued to expand. Podcasting is the medium that will change the way people consume audio. The genre will continue to grow because of the freedom to say what one wants. The RSS 2.0 specification and the enclosure tag set the stage for the remarkable explosion that we continue to see.

RSS: The Glue That Holds Podcasting Together

When Dave Winer incorporated the enclosure tag into the new RSS standards, I am sure he had a pretty good idea, and, luckily, his evangelism of RSS has made the standard a mainstay of website content delivery worldwide. Not only has RSS allowed people like you and me to create and distribute media files, it has also transformed the way millions of people consume news and information.

Since the explosion of weblogs, the growth rate and adoption of RSS all over the Internet continues to expand; there are almost too many applications that consumers use to read the data that lies within those RSS files to count. Personally, I rarely read information directly from a person's website. My RSS aggregator does it for me automatically on a periodic basis, and then I am presented with the new information that has been published in a newspaper-style format.

I am able to review hundreds of sites a day, yet not spend a lot of time doing so. The old publishing model relied on people visiting your page directly. Today, if a website doesn't have an RSS feed, I never see it. I have followed links to great sites only to find that they aren't RSS-capable, which is too bad, because it will probably be the last time I ever visit them.

My weblog at Geek News Central is an average weblog. Over the past three years, I have seen consistent growth at the rate measured in direct hits on my main site of about 8 percent per month. This is nothing to get very excited about, but my RSS feed is a different story. Since allowing my readers to read the full post via their aggregators, I have seen a consistent 15 percent per month increase in the number of times the file is read.

Some aggregators check on an hourly basis, and some are nicer and only hit the site three or four times a day. So, it is almost impossible, without heavy parsing of my log files, to determine how many unique aggregators I have hitting the site, but I have a pretty good idea. Before I parse any data, I typically see nearly 7 million hits to the RSS feed each month. The differential between direct page loads of the main site to the RSS feed is considerable.

That said, RSS has empowered readers and allows them to visit more than a handful of sites per day. Personally, I can review over 400 sites in just about an hour. Because I can consume a large number of sites containing only text, my podcatcher can load enough audio programming while I sleep to allow me to listen to 8+ hours of content every day.

Podcasting will enable companies I associate with to include not only text but also audio sound bites in their RSS feeds. This process can even move into video. If the bandwidth of the average day consumer were large enough, you could actually use RSS with enclosures to have all video and multimedia delivered automatically through the same distribution channels.

Think of the power this offers: companies could provide private feeds to writers to feed them daily news and tidbits about new product development and so on. The uses are endless.

Every time I type "RSS with enclosures," I feel like I am writing a menu for a restaurant. Imagine a chef saying "Sir, would you like your RSS feed with enclosures?" Kind of like ordering a burger and then being asked whether you want the bun. In content distribution, a.k.a., podcast delivery, not having the enclosure is like getting a burger without the bun. You just have to have it.

RSS Structure

Up to this point, I have wanted to avoid giving you a deeply detailed explanation of RSS. I wanted you to understand that it is important to let the software tools do the work. The last thing I want you to do is have to code RSS by hand. First of all, that's sheer stupidity, and second, you'll waste a heck of a lot of time.

If you want to dig in deep and understand the actual structure of RSS, I recommend you buy a book or do some searching on the Net. Experts have written books the same size as this one devoted entirely to RSS, and let's be honest, do you really want to know the inner workings of Real Simple Syndication?

For the sake of review, let's talk about RSS again. On various websites, although primarily on weblogs and news sites, you will see an icon that could be labeled RSS, RSS .91, RSS 2.0, or XML. They are typically small icons with white letters on an orange background. These icons are linked to an extensible markup language (XML) file. The site `http://webreference.com/authoring/languages/xml/rss/intro/` offers a detailed discussion of RSS.

All you really need to know about RSS is that it enables you to share content across the Internet, and you must be able to create or have an RSS 2.0 with enclosures feed someplace on the Internet that your listeners can subscribe to.

I did indicate in the last chapter that I would talk about creating an RSS feed for those of you who prefer to not use an RSS-enabled publishing application. Thus, by reviewing which information you will need to create an RSS file using a manual software tool, I can help you understand how the file is structured without getting too technical on you.

Only a few stand-alone RSS creators on the market today support enclosures. They all work about the same way. I picked the one that would be easiest for me to help you understand the different elements, while at the same time instructing those of you needing to create your own RSS feed.

Manually Creating an RSS Feed

I used the Windows application FeedForAll (`http://feedforall.com`), available for $39.95. For the Mac, I highly recommend Feeder (`http://reinventedsoftware.com/feeder/index.html`), available for $24.95. Figure 12-1 shows the main screen for FeedForAll, the Windows application.

This will be the output filename!

FIGURE 12-1: FeedForAll standalone RSS creator.

This application has a Preferences section where you can set up defaults that you will be able to start with as a baseline each time. It also enables you to create an RSS file with multiple items within a single file, which is critical.

I will discuss in detail what an *item* is. But let's start with the Feeds tab. The Feeds tab shows you the *required items* that absolutely have to be in the file. These items are commonly referred to as the *channel* or *head element*. This data will not change from podcast to podcast.

- **Title:** The title of your website, not the title of your podcast entry.
- **Description:** The basic description of your website.
- **Pub Date:** The publication date of the RSS file (today's date).

You will see an Optional tab with optional entries that are self-explanatory. I personally populated only the Language and Copyright fields under the Optional tab. I have the output file to show you the corresponding sections in Listing 12-1.

Figure 12-2 shows the Items tab and the editor for the Description field.

FIGURE **12-2: Items tab.**

An *item* is a single entry on your weblog. For each and every show, you will be able to add a new item to this list. Thus, in the left column you see GNC-2005-03-25. When you add a new item, the listing for GNC-2005-03-25 moves down a notch, and you will have clear fields for adding a new item.

Required item fields include:

- **Title:** The title of the podcast entry.
- **Description:** Can contain show notes and fully valid HTML, as discussed in the note that follows.
- **Link:** The link to the page that contains the entry for the show.
- **Pub Date:** The date of publication and time of show release.

Note This application has a mini HTML editor in the Description box that will give you limited word-processing capabilities for editing and adding typical HTML components. This alleviates the need for you to know HTML tags.

Next, you click the Optional tab. Figure 12-3 shows the Optional Information tab, where you will enter the enclosure location. The enclosure will be the URL link to your podcast.

See Figure 12-4

FIGURE 12-3: Item tab Optional window.

You will notice an overlapping window. This is a pop-up window from the application. Even though this is the Optional section, in order for your podcast to be downloaded automatically by podcatcher applications, the enclosure entry must be filled out.

Optional entries include:

- **Category:** This can be anything; it does not need to be limited to podcasts.
- **GUID:** This should also be the permanent URL link to the article (optional).
- **Enclosure:**
    - **URL:** The full URL of the file location.
    - **Length:** The file size in bytes (see Figure 12-4).
    - **Type:** .mp3 (audio/MPEG), .wma (audio/WMA), .ogg (audio/ogg), or .torrent (audio/x-torrent).

Figure 12-4 shows how you determine the audio file size in Windows.

In Windows, go to the location where your file is stored, right-click the file, and choose Properties. When the dialog box opens, you will want to write down the number listed in the Size field. In this example, 19016419 will be the entry that you put in the length column in Figure 12-3.

Length

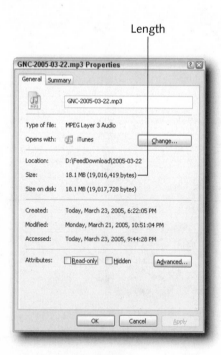

FIGURE 12-4: File properties.

For Mac users, click the file, and in Finder, select File ➪ Get Info. The file size will be in the general section.

After you have entered these parameters and saved the entry, you are ready to upload the RSS file that has been created to a public directory on your website. If you look at Figure 12-1, you will see the filename with the information you have just saved. I proceeded to upload that file to my web server. The contents of that file are shown in Listing 12-1.

Listing 12-1: Raw text of sample.xml

```
- <rss version="2.0">
- <channel>
<title>The Name of My Site</title>
<description>This is the description of my Site</description>
<link>http://www.anydomain.com/</link>
<copyright>http://creativecommons.org/licenses/by-nc-
sa/2.0/</copyright>
<docs>http://blogs.law.harvard.edu/tech/rss</docs>
<language>en-us</language>
<lastBuildDate>Wed, 23 Mar 2005 21:53:55 -1000</lastBuildDate>
<pubDate>Fri, 25 Mar 2005 01:09:11 -1000</pubDate>
<generator>FeedForAll v1.0 (1.0.1.0) unlicensed
version</generator>
- <item>
<title>GNC-2005-03-25</title>
- <description>
Our 50th show tonight with lots of great highlights and the
winners of our contest be announced live.   <br>
<a href="http://libsyn.com/media/geeknews/GNC-2005-03-25.mp3"><br>
GNC-2005-03-25.mp3</a><br>
<a href="http://www.geeknewscentral.com/podcast/GNC-
2005-03-25.wma">GNC-2005-03-25.wma</a><br>
<a href="http://www.geeknewscentral.com/podcast/GNC-
2005-03-25.ogg">GNC-2005-03-25.ogg</a><br>
<a
href="http://www.geeknewscentral.com/torrent/btdownload.php?type=t
orrent&file=GNC-2005-03-25.mp3.torrent">GNC-
2005-03-25.torrent</a><br>
/description>
<link>http://www.anydomain.com/link-to-article.html</link>
<category domain="">Podcast</category>
<enclosure url="http://libsyn.com/media/geeknews/GNC-
2005-03-25.mp3" length="19016419" type="audio/mpeg"/>
<guid
isPermaLink="true">http://www.anydomain.com/permlink.html</guid>
<pubDate>Fri, 25 Mar 2005 01:09:11 -1000</pubDate>
</item>
</channel>
</rss>
```

If you look closely at this file, you will see the correlation between the entries that I inserted in the example and what was created. See, this isn't rocket science. But I'm not done yet; I need to make sure that the file I created is valid.

Validating the RSS File

The most important thing you should do, whether the file was created manually or by hand with an external tool, is validate the results. RSS is funny; you may use some HTML markup that looks great in a browser or in the raw text file but causes an RSS aggregator or a podcatcher application to abort because of some malformed character.

Note Always validate those feeds with Feed Validator (`http://feedvalidator.org`).

Figure 12-5 shows the simple web-based interface for Feed Validator.

FIGURE 12-5: The feed I created has been validated.

After you've uploaded the file to your web server, you can validate the file. You can see that all I did was point Feed Validator at the URL to the location of the uploaded file. This validation process guarantees that you have a feed that can be connected to and aggregated without causing any issues with the software reading your feed. If Feed Validator could not validate this feed, it would have pointed out the line and area that was invalid by highlighting the invalid code.

Summary

In this chapter, you've gained a little insight into what is contained in an RSS feed. You now have the tools to publish a valid RSS feed with enclosures, which is like getting that burger with the bun. They just go so much better together.

Some individuals will decide that they want to code their RSS feeds by hand. Don't do it. Use one of the tools I have recommended, or better yet, enable your website to be published with one of the applications we talked about in Chapter 11.

Following are the key points covered in this chapter:

- The mechanics of RSS are not important.
- There are software tools for creating RSS feeds.
- Always validate any RSS feed that has been updated, whether created manually or automatically via the software on your website.

Well folks, it's show time, and in Chapter 13, you get your show posted for the world to see.

It's Show Time

part

V

Uploading Files and Publishing Your Show

Can you believe it? It's time to upload your podcast. I hope the process has been fun, because now it really gets exciting. You have probably been getting everyone you know and those who are reading your website prepared for the launch of your podcast. It is time to make a splash in the podcasting community and say, "Here I am, world!"

Much of what you've done in preparation for putting together your first show will now set the stage for promotion and growth of your listening audience.

Uploading the Podcast

This almost sounds like "beam me up Scotty," and in a sense, it is. This is the time when you will take that carefully created show and send it off to your hosting provider. Depending on what hosting solution you went with, you may be uploading to your new hosting service, so you want to choose wisely where you will be placing that first show.

The reason I say this is because the podcast needs to be easy to manage so that when you've uploaded your 100th show you're not saying, "Man, oh man, why did I upload to that section of my website?" You never want to store your podcast in your top-level directory.

When I say *top level*, I mean the directory that a web browser reads when you type, for example, www.techpodcasts.com. Instead, you want to create a directory in which to place your podcasts. In Figure 13-1, I've created a new directory with the FTP client.

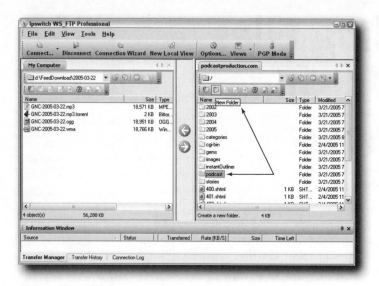

FIGURE **13-1:** Creating a new podcast directory.

Creating the directory is as simple on your host server with a FTP client as it is in Windows or on the Mac. After the directory is created, you want to make sure that the directory has the correct permissions. What I mean by *permissions* is that you need to set rules on each directory for what is allowed to be accessed, modified, and so on.

If you are logging into libsyn.org with your FTP client, you will be required to store your files in the top-level directory. The same may be true with other services, such as archive.org. When you use a secondary service to store your files, you should follow any site-specific instructions.

Some of you may want to try to upload the files using your hosting provider's interface. I do not recommend this, because FTP programs have bit checking. By using a web-based upload interface, you could end up with failed uploads or partial files on your server.

You will hear the word CHMOD used sometimes. This is the Unix command to change directory permissions. Luckily, all modern FTP clients have a utility built in to modify permissions for you.

Click the new directory in your FTP client to select it, then right-click and choose Properties. In Figure 13-2, you see the properties of a directory.

The directory should be set to 755. When this is done, click OK, and you are ready to upload your podcast onto the server and into that directory. Some of your FTP clients may require a different keystroke sequence to bring up the Directory Properties. You should be able to search for help on directory/file properties to find the menu item in your FTP client. By setting to 755, you are basically setting the access permission. For detailed information on UNIX file and directory permissions, visit http://csun.edu/itr/guides/unixpermissions.html.

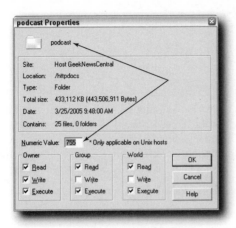

FIGURE 13-2: Folder permission settings.

Because this is an audio file, you will want to set your FTP transfer type to Binary. Uploading in ASCII will result in file corruption. Figure 13-3 shows the files uploaded onto the server.

Because I use several servers to distribute the bandwidth load, I have uploaded the WMA and OGG file to my primary server and the MP3 file to a secondary one. You will want to check the permissions on the files you have uploaded. They should be set to 644.

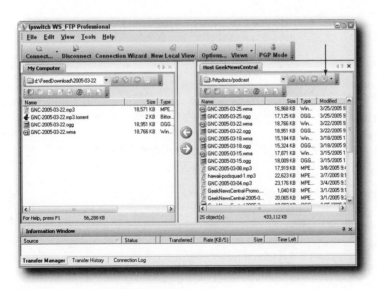

FIGURE 13-3: Files uploaded to the server.

Once the files have been uploaded, it is time to publish your show notes with links to the media files on your weblog.

Posting Show Notes

As I discussed in Chapter 4, it is important to develop a format for your show notes so that they will easily transfer to the website. I find it is extremely critical to put up some information on the show in the same post to which you link the audio file. People will come back to that information after they have listened to find a link to a website you have talked about, or, if they are new listeners, they will want to know what your show is all about before downloading it.

Over time, I have come up with a format that works for me. I transcribe those notes to make the actual show posting.

I feel you have to find a balance in the content of the show notes; give your audience some teasers, but not a spoiler. I do link to the majority of the sites I talk about. But giving readers too much information in the show post may result in people not listening to the entire show.

Some people will put in only a sentence or two and then a link to their audio files. You need to ask yourself what kind of impression that makes. You've gone to all this trouble to create a great show, and then you dress it down by not providing information about what the show is all about. On the other side of the fence, people put excruciating detail on their shows — some include to-the-second details about where each segment is. I never provide the specific time of the segments because I want people to listen to the whole show; also, I may rearrange the sequence of topics I talk about on the fly.

So, what does your podcast look like when it goes up on the web? Figure 13-4 shows my final product.

Website Show Note Format

My show notes include the following:

- One or two paragraphs containing highlights or general announcements.

- The actual MP3 Links (GNC-YYYY-MM-DD.MP3) and URLs.

- Sponsor information (advertiser's name and domain link).

- Special announcements.

- Show topics linked to websites discussed.

- Independent music and link to artist's website.

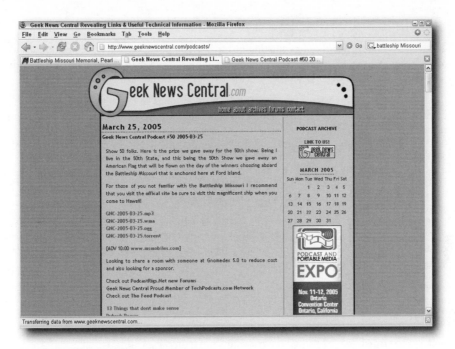

FIGURE **13-4: My website's published format.**

If you compare my website post to the show note format I discussed in Chapter 4, you will see how I laid out the show notes. I encourage you to visit my website and look at the formatting (www.geeknewscentral.com/podcasts).

Triple Checking

I always do a review of everything I have posted and double-check the links. I click each of my audio links to ensure that they point at the correct files. To save time, sometimes I cut and paste the link information from previous shows. All I have to do is make a date change. It is best to make sure that you have not mistyped.

I also have the podcatcher client set up to download my own show, and I launch that and make sure it is not having trouble. As I recommended in Chapter 12, you should validate your RSS feeds.

Pinging audio.weblogs.com

There is a special service that has a listing of the last 100 podcasts that have been published. If you are using MovableType, it will automatically ping the site with the required information when you publish your post as long as you are using the Podcast category.

If you are unsure about whether your weblog application pings `http://audio.weblogs.com` automatically, you will want to ask around on your weblog support forums about how people are doing it automatically.

You can also manually ping the audio.weblogs site at `http://audio.weblogs.com/ pingform.html`. This site offers a form you can fill out — simply enter your site's name and URL. The site shows only the last 100 shows, so the length of time your show stays in the 100 last shows depends on how many new shows come after yours.

Some of you may be saying, "Ping? What are you talking about?" It's simple. When weblog applications ping a site, they send some data to the site they are pinging and say, "Hey I just updated my site and here's some information about what I updated." In turn, the site receiving the ping takes that information and updates their site's newest show listings.

Summary

You have uploaded your show and posted your show notes, providing:

- A one- or two-paragraph show summary.
- Links to your podcast.
- Links to sites mentioned, with inviting titles (teasers).
- Credit to any musical artists and links to their sites.

The hard work is over; now, it's time to build your audience. In Chapter 14, I will show you ways to drive your listener count through the roof.

Feedback, Promotion, and Paying the Bills

Your podcast has been published, and the next phase of the journey begins. With all this hard work, you will want to find out exactly what your audience's opinions are and make adjustments to your show as necessary. It will take some time to grow your audience, and with that time you can adjust your show as you receive feedback on your content.

You will want to get your site listed in the various podcasting directories, as well as get your podcast reviewed and, with any luck, promoted by other podcasters. The ultimate goal for some of you may be to attract sponsors/advertisers, and with that in mind, certain issues must be considered.

Collecting Feedback

The single most important thing my listeners can do is use the lines of communication I have set up to send me feedback. It has been essential to my show's success that there is a two-way dialogue of sorts through e-mail, my mailing list, skype, and voice mail.

The majority of changes I've made to my show resulted from recommendations from my listeners. They told me my audio was too low, my background music was too loud, there was too much initial chit chat, and so on. I modified my show's format by fixing the audio levels, removing background music, and shortening my introduction.

It's apparent to me when I have implemented something people do not like, because I get immediate feedback; the same goes for positive changes. You will find that it may sometimes be a challenge getting listeners to e-mail you about what they do like because it is human nature to speak only when there is something we don't like.

Mailing Lists

On top of posting the show notes on the website, I also started a mailing list. I simply e-mail the show notes to the list's participants. This is another way for me to reach my listeners and a way to introduce each new podcast. This also provides an easy way for them to provide direct feedback. My listeners are part of my family, so just as I would listen to a family member, I also listen to my podcast family. I can also send polls to the mailing list to better understand what my listener demographics are.

Doing a podcast also means that you will be opening up lines of communication to yourself that people you do not know will use to contact you. I recommend setting up a separate e-mail account, possibly one on `http://gmail.com`, `http://yahoo.com`, or `http://hotmail.com`. This will allow you to isolate podcast e-mail.

Skype

Skype (`www.skype.com`) has revolutionized the way I communicate with people around the world. The service allows users to make computer-to-computer calls, computer-to-traditional phone line calls, and traditional phone line to skype calls. The best part of all is that some of those services are free. Figure 14-1 shows the skype interface.

FIGURE 14-1: Skype interface.

Skype recently introduced a for-pay service that is basically an Internet-based voice-mail service. I encourage my listeners to call me on skype and give them my skype address. I was initially worried that I would spend all my time answering skype calls, but it turns out that I am usually not bothered very much. Some of the top-ranking podcasters have had to start filtering calls. If I am busy, I put the application on Do Not Disturb and let voice mail pick up the call. I have saved hundreds of dollars in regular long-distance charges while doing research for this book by calling developers of applications on their landlines via skype at very low international and domestic calling rates, or for free skype to skype. So, if you're looking to stretch your budget further, use the technology to your advantage.

Voice Mail

Many of your listeners will not have skype or may be someplace where it cannot be used when listening to a show. I have a separate dedicated voice mail line that is just like a standard answering machine. The main difference in this service is that when the caller is finished leaving a message, the voice mail service e-mails me a WAV file of the actual recording. This allows me to easily incorporate listeners' calls into the show.

This is also a way to avoid having your home phone ring at all hours of the night. I would never recommend giving out your home phone number. A large number of podcasters get their voice mail at a free service originating in the 206 area code. You will want to visit K7.net (www.k7.net). They have vanity numbers available, and some podcasters have been very creative in finding a number that easy to remember. Figure 14-2 shows the K7.net website.

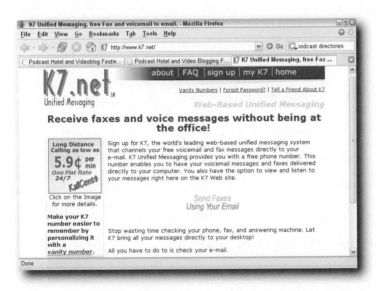

FIGURE 14-2: The K7.net website.

The K7.net service is nice, but I find it somewhat low on audio quality. I chose to go with a commercial service because the recorded message was of a higher standard and could better be reproduced on the show. However, I can't complain about the free service K7.net offers.

Promoting Your Podcast

Let's face it, most of us don't like to toot our own horns, but I'm here to tell you that if you don't, no one will. With new podcasts breaking out every day, you need to be aggressive and work hard. I am going to give you several steps to take that will place you ahead of the pack when it comes to getting the attention of listeners and podcasters.

Getting Listed in Podcast Directories

As soon as you have your first podcast up and you're sure that your RSS feed is validated, start submitting your show to the major podcast directories.

Before you do, though, you will want to take some time to come up with a detailed description of your show. I try to specify who this show is for and what it is about in the first paragraph. If you still have potential listeners' attention, you can list some personal stuff and more details.

If the directory allows you to put 255 words in the description, use all 255. You want to provide as much detail about your show in your description for search engines, either the directories' or spiders from the major services. Most of the directories allow you to add 10 keywords; again, think those through. Typically, most of us can come up with four to five very easily, so imagine what you want to enter in a search engine to find your listing. Along with that, you need to choose the proper category. Most sites allow you to pick two. Make sure that the category in which you put yourself is the correct one.

Note When you enter the URL for your podcast feed, make sure it is one that you plan to stick with. If you have not created a dedicated RSS feed for your podcast, STOP and do that before submitting. It is much harder to get something changed once you have entered it.

If you subscribe to the podcast mailing list at `http://groups.yahoo.com/group/podcasters`, you will find that announcements for new shows are made all the time. Sure, I think it's great that people do that, but the true secret is to list the tidbits of information that listeners may not find otherwise. It seems like people are announcing new services and software updates on a daily basis. Following are some directories that are definitely sites where you want to be listed:

- Digital Podcast (`http://digitalpodcast.com`)
- iPodder (`http://ipodder.org`)
- iPodderX (`http://ipodderx.com`)
- Podcast Alley (`http://podcastalley.com`)

- Podcast Bunker (http://podcastbunker.com)
- Podcast Central (http://podcastcentral.com)
- Podcast Directory (http://podcastdirectory.com)
- Podcast Net (http://podcast.net)

Revisit those directories often, and be a participant in their forums. You want the directory manager to know who you are so that when it comes time for him to highlight a show, he remembers your participation in the forums.

Distributing Show Promos

Take the time to create a very good 15 to 30 second audio and written promo for your show. A promo is something that really gets everyone's attention. The best way to get your promo played on other people's shows is to play their promos. So, don't be bashful in asking for someone's promo, and once you've played it, make sure that you let them know which show it was played on and where in the podcast the promo you played it. Provide a courtesy link to your show and the link to your promo.

My news show promo goes something like this: A siren sounds to get people's attention; then a voices comes on that says, "Your attention please, a new edition of the *Geek News Central* podcast is online now. Be sure to visit Geek News Central at www.geeknewscentral.com to subscribe or pick up the latest show. You can call the voice mail hotline at 619-342-7365 to have your comments heard, or call the host directly on skype at "geeknewscentral." As always, this is a show that you are not going to want to miss. Once again, a new podcast by the geek at Geek News Central is online at www.geeknewscentral.com."

My goal with that promo is to get people to come and check out the show. I could have gotten into details, but I wanted the clip to be less than 30 seconds. You have to get your message out quick. I sometimes submit that clip to http://openpodcast.org, but not every show, because people can become annoyed if they hear it too often. Every couple of weeks is more than enough. They are very effective, because I often hear from listeners that they heard my promo on such-and-such a show.

A great service that was recently launched is a clearinghouse for people looking to share their promos; it's called Podcast Promo and it can be found at www.podcastpromos.com. This service allows podcasters to post a note with a link to their promo; then podcasters simply exchange promos. It is purely voluntary, but people get exposure on shows where they would not normally.

If someone is doing a tech show and they send me a promo, I find it easier to play it because it fits into my content. I actually like playing people's promos, and because you have purchased this book, if you send me a promo at podcastbook@gmail.com, it will get some free airplay. I will play your promos on my show as I can fit them in.

Finding Gems in the Sand

With the large number of podcasts being launched, it is difficult for new podcasters to get the type of exposure they deserve. Some of the best content I have found to date is from unpublicized podcasts that are relatively new. A small number of early adopters continue to get the lion's share of the press. The early adopters deserve the credit they get, but they had better not be resting on their laurels because lots of new podcasts are waiting to be found.

Note

This offer is only for noncommercial podcasts. Those of you creating commercial programming will be able to find plenty of podcasts to play your advertisement for a small fee. I will talk more about that later in this section.

If you are creating noncommercial content, there's no reason to pay someone to play your promo; the spirit of podcasting thus far has been pretty open.

Getting the Word Out

Besides producing a promo and getting listed in directories, do your best to publicize your podcast in and around your local community. I have been able to score front-page publicity in the local newspaper, just because I was active with local podcasters. This, in turn, drove my local listenership up and has opened up some consulting opportunities to help local companies get dialed in with podcasting.

You have to sell the sizzle of your podcast, and with a few well-placed announcements, you will grow listeners. I also suggest that you go outside the podcast channels and promote your show in appropriate news groups. You may be surprised how many will tune in and be hooked because the format is different from what they are used to hearing.

I have a mailing list for my listeners and I ask them to spread the word in forums in which other podcasters hang out. You can submit your website for indexing with Yahoo! and Google. A few well-placed links by other podcasters to your main site will help get the search engines to index your page. Some podcasters have hired search engine placement specialists to help get their podcast higher in the Google rankings. I used to buy into that thought process, but, honestly, content is king. If you have good content that gets updated often on your website, your site will get indexed on a regular basis by the search engines. When you have a big event like a milestone show (e.g., 10, 25, 50, 100), send out a press release to all the podcast directories that feature your site.

Advertising and Accepting Advertisers

Some of you won't want to go to the trouble of advertising or getting advertisers, but read on so that you have an idea about the potential for advertising.

When I decided that I was really getting serious about podcasting, I started advertising my show on other sites. There is no better way to get the word out on your show than to advertise with a podcast directory or even on another podcast. I had run into trouble trying to get my promo played on a few shows, so I used the almighty dollar to buy some advertising time. Another podcaster will be happy to take in some revenue, and it will introduce you to that person's audience. Plus, the cost of entry to some shows is pretty low.

Some podcasters are doing a good job of isolating themselves and only cross-promoting a small number of shows. This is a tactic used to try to corner a larger market share and shut others out. I feel that to be totally diverse, you need to go digging to find the gems in the sand. Nothing will make you happier than to have helped a fellow podcaster or to have been helped by someone.

Advertising on sites and in podcast directories allows you to build good community and personal relations by sponsoring other shows.

Some of the podcasters that had backgrounds in marketing have been able to use traditional advertising techniques that have caused their show's popularity to sizzle. So, watch what the top-rated shows are doing and pick the pieces that work well for you in developing your audience.

Accepting Advertisers

Many of us are still establishing what podcasting represents to companies looking to get the word out on their products and services. Current podcasting advertising rates are a very good value to companies. What other medium can put hard numbers on downloads of files and web traffic? The traditional radio market uses a lot of hocus-pocus to come up with extravagant numbers.

My guess would be that podcasters have a better handle on total numbers than anyone in the market today. I can tell you exactly how many unique downloads I have had and explain in detail what the potential show audience is. I have log files, and I can prove exactly how much traffic has been moved, factoring out duplicate downloads and so on. I know I can say within 2 to 3 percent exactly where my numbers are.

The streaming services can detect how many streams were started. Although, as with traditional radio, no one can be certain how many of the people who download or tune in really listen. I bet we have a pretty high take up, and this makes those listening to podcasters valuable. We may not have the razzle-dazzle of a radio station, but when I tell people I like something, or I stand behind a product and they are listening to show, don't you think that has an impact?

That said, I take advertisers and support products. I have that luxury. Since October, I have turned away over 20 advertisers because I didn't agree with their campaign.

I was somewhat naive about the power I had when it came to negotiating the selling of the single advertising spot on my podcast. I severely undercharged for my spots early on. I was looking through a straw when I should have been sampling what was happening in the real world.

I started talking to podcasters and marketing people, and they told me I was getting robbed. Heck, I had no idea what 8,000 targeted listeners were worth. Hopefully, the seminars and classes that are starting to be held will help us become better informed as to the true value of advertising on our podcasts. I cannot to this day tell you exactly what 8,000 listeners are worth, but if we use some standards from streaming audio services that claim to have 10,000 listeners, we should be able to charge a minimum of $1,000 a month, of course, there are a lot of factors to consider, including the number of shows you produce, and so on.

I highly recommend that those of you who want to take podcasting to the next level and see what all the hype is about attend what I hope will turn into an annual event: the Podcast Expo (www.podcastexpo.com).

Many of you will be happy to just cover the cost of producing your podcast. You will know the momentum of your show is gaining speed when you start getting unsolicited offers for advertisements.

I personally want to make my advertisements unique so that each ad gives something to my listener. Some podcasters have been sneaking in advertisements without saying that they're advertisements. Having run a Geek News Central weblog long before a podcast, I always included a disclaimer when something I was writing about or reviewing was a paid spot or if I had gotten the product for free. I feel that full disclosure is critical if you want to stay credible with your audience.

These values have been incorporated into my podcast advertisements and into the way I have developed my show. I always thank the sponsor after running the clip or reading the spot. I also give the advertiser/sponsor the best effort possible in making sure their ad is heard. Some podcasters place their advertisers' ads at the end of the show. I don't agree with this and think that advertisers will soon be demanding to have their spots run in the middle of the show. What value are you providing by putting an ad at the end?

My listeners have been very supportive of my running ads because they know I am a dad with kids, a car, a house, and the like. This is fun for me, but I am not going to dig into savings to support 10,000 listeners on my own dime. That said, I run only one advertisement no longer than 30 seconds during a 45-minute show. This is podcasting—we don't want to turn it into radio.

I am asked all the time by podcasters how to set advertising rates. Quite honestly, I think we are still working that out. I knew when I published my rates and had a huge influx of potential advertisers that my rates were too low. But finding that sweet spot has still been a challenge.

Note The job of the marketing person who calls you is to get the most bang for the buck. If he thinks you're weak and he can talk you into running his ad for a $100 per month, then he'll go for the kill. If you have your act together and tell him that your rate is a $1,000 per month and why, you will have greater success in selling a higher advertising rate, even if you have to negotiate downward.

Endurance Radio (www.enduranceradio.com), which has been wildly successful in selling advertising spots, is rumored to charge as much as $4,000 per month. They have attracted sponsors such as Gatorade and Fleet Feet Sports. It's not that they have a huge audience, but their audience is targeted.

Don't Forget Branding!

You want people to know who you are and what your show is about. I am now commonly referred to as "the Geek from Geek News Central," and I do a technology-based podcast for the common man. I have done this on purpose. I want people to know I am a hip tech guy, and when I talk tech, I talk at a level that enables any listener to get a lot of information.

My site is unique. There is no other site on the Net thus far that has the color scheme my site has, and that is on purpose. I want people to have no doubt that when they leave my site, they are no longer on the Geek News Central website. When they arrive, my unique website design greets them. People used to ask why I chose those colors. Simple; no one else was brave enough to scheme their colors the way I have.

Endurance Radio was smart in that they branded their site in a way that is advertiser-friendly. You will see their sponsor's ad on the main page. It actually looks as if the site was built around the ad.

Endurance Radio contracts audio advertisements to a professional voice-over person. They have put together a professional media kit that they can present to potential sponsors.

This media kit covers the following:

- **General information:** This talks about what makes Endurance Radio unique and what they do, along with their mission and how their media content is made available.

- **What sets them apart:** This explains why their site has a unique targeted audience.

- **How they attract listeners:** This talks about their paid search engine placement and the advertising they do to promote the show.

- **Advertising rates:** This explains how their ad is placed and their brand blended into the Endurance Radio site.

- **Additional Information:**
    - How sponsoring the show will sell more of the advertiser's products.
    - An example of how the site would look with the advertiser's branding.
    - A link to a study on the effectiveness of advertising on Internet broadcasts.
    - Listening statistics.
    - Listener demographics.

You can review the media kit by downloading it from `http://enduranceradio.com/ERMediaKit.pdf`.

When I saw the media kit and the number of listeners, I realized that a large number of podcasters could be generating real revenue, not just covering costs. Thus, my advice to you is to do some homework and be prepared when that Fortune 500 company comes calling.

I recommend that you visit Endurance Radio's site and look at what they've created so you can understand the type of commitment it will take to generate serious advertising dollars. Don't undersell your show, but ultimately you will have to decide what is best for you and what you think you should charge. I wish I had a magic number that said every listener is worth X amount, but I don't have the professional background to lay out that kind of information.

I have been able to sell ads on my show and cover all costs since about January 2005. I will be honest and say that I was just putting it together as I went. If some geek can do this and pay the bills, you can, too.

Targeted Audience

The majority of podcasters have targeted audiences, whether we think so or not. Unless you are just rambling on about life, you will find that people tune into your shows for that something special you like to talk about.

Some of the shows are very targeted: The Catholic Insider (www.catholicinsider.com) is of great interest to Catholics and will likely be followed by Christians who want to learn more about the faith and happenings at the Vatican. The death of Pope John Paul II drove that site's listenership into the stratosphere overnight. You never know when an event will cause your show to become the center of attention.

If you have a targeted audience, you will definitely want to target companies that sell products to those audiences. If you don't know what your audience demographics are, find out.

Polls

Run informal polls to develop a rough idea of who is listening to your show. I would not recommend that you perform a poll every week, just once. If you have a mailing list, you can point those on it to an online poll location to answer the questions. This info can be used when you are ready to develop a media kit.

Strategies for Paying for Bandwidth

You may not be comfortable taking on advertisers, so consider finding an underwriter or working out a barter arrangement with a hosting company. Many podcasters went to the hosting providers they are with now and worked out a deal in which the hosting provider covers the bandwidth, and the podcaster puts a post on their site saying, "My website, hosting provided by *XYZ*."

Work with those with whom you do business, offering a special deal only available through a referral from your website or podcast. I love giving my listeners a link to a good deal if I can save them a buck or two. They will keep tuning back in; meanwhile, I may earn a commission from that sale and/or keep the person I am bartering with happy.

Many podcasters have been successful in throwing out a tip jar. Based on what your hosting costs are, it would not take many tips in a month to pay for your hosting and your content and maybe have enough left over for a beverage of your choice. I always appreciate the $2 tip in the tip jar. It shows that the listener cared and took the time to go over to PayPal and throw me $2. Heck, if every listener to my show gave me a dollar a month, I would produce seven shows a week. I could literally give up my day job.

Google or Other Similar Ad Programs

For three years, I resisted putting a Google Adsense ad on my site. Google Adsense is an advertising program that places a small link on your site and serves up ads relevant to your content. When people click them, you earn a small commission. As near as I can figure it, after having a Google Adsense ad on my site for the past two months, if I had had one from the beginning, I could have paid for all my web design work and hosting costs for three years and still have had enough money left over to contribute to my IRA. Seriously folks, I was amazed at how quickly just a few clicks a day by site visitors have been able to raise funds through Google Adsense. Even if you have a site that you're just getting started, opening an account with Google should pay off in the long run.

Tax Liability

If you will be accepting advertising, you may as well register your podcast as a small business so that you can claim certain expenses. When the advertisers started knocking and other opportunities presented themselves, I started a new company.

Folks, keep track of your income and expenditures, because Uncle Sam will want his share, and you will have to file those expenses and incomes even if you don't make a profit. Get some financial advice from a tax planner or lawyer. There are also some tax and legal advantages to registering a sole proprietorship or limited liability company (LLC) or creating an incorporated company.

Summary

The task has been set: to get out and promote your show. Sell that sizzle that you have worked so hard to create. It will pay off in the long run. Here's that short list of things you need to do:

- Seek feedback.
- Get listed in all the major directories.
- Create a short promo and play other podcaster's promos in exchange.

It may be wise to advertise on other sites, and you are now equipped with some knowledge about what to prepare for when you are ready to start accepting advertisers. All in all, putting together a media kit is a lot of work, but the resulting reward could be significant.

The road ahead is exciting, and I will talk about where we are headed next.

Where Do You Go from Here?

Podcasting's distribution system is but a baby that has barely learned to walk. With wild publicity, this year is shaping up to be the year of the podcast. From the very first time I listened to a podcast, things have moved so quickly that being along for the ride has been fun.

I think that as we move down the road a year or two and start gaining market share, and as more people start creating content, we will reach a point where traditional radio stations have to go back to their 10-year projections and draw a diagonal line heading in a southerly direction.

Mainstream Radio

I am not one to buy into the hype that podcasting will destroy traditional radio. But I do buy into the notion that traditional radio has not kept up with technology, and it has not listened to the cries of those who want to hear something new instead of that same old, tired Top 40 list.

Public radio used to be a pretty good outlet for getting your independent message out. But that's not necessarily the case today. Part of the problem is that public radio has always struggled for funds, and many stations run on shoestring budgets and have to rely on national programming to supplement their budget. We're lucky just to get the small number of public radio stations that we have on the air today. However, moving content that originated online to public radio is going to be a tough sell.

When you have energetic teenagers sharing their play lists for their MP3 players and understanding technology better than most adults, you know the big media executives have to be worried that the wide spread of broadband, and innovative sharing techniques, will give more people the opportunity to nibble away at traditional radio's market share.

Even though I have a small audience, it is growing daily; people are tuning into my show, and they spend 45 minutes with me. That is 45 minutes that they do not spend listening to traditional broadcasting.

Has my podcast made an impact on reducing radio market share? Probably not, but with 4,500 podcasters worldwide, and that number growing each day, as a group we start to take away a still undetermined percentage of market share. Where will that market share be in several years?

Satellite Radio

XM and Sirius have a great product. I think these carriers are best suited to syndicate podcast communities on their satellites. Focused podcasting distribution groups that build a network of podcasters who provide consistent programming will be powerful contenders when these two companies realize that they need to tap podcasters for inclusion on their satellites.

Distribution

As media devices such as the iPod, iRiver, Samsung Yepp, and the hundreds of other MP3 players become more sophisticated, I hope that retailers realize that they need to have all their devices WiFi-capable and smart enough to know what podcasts the user subscribes to, so that any time the device is synced up with a WiFi hotspot, it loads the latest podcast for the user.

That way, people on the go, like me, can stay synchronized with the latest shows throughout the day, as opposed to being synchronized only when they can physically plug into the Net.

Because a podcaster's audio file can be played at the same time it is being downloaded, in a sense podcasters are already streaming audio. Those who have streaming services will say they aren't, but in a way they are. Giving credit to the streaming services, some podcasters are porting their feeds onto old-school streaming services. This has not been widely adopted by podcasters, and here is why.

Techpodcasts (`http://techpodcasts.com`) recently did a survey and found that nearly 75 percent of the people listening to podcasts are doing so with portable media devices. Fifteen percent are using their laptop or desktop computer, and the remaining 10 percent are using a PDA.

So, this tells me that of the 1,200 people who participated in the survey, 85 percent of them understand and are using the delivery vehicle that has made podcasting so popular. Thus, given this single poll, I think we will see a shift away from streaming services to a podcast model.

Podcasting: Let the Commercialization Begin

I almost hate the word *commercialization*. What I am doing now is so much fun that I can hardly call it a commercial endeavor. From the day I started my podcast, it has been about having fun. The majority of us are having a blast, but we have to realize that the commercial companies are going to start looking at podcasting as an opportunity.

Positive and negative issues surround such an opportunity. I feel that it is important for a number of reasons to begin an association that has podcasters' best interests at heart and that can act as an industry watchdog and advocate podcasting, but to date this has not happened. Without such an organization, some podcasters might not be fairly compensated when the big boys come knocking.

There are, however, small groups forming and getting organized as focused distribution groups.

Focused Distribution Groups

With 4,500+ podcasts being listed in podcast directories, some of the directories' categories have begun to get so large that new websites are being launched that focus on a specific category of podcast.

I call these *umbrella groups*, which probably is not the correct term for them. I liken them to a type of coop or community organization. These groups have formed with mission statements, core value requirements, and membership/affiliation/participation requirements. Within these groups is an understanding of what is coming down the road in terms of public and commercial scrutiny along with commercial opportunities.

There is no rating system for podcasts. Podcasters across the board have been wary of implementing a rating system. Some podcasters have provided disclaimers or warnings at the beginning of their shows on the suitability of the content, but not all by a long shot.

As for the commercialization of podcasting, it is confusing territory for companies that want to develop advertising relationships. I highly doubt that a company with strong moral values would partner with a show that turned out to be risqué.

These umbrella groups are setting the standards that companies can use as a reference or tool to determine with whom they will associate their advertising dollars. These umbrella groups will also serve to help consumers find content that they can turn their kids onto.

These groups obviously have wider agendas and goals than to provide a broadcast standard that people can trust. They also are having their members scout for new talent that is being missed in the shuffle and to align with those who are like-minded. Ultimately, I see these umbrella groups as the pathway to bigger and better things.

I personally have advocated for umbrella groups quite heavily and was one of the first to launch an umbrella/focused distribution group for technology-based shows. The benefits are enormous, and having a group work toward a common goal allows us to build communities more quickly.

Funded Commercial Podcast Ventures

Several companies are working on the commercial side of things. BoKu Communications (http://BoKu.com) is positioned to sign podcasters to real money deals. Rumors have it that they are signing a select group of podcasters and putting them on the BoKu payroll. Because the majority of what is being developed by Adam Curry and his partner has been a secret, I can only guess what they have planned. By the time this book is released, hthey will hopefully have launched their new company and more details will be available.

Other groups, such as Odeo (www.odeo.com), are rushing to make podcasting as easy as opening your web browser. Currently in a closed beta test, Odeo's offering should also be launched and operational.

One company that has a product available today is Audioblog.com (www.audioblog.com). They have a low-priced service that allows podcasters to create short podcasts and have them hosted on their site.

All these approaches are working toward the dream of true worldwide take-up of podcasts. The current distribution method of podcasts makes content easily available, and, hopefully within a couple of years, we will have millions of people tuned into a podcast network that will continue to have no barriers for entry.

Syndication

I use the term *syndication* loosely. Traditionally, the term implies that you have hit the big time. With podcasting, you are syndicated from day one. All you have to do is wait for the audience to catch up. The time will come when podcasts rule the online content community, and we will reach the millions of people who are starved for news, entertainment, independent music, educational material, and the like.

The iPod Generation

Let's face it, without the Apple iPod and the millions of other mobile media devices that can play MP3s, combined with the public's appetite for downloading anything that has an MP3 on the end of it, podcasting would not have exploded the way it has.

All age groups are tapping into content that they can download from the web, be it audio-books, music, and now podcasts. The iPod generation, which covers the youth of today up to those 25 years old, don't listen to the radio very much. They download mashups on the Net, share music they are creating, and share RIAA-controlled music. Instead of having friends over as I did when I was a kid and duplicating cassette tapes, because I did not have $14.95 in allowance money to buy my own, they are now creating music on Windows- and Mac-based computers themselves. They understand and use these tools, creating some amazing things.

The youth of today ask for credits on their music accounts and buy the latest singles as we all did. With the RIAA cracking down on P2P, many kids have no alternative but to look for independent music and tracks on sites like GarageBand.com.

The number of mobile media devices being used by all generations is increasing. I see more and more men and women my age, younger, and older plugged into a mobile media device and listening to content they want to listen to.

The question now is, do you want to take the information I have provided and get your message out to the masses, distributed in ways that were never possible before? I encourage you to join the Podcasting Revolution and help transform the way media in today's society is distributed and consumed.

I wish you the best of luck, and as with all things, send me your feedback, positive or negative, at podcastbook@gmail.com.

Finally, if you're not having fun while podcasting, then you're not doing it right. Enjoy!

Index

X–Y–Z